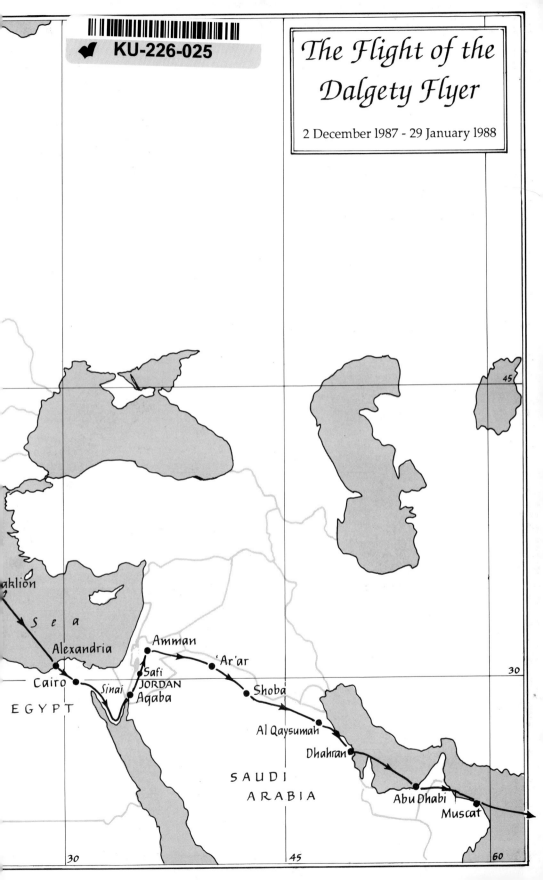

THE DALGETY FLYER

THE DALGETY
FLYER

Brian Milton

BLOOMSBURY

First Published in Great Britain 1990

The moral right of the author has been asserted

Copyright © Brian Milton 1990
Back jacket photographs: Dalgety
Author photograph: TV-am

Bloomsbury Publishing Limited, 2 Soho Square, London W1V 5DE

A CIP catalogue record for this book is available from the British Library.

ISBN 0 7475 0599 3

Photoset in Linotron Sabon by
Rowland Phototypesetting Limited, Bury St Edmunds, Suffolk
Printed and bound in Great Britain by
Butler and Tanner Limited, Frome and London

For most people, flying to Australia involves nothing more dangerous than boredom and cramp. Brian Milton did it differently – by microlight. In an epic two-month journey, reminiscent of the great flights of pioneer aviators like Amy Johnson, he flew his tiny plane through some of the most inhospitable skies in the world. On the way he:

– got totally lost in thick cloud in France
– was blown upside-down on a Greek island runway
– had engine failure at 5,000 feet trying to cross a 6,000-foot Jordanian mountain range
– crash-landed in the middle of the Persian gulf with a grandstand view of an Iranian attack on two oil tankers
– landed on the only track through a Malaysian paddyfield
– was nearly blown out of the sky by a 'playful' military helicopter
– at the end of his longest leg – ten and a half hours – landed in the dark in the Australian Outback between three lightning storms in time for a major earthquake

In all, Milton made nine emergency landings. Even when everything went right – such as during the white-knuckle flight over the shark-infested Timor Sea – he could rely on nothing but his own courage and the flimsy support of an aircraft a mere twenty-one feet long powered by a forty horsepower two-stroke engine.

But he made it. His is a thrilling story, one that will appeal to armchair adventurers everywhere.

ACKNOWLEDGEMENTS

There are four groups of people I would like to thank for giving me the greatest adventure of my life:

First, the leaders in Dalgety: Terry Pryce, the Chief Executive, Sir Peter Carey, the Chairman, and Tony Spalding, the Chief of Public Relations. They had the corporate courage to back me, and I could not have had better sponsors.

Second, my engineer, Mike Atkinson, and project co-ordinator, Neil Hardiman. Mike glued the Flyer together whenever I bashed her or took her swimming, and he never let me down. Neil cleared us both through some of the most difficult regions of the world – without a hitch.

Third, those I met en route, like HRH King Hussein of Jordan, who became patron of the flight; Sheik Mohammed Ben Zayed of Abu Dhabi, and his emissary, Rachid Abbad, who helped me to get going after ditching; Emirate Air Services; Group Captain Deshmukh of the Indian Air Force; Captain Tei of the Royal Malaysian Air Force; and a great many more.

And fourth, my family: my son Jamie, who thought I was mad, and my daughter Tracey, who wished I would not do it but who knew I had to. And thank you to my wife, Fiona Campbell, for whom I am going to ration all my new stories so that she doesn't send me out too quickly on the next wheeze.

CONTENTS

LIST OF ILLUSTRATIONS

'Those people who had the opportunity to fly slow and low were able to share in a unique experience. Today there are few spots where man's foot has not trod, or over which the shadow of an aeroplane has not fallen. But half a lifetime ago . . . the earth's great vastness stood as a challenge to pioneering flyers. I am thinking I was fortunate enough to be one of them.'

Hans Bertram, Flight Into Hell.

Chapter One
The Fall

When you fall 250 feet, it normally takes three and a half seconds to hit the ground.

You accelerate at thirty-two feet per second and after three seconds you should be travelling at 76 mph.

Hitting the ground at that speed, there should be no question about whether you live or die, which is certainly how I felt when I began my fall on 13 November 1978.

At that time, hang-gliding had passed through its most dangerous phase. We had learned how to build machines so they didn't stay in a dive when put into one, and didn't break up in the air. Accidents occurred more because of pilot error than for any other reason. But a small number of us were sticking engines on hang-glider wings in order to discover the best way to fly them without having to jump off a hill.

One of the pioneers of British hang-gliding, Len Gabriels from Oldham in Lancashire, had built a wing called the Skyhook Silhouette, and I was making my test flight on the single-engine powered version. My wife Fiona Campbell had already set up a sponsorship company, and found a sponsor in Bluebird Toffees for our latest 'wheeze', which was for me to become the first pilot to fly a powered hang-glider from London to Paris.

My experience with flying powered wings had not been an altogether happy one, but I was stubborn and persevered. My first flight had been earlier in 1978, at Winter Hill in Lancashire, an established hang-gliding site dominated by huge TV aerials, where I had flown for the BBC *Tomorrow's World* cameras on a wing with two small 98cc engines, one on either side of me. Len had built that too. Both throttles had been on the bottom of the control bar, and had had to be thrown open while balancing the wing on my shoulders. On this first occasion, Len told me to be ready to run like stink. The aircraft flew faster than I could run, he said, but if I threw myself forward quickly enough, I could get safely into the air.

On the hill as I lined up to fly had been a friend called Mike Atkinson, a fisherman from Plymouth and, like Len, one of the founder pilots of the National Hang-gliding League which was to take Britain to a World Championship gold medal years later. Mike helped me into the harness and attached me to the kite. Len started both engines, the BBC cameras whirred, and I threw open the throttles and legged it over the edge of the hill. Frightened silly, I was dragged into the air, and found myself roaring higher and higher away from the hill, trying desperately to work out how to control what was happening.

The next five minutes I will remember vividly for the rest of my life, as I scuttled from one side of the control bar to the other, adjusting the throttle to each engine. Control was by weight-shift, so the glider turned left or right every time I moved. Sometimes the engines thrummed, which meant they were synchronised and working as they should. Nevertheless, I thought something was wrong and fiddled with the throttles again. In this way, never deliberately initiating a turn since I had no faith the aircraft would straighten again, I roared all over the sky, looking with great longing at the ground and wishing I was there again.

Then the right wing was caught by a thermal which turned it slowly and involuntarily toward the hill. Realising that I was going to hit the aerials on top of Winter Hill, I threw my weight to the right to avoid them. Nothing happened. As the aerials loomed up at me, I watched in horror and thought my last moment had come. Another desperate heave to the right still had no effect. Then I leaned left and the machine whipped around, facing away from the hill but over high ground. Cutting the engines, I slid in for a normal top landing.

Friends came running over to congratulate me on the flight while I sat under the wing, pulling desperately on a cigarette, glad to be alive. I wanly acknowledged all the enthusiastic comments, while inside me a voice was telling me, 'you are going to die doing this!'

But the odd thing about fear is that, given a little time, it goes away, or I can persuade myself that I'm not as frightened as I thought I was. Later that day I had another flight. The second flight went better, enough for me not to discourage Len from sticking with the two-engine format. It took another few flights like the first one to make me suggest, diffidently, that I would rather have a single-engined machine if he was building one. He was.

We agreed that my first test flight on the new machine should be at the ancient hillfort bowl at White Sheet Hill, at Mere in Wiltshire. It took place about two weeks after I came back from the triumph of the first American Cup, where I had coached a British hang-gliding team which, against all the odds, had thrashed the mighty Americans, and produced what the French called a 'watershed in the sport'. Len Gabriels came down from Lancashire, and there was another film crew there that day, this time from the BBC *Nationwide* programme, who were going to follow the whole story of the Paris flight. The producer, Peter Gilbe, wanted me to make a number of flights for the film crew to stock up library film, especially in-air shots.

White Sheet Hill has a south-facing bowl. It was a fine day, with fluffy clouds in the sky and the wind starting from the south but moving to the west in the afternoon. Rodney Coward, the farmer who owned the field below, had ploughed it the previous day, and it had rained overnight. All these factors combined first to start the fall, and then to save my life.

Three flights were made in all, and I was so absorbed in what I was doing that I did not notice the wind change direction. On the first flight, I carried no cameras, took off safely, and swanned around getting experience in the air. The engine was mounted on the keel above my head, driving a long shaft which stuck out the back, attached to which was the propeller pushing the aircraft through the air. (Conventional propeller-driven aircraft are pulled through the air.)

One problem with the Bluebird wing was that I had two separate throttles to control the engine. On the take-off run I needed both hands to hold the control bar, so one throttle was a large peg. I had to bite the peg, which opened the throttle, and run off with my teeth clenched. When I was safely away from the hill and in my harness, I spat the peg out, and flew on a hand throttle attached to the bottom of the control bar.

On the first flight, after I had gained a few hundred feet, I flew back over the top of the hill, turned the engine off, and tried for a top landing. But I was unfamiliar with the machine, and fluffed it. I shot over the ridge and floated down to the glutinously muddy field below. It took an hour of hard physical effort to struggle up the hill again with the aircraft, and as I lit what was to be the last cigarette I have ever smoked, I resolved not to do that again.

The second flight ended safely back on top, this time carrying on-board cameras. My problems started on the third flight.

The 250cc engine over my head was screaming noisily, the throttle wide open, when I flew away from the hill, but I had difficulty climbing. Struggling for control, I flew in circles, moving further out into the bowl. The southerly wind was no longer coming cleanly into the mouth of the bowl, and was now a southwesterly, crossing the right-hand ridge and rolling turbulently over where I was flying. In addition, the Accident Investigation Branch of the Civil Aviation Authority later deduced, a *sheer* line had been approaching, an invisible line between two masses of air moving at different speeds.

My last coherent memory was of looking right and seeing hang-gliders in the air on the other side of the bowl, soaring on a southwest wind. I remember thinking, I should fly south and head around the outside of the bowl to join them and to gain height. Then the glider tipped forward, I did a handstand on the bar, fell backwards into the sail, and the next thing I knew I was hurtling towards the ground 250 feet below.

There was no question. I was going to die.

There is a myth that people falling a long way black out before they hit the ground. I do not believe that myth. I can remember every one of the five seconds it took me to hit the ground from a height of about one and a half times as high as Nelson's Column. The exact timing came from the film of the fall, which was transmitted by television stations all over the world.

Halfway down, I pulled the parachute from its bag on the front of my flying harness, and threw it. Unlike conventional parachutes, there was no ripcord. Hang-gliding parachutes are hurled away from the pilot, and are supposed to open and lower the pilot and aircraft to the ground. But even as I threw it, I knew the line would catch on the propeller roaring behind me. The ground came rushing up to me, and then I hit it, right shoulder and face first.

When I came to, I was lying on my back, looking at the hill from which I had flown. White fluffy clouds still drifted across the sky. I must have bounced, because I was lying on my back, and had great difficulty breathing. Two years previously, one of my best friends – Tony Jones from Shropshire – had drowned in blood from his injured lungs after banging his chest in a heavy landing. Dreamily, I thought that this was happening to me.

As at other times of mortal danger, I felt myself splitting into two. One part of me was dying; the other part of me was in a very detached state, just watching. What is so frightening is how easily one can accept dying, without struggle, even without fear.

After a long, long time, I moved my legs, first one, then the other. Good, I thought, my back isn't broken. Then I moved my arms, and my head, and was pleased in an odd way that my neck was not broken. Odd, because if I was going to die anyway, what did it matter what was broken? The blood roared through my veins, a sensation I could feel vividly, much as people who have had acid trips are said to feel. Someone groaned loudly. When I heard the noise, and realised it was me, I groaned again to experience more fully the sensation of being alive.

Another long, long time went by, and then a face loomed over me, red-cheeked with a mass of frizzy hair and two very intent eyes. Ashley Doubtfire, another Hang-gliding League pilot, had been with me at the top of the hill only a few minutes earlier. He had jumped into his hang-glider and flown down to where I lay.

'Don't let me lose consciousness, Ashley,' I croaked, fighting for breath.

I still thought I was going to die, and if I lost consciousness I would have no chance to fight against it. The part of me that was watching the rest of me die had decided to start struggling. I lost my sense of detachment.

An ambulance was called. Coats were put over me to keep me

warm, and my breathing became very slightly easier. The BBC crew struggled down the hill, stopping now and again for long and medium shots, and then staggered over the loose, sloppy soil to where I lay. Ashley appeared again.

'Can you give the BBC an interview?' he asked.

As press officer for the British Hang-gliding Association, I did not think anything I could say at the time would improve the image of the sport.

'I don't think so,' I whispered hoarsely.

The crew contented itself with getting close-up shots of my face, battered all down the right side. My jacket had been cut open to see what horrendous injuries I was suffering, but my upper right arm had just a simple spiral fracture. There was quite a bit of blood coming from a deep gash on my chin, which later needed fifteen stitches.

Why had I not been killed?

First, the field was soft from ploughing, and this was helped by the overnight rain. I had been lucky in my landing as only twenty feet away the ground was hard as iron. Secondly, during the fall, I had had so little hope of staying alive that when I hit the ground I was not braced for the impact, and was thrown around like a rag doll. The fall did not kill me, and the engine did not hit me from above nor did the propeller, or the thick iron shaft, or the hang-glider wing.

Looking at the film later, it is obvious that I somersaulted once before falling. The line of thrust through the engine and propeller, as we had it rigged, was along the glider itself. This thrust line was counterbalanced by my weight hanging in the harness underneath. Struggling with the turbulent air, trying to get the machine to climb, I had the engine flat out and the nose up, just off the stall. The CAA said I hit a sheer line, but whatever it was, it caused what is technically known as a power stall. My weight went off the harness, and the engine, at full power, immediately drove the wing upside down, as if I was a fulcrum around which the wing was swinging. When I fell into the sail, which was not built to be flown upside down, the outside part of the wings collapsed. But – and it saved my life – the inner triangle remained intact, and this broke my fall.

The Fall

It is estimated I hit the ground at about 35 mph, and not the 76 mph I could have achieved in a free fall.

At the hospital in Salisbury a very unsympathetic doctor looked me over and thought I might stay the night. He had no time for hang-glider pilots. The deep gash on my chin was stitched up, and I was sent through an X-ray, which diagnosed a broken right arm and very severe bruising. Meanwhile, the BBC crew tore back to London with film of the whole flight, and the assistant cameraman who had started his camera rolling three seconds before the fall earned promotion to full cameraman. ('Why did you choose that moment?' I asked him later. 'You looked like something was about to happen,' he replied.)

Fiona and the children were intercepted near Mere by Ashley Doubtfire, who greeted her with an all-time classic line in reassurance: 'Fiona, Brian has had an accident, but don't worry, he's still talking.'

(As a coincidence, it was ten years to the day since I had set off in a 1937 Austin 7 Ruby called Alexa to drive across Africa to Johannesburg, where I was going to marry a girl called Fiona Campbell. Alexa beat six landrovers across the Sahara Desert – solo – in eighteen days, and I succeeded in driving her as far as the northeast Congo, only 300 miles from Uganda. This was during a particularly troubled period in what is now Zaire; it was only four years after a terrible rebellion during which vanquished enemies had been eaten in triumph by their captors. For the last 2,000 miles of my journey, before I left my wrecked car in a place called Mungbere, Alexa motored on only three pistons, without even a plug in the fourth cylinder. For the last 900 miles, she had no brakes, and every evening I went around the jungle in circles, with my foot out the door, to stop her.

I married Fiona in 1970, but it had to be in England, because on the night we were writing our wedding invitations the South African Special Branch turned up at our house in Johannesburg to expel me from the country. They never said why they wanted me out, but in those days, six priests and six journalists a year were expelled. My expulsion was Class of '69. In 1975 Fiona gave birth to our son Jamie in St Albans, and earlier in 1978 to our daughter Tracey.)

When Fiona found me in the hospital, still waiting for a bed to be prepared, I whispered hoarsely that I would live, and that my breathing was getting better. She went off to a hotel, and that evening watched the first showing of the film of the fall at the end of the BBC *Nationwide* programme. It was also run, heavily trailed, in the nine o'clock news that night, introduced by Angela Rippon with the cue line, 'The luckiest man alive'.

The fall is quite dramatic, and stops your breath when you see it for the first time. Friends told me they jumped out of chairs and shouted with alarm. If you don't listen to the commentary, you are quite convinced that the little tumbling figure on the screen is falling to his death. When I look at it, I find it hard to think of it as being me.

But as a result of the BBC film, the Salisbury doctors allowed me to stay in the ward two whole days extra. It was not wholly humanitarian. Experts came in from various parts of the country and demanded more X-rays, to see if there was something about the way I'm built which enabled me to survive such a fall. During one such X-ray it was discovered that my left wrist was fractured. I hurt all over, so there had been no particular pains to suggest a fracture or any other breaks.

One news reporter spent half an hour sitting by my bed, as I lay strapped up and defiant, urging me to say that it was a miracle I was alive. 'Surely God was looking after you,' he whispered, eager to get me to say yes. Some perverse honesty about my own beliefs would not let me do it. He was honest enough not to use the 'miracle' line, whether I had said it or not, even though it would have made a simpler story.

Meanwhile, Fiona was so upset by the fall that it affected the milk she gave to Tracey, who was sick for the only time ever during breast-feeding. Jamie, however, took to jumping off the hotel radiators half the night, shouting 'Look at me, I'm Daddy', and falling on his head.

Because of the American Cup victory, I was due to meet Prince Charles within ten days of the fall. It was at a Royal Aeroclub meeting in London, and I went with my right arm in a sling, my left wrist in plaster, both eyes blacked, the right side of my face covered in bruises, and fifteen stitches in my chin. I was not a great advertisement for the sport.

Inside hang-gliding, there were groans all around at what I had done to the sport's image. There was a thinly veiled suggestion by Garth Thomas, then editor of *Wings!*, the hang-gliding magazine (and no champion of mine, I'm afraid), that I had fallen in the first place merely to provide a better piece of film for the BBC.

Len Gabriels rebuilt the Bluebird wing from the pieces sent back by the accident investigators, and flew it from London to Paris in August 1979, chasing another pilot called Gerry Breen, who was actually the first to fly a microlight from London to Paris. Recovered from my accident, I followed Len in a helicopter across the English Channel and down through France, where we were held up by aviation officials because our paperwork was not up to scratch, and in the end had to abandon the flight. The Bluebird wing, however, may now be seen in a museum, as an early example of soft-wing powered flight.

Within fourteen weeks of the fall I was back hang-gliding, with the daily help of the lovely physiotherapists at St Alban's hospital. My first flight, in February 1979, was a day before the new League competition season began, at Hay Bluff, a 600-foot hill in South Wales. For an hour and a half I struggled up the hill in deep snow, with the glider on my shoulder, and I rigged it as the light was fading. By the time I was ready there was no time to contemplate whether or not I had the nerve to fly again; I couldn't face the walk back down in the dark.

But there were long-term effects from the fall. It made me nervous about flying, no matter how much I enjoyed individual flights. I was thirty-six years old when I hit the ground, past the first flush of youth, and it was no longer possible to believe, in the way most of us do, that dying was not going to happen to me until I was old enough to do it decently in bed.

The fall also had a profound effect on my attitude towards heights. At any height above a thousand feet, I became nervous. However illogical, one part of me said, 'You can survive a fall from low down, so stay there.' In fact, there is more safety in height, because if anything goes wrong you have more time to put it right. But logic was no comfort.

Though I continued to fly, and could not contemplate life without being in the air, after the fall a bit of me started to hate it, and was frightened by the whole experience. It was not something I would admit to anybody, but it was to haunt me later, particularly flying over India.

Chapter Two
Origins of the Flight

A number of separate events led to the microlight flight to Australia. These included landing a television presenter's job, taking a girl for a joy ride, the sale of a billion dollars' worth of assets by one of the world's richest men, and three men with the corporate courage to back a good idea.

At the time of the fall, I had been working for BBC Radio London, but after ten years there, I moved to TV-am in 1982, joining the breakfast television company before it was even on screen. My career at TV-am was a chequered one: taken up by one faction, dumped by the next, tossed around indifferently by a third. I worked in production for nearly a year, through the period known as the bloodbaths, when Anna Ford and Angela Rippon left, before being transferred to on-screen reporting rather against my will. But it was either that or no television job at all, and there was a lot about the techniques of producing picture stories that I had to learn.

Hang-gliding was no longer the dominating obsession it had once been. But through a series of chances, at the end of 1984 I found myself owning a large two-seater, soft-wing microlight. Microlight flying was by this time becoming regulated, and I had not obtained a licence under the grandfather clause that enabled other hang-glider pilots to continue with powered flight. But I had obtained a pilot's licence on Tiger Moths back in 1960, and with ten years' experience hang-gliding, I taught myself to fly microlights during the winter of 1984–5.

Any nerves left over from the fall had to be overcome when I became involved in another wheeze, a flight I felt I *had* to make: to follow the course of the first ever air race held in Britain between Louis Paulans and Claude Graham-White on 27 April 1910. Judy Leden, the women's world hang-gliding champion, joined me to fly in the opposite direction to the originals in April 1985, exactly seventy-five years to the day after they had done it, landing in the same fields, even stopping overnight at the same hotel. It got me back into microlighting, but it was still just a hobby.

One weekend, a girl called Kathy Rowan came to stay at our home in Bristol. She worked with me at TV-am; we had lunched together a few times, and were companions in gossip. I took her flying on the Mendips on one of those still, West Country days in February, when the sky is marked by high curly cirrus clouds, and the ground is hard and white with snow. We flew over country reputed to have been inhabited by King Arthur and the Knights of the Round Table, but Kathy spent the whole twenty minutes staring intently at the back of my head. In a weight-shift microlight, the passenger's legs are wrapped around the pilot, who can feel every squeeze and tremble. Though I flew as gently as I could, it did not help when, circling at 600 feet over some farmhouses, Kathy felt there was nothing between her and the ground but a thin piece of aluminium on the seat.

It was during this weekend that I showed Kathy some brochures I had been drawing up to canvass for sponsorship to fly a microlight to Australia. I have always been involved in 'wheezes' and one of their major attractions to me is the danger. The closer I get to dying, the more alive I feel. Walking along the edge, looking down and seeing that it all could end, and then by daring, stamina and luck getting away with it – there's a feeling afterwards of great calmness. It is possible that I am an adrenaline junkie. In any case, the fall had not turned me to a more sober way of life, and working out 'wheezes', ideas for adventures, is something I have always done when bored at work. Flying a microlight to Australia was the longest microlight flight I could conceive of, and would certainly be an interesting adventure.

During 1985 I continued my search for backing for the flight, and raised some interest in making a film about it, the first step to getting sponsorship. But in 1986, two events happened which put me off the whole idea. The first was that Eve Jackson, a thirty-year-old Englishwoman who came from Thame in Oxfordshire, set off on her own in a microlight she called Gertie. She had just £500 in her pocket, and aimed to become the first person to fly from London to Australia in the smallest of all the categories of aircraft. Like everyone else, I did not fancy her chances of success, but as long as she persisted it was impossible for me to set off after her. The film makers lost interest, and any right-minded sponsor would point out that Eve would get far more media coverage than I could. Before I could go myself, I had to wait and see if Eve succeeded.

The second reason for my losing interest in the idea was brought about by a big Australian called Bruce Gyngell taking over as boss of TV-am. Bruce was put in by the Australian billionaire Kerry Packer, who had bailed out TV-am during one of its more difficult periods. Gyngell was a close friend of Packer, and had his own rather eccentric though sometimes brilliant ideas about television. In 1986 he came up with the idea of screening what was to be the first daily programme of City news on British television. I was chosen to produce and present the slot.

I loved *Money Matters*, and threw myself into it heart and soul. This was in the days before the October '87 Crash, when everyone was interested in the Stock Market. It was very like it must have been in New York in the early months of 1929. The rhythm of the market and its reaction to the economic numbers published in Britain and the US; charting the great power of Japan which was then just beginning to be acknowledged; this was an adventure all of its own, and I treated it as such.

It was an immensely wearing job. I had to be out of bed at 3 am, and in work by 4 am. There were three scripts to write, from raw material left by an overnight researcher, and I had about two hours in which to do them. The main script had to be done by 5.30, and the basis of a one-minute bulletin laid out in the computer. There was always a live guest, a City analyst or economist, always invited in at the unearthly hour of 5.45 am to rehearse the interview, which was tight at ninety seconds in length. My working day was generally over by 7.10 am, and I spent the rest of the day either working out the following day's stories, or in the City.

Whatever surges of adrenaline I experienced during flying were easily equalled under the pressure of three live-television appearances in an hour. I was always responsible for my own scripts, my own graphics, my guest, everything which in other more mature television stations is split between a number of people.

Every now and again, I checked on Eve Jackson's progress, noting how she had been shot at in Yugoslavia; held up for six weeks in Muscat, waiting for the right weather to cross to Pakistan; and the months of delay she'd had getting her engine serviced in India. My own proposed flight had become a back number, perhaps to be done 'one day'. I did not, however, mention this to Kathy Rowan, which became enormously significant when Kathy fell in love with Bruce Gyngell, and married him.

Early in 1987, Kerry Packer sold his entire worldwide interests in television, including more than twenty per cent of TV-am, to Alan Bond, for £468 million. Packer came to England, lodged in his customary suite at the Savoy, and was reported in one newspaper later that week to have lost £8 million gambling in London casinos. One night he had dinner with his friend Bruce, and Bruce's new bride, Kathy. During the course of the meal, Kathy learned that Kerry Packer flew microlights, and actually owned three of them. When my name came up later, my slot being deemed a success, Kathy, not knowing that I had shelved the whole idea, told Kerry Packer that I wanted to fly a microlight to Australia. She suggested that he should sponsor it.

The following day I was summoned to the Savoy to meet Packer's right-hand man, Linton Taylor. The gist of the conversation was this: could I fly a microlight around the world in eighty days, landing in Sydney on 26 January 1988, Australia's Bicentenary Day? This was the first time I heard the date which was to dominate my life for so many months. At the time, I was dressed in my pinstriped City suit, with the prospect of a good lunch ahead of me. I looked at Linton and thought, even if this is possible, I'm not the man to do it. Too comfortable, I thought, too old at forty-five, too set in my ways. Somebody else could take the risk. Nevertheless, I asked for the weekend to think about it, wondering whether I knew anyone else who might want to do it.

The weekend was spent looking at maps and history books, and talking to an experienced microlight pilot, Bob Calvert, a World record-holder and one of the best pilots around. Bob wanted to fly the Atlantic in a microlight, and I was lazily looking for sponsorship for him, but not with a lot of effort. I suggested to Bob that he might want to make Packer's flight, but he phoned back the following day and said it was not possible in a southern hemisphere summer. It would mean leaving Sydney in November, flying north through Indonesia, Malaysia, Thailand and China to Russia, then crossing Canada and the Atlantic in the northern hemisphere winter. After that, there was a mere 13,500 miles to go to get back to Sydney!

But I hated to lose a potential sponsor, and was tickled with the thought of a billionaire backing an adventurous flight. During the weekend's research, I read about the first ever flight between London and Australia, which had been done in November–December 1919, by an Australian called Ross Smith, and a crew of three in a Vickers Vimy bomber. Ross and his navigator–brother Keith were knighted for their efforts, and his two mechanics, Wally Shiers and Jim Bennett, were also honoured. It might be possible, I thought, to race against their ghosts across half the world, and mingle with the ghosts of all those early aviators – Kingsford Smith, Amy Johnson, Bert Hinkler – who tried and sometimes died on the blue riband route. I did not know it then, but this was the beginning of what I came to think of as a noble obsession. It would be a sporting proposition.

Kerry Packer listened to the idea, and we spent an hour telling each other 'there-I-was, upside-down, nothing-on-the-clock, still-going-up' stories. In the middle of one of these, Linton leaned over, told me I had got the sponsorship, and to go off and prepare a new budget!

Packer lasted as a sponsor for six weeks before I was phoned on 1 April 1987 and told that it was all off. He felt, on reflection, that the flight was too expensive, and too risky. The expenses had been batted back and forth between the two of us, each giving a bit here and there, but the budget had crept up to £100,000. Now it was too expensive. The risk was something we had not talked about, and I knew only that I was determined to make a go of it. But impassioned argument was no use in changing the decision, and I was left with a superb idea and no means to make it work.

Fiona said to me that spring: 'Do you know, our stories are growing whiskers? We need some new ones.' I think her words had struck home much deeper than she realised. The Australia flight started to become an obsession, something for which, I found, I would sacrifice almost anything, including, eventually, my job.

One measure of how serious I was that summer was my taking £10,000 in money I could little afford to lose, and putting it on the most risky of all investments, a 'put' option on the US dollar. This was a massive bet that the American dollar would plunge, and taken on the best advice I could find. The advice was correct, but the timing was wrong – I was three months too early. Had I chosen the right time, I would have been able to raise the money for the flight on my own. It is an indication of my state of mind in the spring and early summer of 1987.

However, many of the guests I had on the programme knew people who had access to sponsorship money, and I began gently hocking the idea around some of them. David Brewerton, then City Editor of *The Independent*, now of *The Times*, was one of them. He talked to four men at the top of the public relations field. Two said outright that they were not interested. One, from a big oil company, toyed with the idea before dropping it. But the fourth man was Tony Spalding, soon to be President of the Institute of Public Relations, a man who had originated or expanded some of the most original and exciting sponsorships in Britain, including Ford's motor racing programmes and the Whitbread Round the World sailboat race. Tony had recently been taken on by a large food and commodities company called Dalgety.

He came to breakfast at TV-am one morning, after I had finished my three financial slots, and we took to each other immediately. He was immensely intelligent, and so fast in his thinking that it was soon apparent that he was three steps ahead of anywhere you thought he might be. He listened to the idea in outline, took away my budget, and phoned later on. Dalgety was a company whose roots in Australia went back 140 years, he said; they were interested in the flight and might take half the sponsorship. A week later he phoned again to say that Dalgety were not interested in half measures, and might take the lot. Having counted my sponsorship chickens a number of times in the past, only to lose them when the crunch came, I was cautious.

'You have got to convince our chief executive, Terry Pryce,' Tony told me, and we arranged another breakfast meeting. This time, they would watch *Money Matters* going out. Live television is very exciting, and I wanted to impress Terry with that excitement. It was a wild, romantic aviation idea that I was trying to sell, and I was aware whilst selling it that it came most improbably from a sober, City-suited journalist. My suit lent weight to the proposition.

'What if you get killed?' Terry Pryce asked me at the breakfast table after the programme, while Tony Spalding buttered another piece of toast and left me to make my own arguments. 'What if you fall in the water? What if you're kidnapped? What if you're seriously injured? What if you crash and damage the aircraft beyond repair? What if it all becomes too much for you?'

They were not easy questions to answer! I did not give up easily, I said, explaining how I had driven across the Sahara in a 1937 Austin 7, and how it had only been when the car physically could not move any further that I had left it. As for falling in the water, I didn't think it would happen, but if it did, then I would find some way to get the aircraft out and fly again. (I could not know at the time that this was not an academic question.) Tony ate his toast and watched us both silently.

'Do you know, we've existed as a company for a very long time,' said Terry finally. 'We have always paid dividends, but some have thought us a trifle dull. This is such an exciting idea. Let's give it a whirl!'

That was that! Dalgety financed the setting up of a small company – Windrunner Ltd – to make the project work, and from then until the flight was over, through all the trials and problems, they stuck by me. I learned later that three men at the top of the company were key players in seeing the flight through. Terry Pryce was where the buck stopped, and it had been his decision. But Tony Spalding on one side, and the company chairman, Sir Peter Carey, on the other, made up with Terry a powerful triumvirate of support. I could not have had better sponsors.

Chapter Three
Learning the Ropes

Having been awarded the sponsorship, I had to find a microlight capable of flying to Australia, and learn how to fly it. At the time that I was talking to Dalgety, microlight aircraft were little more than toys. Most microlight pilots kept their machines folded up in barns or garages, and when the weather was right, spent far more time driving them to a field, rigging and derigging, than time in the air. For the overwhelming majority of pilots, a fifteen-mile flight was quite a big thing, and a fifty-mile flight something to boast about. Perhaps sixty or seventy people in the whole country used microlights as real aircraft to transport themselves further than 100 miles. As toys, microlights were not built to fly 13,500 miles, which was what Eve Jackson was doing at a leisurely pace, and what I was now proposing to race at speed!

Very early on I decided, like Eve, to make the flight in a CFM Shadow, one of the most sophisticated of all microlights, and designed by a former hang-glider pilot called David Cook (CFM stood for Cook's Flying Machine). It had three-axis controls like ordinary aircraft, rather than weight-shift control like a hang-glider.

The Dalgety Flyer was the sixty-sixth Shadow built, powered by a 447cc Rotax two-stroke, two-cylinder engine, developing 40 hp. Cruising speed was 70 mph, and VNE (Velocity Never Exceed) was 108 mph. Normally, there is a five-gallon tank for fuel, enough for just over two hours, but the Dalgety Flyer had two extra tanks fitted, to create a total capacity of twenty-eight gallons. The biggest extra tank sat on the passenger seat.

The Shadow is a flimsy-looking aircraft, a high-wing monoplane with a swept-back leading edge and a swept-forward trailing edge. The wing is braced by two struts, and built from foam spars with a wooden leading edge. The monocoque of the body is constructed from fibrelam, an expensive space-age material costing £400 a sheet, and a major reason for the aircraft's high price of £13,500. It is a two-seater, capable of dual control, although The Dalgety Flyer had only one set of controls. The tricycle undercarriage is steered by heel-brakes on the rudder pedals; the nose wheel is not steerable.

The tail of the Shadow is odd to a conventional pilot, with the plane and the rudder inverted. This leaves the control surfaces directly in line with the propwash, and makes rudder control more positive. There are two vertical stabilisers above the tailplane. The aircraft is twenty-one feet long, with a wing span of thirty-three feet. It does not stall, nor does it spin. Handling is light and easy, with a landing speed of around 45 mph.

As I learned to fly it, I added to the basic instruments on board. These included a magnetic compass, an ASI (air-speed indicator), altimeter, a vertical-speed indicator, two temperature gauges, a rev counter and two fuel gauges. With the exception of the compass, all these instruments were lost and had to be replaced after Christmas Day 1987.

Normal radio communication was by two ICOM VHF A-20 radios, both hand held. One I used to talk to air-traffic controllers, while the other served as a radio-navigation instrument. When I left London the Flyer was also equipped with a beautiful ICOM HF radio, trailing an aerial fifty feet out the back. This aerial rigging was used by bomber pilots in the last war, but unlike them, I did not reel my aerial in when I landed, but trailed it behind me instead, like a long tail. The HF radio enabled me to talk to London direct – through Portishead radio near Bristol – while I was airborne thousands of miles away.

As for learning to fly the Shadow, I had a microlight licence, but a restricted one, confining me to within eight kilometres of my takeoff point. To remove the restrictions I needed to go back to school. David Cook recommended the Skyrider School in Coventry, run by a burly, thirty-year-old, red-headed man called Peter Davies, a brilliant pilot. One of my difficulties was embarrassment. How do you explain to your teacher that you are learning to fly in order to make the longest, fastest flight ever made in a microlight as soon as you get your licence? As a result, there were restrictions in the questions I could ask Peter – about how to use an aviation radio beacon-finder called a VOR, for example, an essential tool of modern navigation. Learning the VOR, and some other skills, had to be by trial, error and the instruction book.

If I was going to learn how to fly a new aircraft, I still needed an engineer. Fiddling with engines is not my forte, and I lack the logical patience of a good mechanic. Right from the start Mike Atkinson, an old hang-gliding friend, said he would follow me across the world as my mechanic. He had been one of the fifty-four original members of the British Hang-gliding League, and had shadowed Judy Leden and me on our Manchester to London flight. Mike and I knew from the start that there would be problems flying a micro-light at speed to Australia, but we did not know what. He was an insurance policy in case anything went wrong. Aside from being physically tough and full of stamina, Mike can fix anything, and if the repairs don't look pretty (and they don't), they always work. He had jumped at the chance of an interesting winter.

As far as the route was concerned, I had decided that because of the Bicentenary, I wanted to touch the history of Australia in every way possible, picking the route for the flight so that the places I passed through would be part of Australian folk memory, even if buried deep. If the flight reminded people of their own history, then I hoped they would see its significance, and not simply dismiss it as a small, unsuitable aircraft struggling against adversity over half the world.

My first projected route was via the Somme River in northwest France, where thousands of Australians had lost their lives in World War One. I also wanted to take in Gallipoli, where I planned to stop and film for a day, and swotted up my history for when I walked the old battlefields. Unfortunately the route later had to be modified to cut out Gallipoli, because I did not have time to get Turkish permissions, but I remained faithful to the original intentions. In Egypt, I wanted to go via El Alamein, because there were Australian regiments in the Desert Rats, and via Cairo, where countless Australian troops had left their graffiti. Crossing the Sinai Desert, I knew I would fly over country where Ross Smith and the Australian

Light Horse had stopped the Turks from seizing Cairo. At Aqaba in Jordan, I would look down on the same land as Ross Smith had in one of his wartime jobs as personal pilot to Lawrence of Arabia. Later, I planned to go through Burma, where the 'Forgotten Fourteenth Army' fought under General Slim, an Australian.

My wife Fiona suggested that as my own individual 200th birthday present, I should bring a Birthday Book to Australia, signed by people in all the countries through which I flew. Collecting the signatures from the great and the obscure would also provide an opportunity to talk to people about the Bicentenary. The flight, as I saw it, would be the aerial version of the Tall Ships leaving England for Sydney, but more appropriate than Englishmen carrying English convicts because it had been Australians who had pioneered the air route out.

At the beginning of July 1987, on Mike's recommendation, I hired as organiser a twenty-four-year-old called Neil Hardiman. Neil was an instructor at Mike's Devon School of Hang-gliding, and had a Masters degree in Engineering. The job had to be what Neil made it, and the only brief he had was to make sure that there were no paperwork problems of any kind for Mike and I on our way to Australia.

Neil was wary about the job. He had serious doubts about whether he could do it, and also whether or not the flight could succeed. His responsibilities would be wide: flight clearances, visas, securing equipment, travel, maps, accommodation, routings and fuel. He was required to be a bureaucrat, with the soul of a flyer. He turned out to be an inspired choice. He had charm, intelligence, diplomacy and tenacity. The wilder the rest of us became, the more cautious he was.

There were tremendous problems putting together a microlight flight to Australia at six months' notice, and I did not possess the skills to deal with them. Neil had to find the questions to ask, as well as the answers. He travelled regularly between Bristol and London, and at meeting after meeting was always calm and methodical, never a prima donna about the work that piled up on him.

His liaison with me was sporadic, at first because of the daft hours I worked at TV-am, and the daytime sleeping I did at weekends to recover. After I resigned in August 1987, following a spat about resources for the programme, I had to concentrate on getting experience in the air. Neil worked on his own, and there were no problems in his area of expertise during the Dalgety Flight, which was just as well, considering what happened elsewhere.

At Dalgety, Tony Spalding wanted a professional public relations firm to handle the media throughout the flight. He put the word around three top agencies, who submitted their proposals for handling coverage. Representatives from all three agencies made a pitch for the business, but one – Shandwick – stood out well above the others. Their proposal had been written by a slim, intense, would-be pirate figure called Simon Newlyn, who had researched the flight almost as much as I had, and saw some wonderful ways of attracting publicity. He had handled a stunt for the Dangerous Sports Club when they 'walked' a large plastic ball down the Thames. An account of the event by the Club's founder, David Kirke, endeared Simon to me.

The link between Dalgety and Shandwick was provided by a girl called Patti Hewstone, who lived in our house in Bethnal Green and was involved in the Dalgety Flight early on. She and Neil would be my points of contact in London when the flight began.

Patti took her job very seriously. There was a time when we believed that if I carried cameras on the flight, I would run the risk of imprisonment. Patti, newly appointed, gave me a public wigging on the subject, saying I could not run this sort of risk and she was warning me on behalf of Dalgety that a dim view would be taken. Six weeks later, when we had fixed target newspapers for our photographs, Patti gave me another public telling off, saying quite the opposite, that a dim view would be taken if I did *not* carry cameras. In the event, I did carry cameras. I had always intended to anyway, having failed to get many photographs of the journey by Austin 7 across Africa twenty years earlier. I was not going to make that mistake again.

It was Patti who conjured up the embassy letters from the countries through which I would be passing, which were to be so helpful during the flight. And it was also Patti who decided that it would be a good thing if I left a week before the anniversary of Ross

Smith's arrival in Australia – 2 December instead of 10 December – just in case anything went wrong.

My flying training, from the beginning of September to the day I left in December, was characterised by purple patches. I put in a hundred hours in the Dalgety Flyer, many of which I hope never to have to repeat again.

One experience I remember as The Four Frights, when Peter Davies and I set out to fly to the Orkneys in preparation for an assault on the World Distance Record for microlights, which then stood at less than 500 miles. We left Coventry on 14 September in westerly winds forecast to climb to 50 mph. Peter was the leader and navigator in one aircraft, while I flew formation with him in the Flyer, not at all confident of my flying skills.

The first fright occurred as we flew over Morecambe Bay and entered the Lake District. We were thrashed around, hacking over Coniston Water and up past Keswick.

'Just around this ridge,' Peter radioed, 'and we can turn downwind and make it to Carlisle Airport, where we'll stay the night.'

As we flew around the corner, my canopy covered in raindrops and visibility getting poorer, the engine died. It did not go completely but all power was lost. Nervous about losing my engine, I sent out a Mayday (from the French 'M'aidez') a distress signal about which I later felt deeply embarrassed. Then the engine came back and I followed Peter, full of fear and sweat, over the countryside towards Carlisle. The engine died again, and again came back, but when it died a third time it stayed dead. In the silence and the rushing wind, I was looking around frantically for somewhere to land in the gloom and rain, when I heard a voice in my ear:

'There's an aircraft crossing the threshold of our aerodrome!' It was the Carlisle controller.

Just to the left of vision below me was a runway. I approached it downwind, wallowing and stalling. Realising I would crash if I continued like this, I stood the aircraft on its wing like a hang-glider and turned into wind to land safely on the grass, but my heart was thumping and I wondered, is anything worth this? Later I discovered that small plastic particles in the new sixteen-gallon tank had collected in the fuel filter and blocked it.

The second fright occurred the following day when, making our way north of Glasgow, we came to the western Highlands. There was cloud all around, obscuring the mountain peaks and drifting into the valleys. Peter chose to head in between two mountains and descended into the gloom. With my heart thumping wildly, I followed him. It started to rain, and I found I could see very little because the windscreen had misted up. We were in a valley surrounded by mountains, and only just below cloud.

'If I lose you, Peter,' I quavered on the radio, 'I am a dead man.'

'Follow grandad,' he replied laconically. 'I am turning slowly left. I think there is a way through there.'

Blind, frightened and sweating, I turned left with him and slowly conditions began to improve. Soon I could see the valley floor again and then the surrounding mountains, and my fluttering heart began to calm down.

The third fright happened during the record attempt itself. It was the day after my forty-fifth birthday, which Peter, an Orcadian friend called Stanley Pottinger, and I, had celebrated too well. We had been told that the weather on 18 September would rule out a record attempt, with winds strong enough to blow us over, but on the day itself the forecaster changed his mind and said we should go as the weather would only get worse. Because of the muddle, we didn't leave until late in the morning.

Conditions were so rough on the airfield that we had to be walked down the runway, a fireman at each wing tip to stop us from being blown over. In a strong westerly wind we crabbed southward, thirty miles to the mainland, and another fifty miles over the sea to Lossiemouth. We had no dinghies, no life jackets, and our hearts were ready to jump out of our mouths. I spent much of the time watching an oil rig and wondering how close to it I could ditch if the engine failed.

The flight over Scotland and northern England was smooth and uneventful after Lossiemouth, but we had no chance of making it to Portsmouth, our goal for the record and 558 miles away. The furthest we could get was Liverpool, and the third fright began while we were still in the air as the sun went down. In aviation, night officially begins thirty minutes after sundown. At Liverpool that day sundown was 7.33, but we flew over the darkened city at 7.50, barely able to see each other, and looking for the city's airport. Peter radioed that it was on my right and then disappeared in the darkness.

How can I describe rushing through the night air at 70 mph, a thousand feet over a great city, with no lights and having lost my guide?

The local air-traffic controllers were not happy when I said I could no longer see Peter, but then he heard me on the radio and turned in the gloom. I vaguely saw him again but then he was lost once more. This time, I decided I was not telling anybody and I flew on, frantically looking for a runway. A long minute later I found it and landed in the dark, covered in sweat.

The fourth fright happened the following day as we headed back to Peter's home base of Coventry. A weather front moved north, bringing in low cloud, mist and heavy rain. Both Peter and I had been tired and irritated at flying for eight hours the previous day and failing to get a record, and we had neglected to recharge our radios. He took me over the M6 and east to a railway line and then south following a radio beacon to Coventry. Rain covered the outside of my canopy, and fear made me sweat and mist up the inside. Then, after two hours of sustained terror, I lost sight of Peter in a wisp of cloud.

In a garbled way I got a message through to him. He told me to land wherever I could. Through the mist and cloud below me I saw a football field and instantly decided I was going to land there. My hang-gliding past took over and I spiralled out of the sky, watching the field, and hung around downwind of it to lose height. When I turned on to a final approach, I was set up so that if I overshot the football pitch, I would still have the cricket pitch behind to land on. In fact my wheels touched down at the wicket and the tracks went for seventy-five paces in the wet grass to the boundary. Both my feet had been hard on the brakes.

My landing field was a miner's Social Club at Dordon, just north of Coventry. It was the most important landing I ever did in the

Flyer, because it removed the fear of landing out. The experience that day was repeated more than half a dozen times on the Australian flight itself, but never again in the same terror-stricken way.

The four frights were a great shock. Until then I had lived with an illusion about my flying skills. The frights killed all pretence. I spent the weekend after in a miserable funk, trying to work out how quickly I could acquire the flying skills that Peter Davies had. After a lot of thought, and a pep talk from my friend Judy Leden, I was able to see that my real problem was navigation. Not knowing where you are in the air is fatal. As soon as I knew where I was, a lot of the fear went away. I toyed with the idea of asking Peter to come with me to Australia, but that would not have worked. If I lost him somewhere, I would still need the skills to go on with the flight. I had to fly alone.

That weekend I stopped looking for a new job, following my departure from TV-am. If I was going to fly to Australia, I needed all the practice I could get. This also meant turning down an £800-a-day offer from a London stockbrokers to teach their analysts how to appear on television. It was either earning money, or getting killed in early December.

Peter Davies and I had another attempt at the World Distance Record two weeks later, flying from Southampton to the Orkneys. The 558-mile flight took seven and a half hours and was sixty miles longer than the official record. It was an uneventful flight, just long and claustrophobic. But months later we learned that an American had flown eighty miles further than we had only four days before our flight. We could only claim a British and European record.

The record attempts taught me the lesson that I hated flying with other aircraft because I was so nervous about midair collisions. From then on, I flew alone, the way I would have to fly to Australia.

It was not long after Peter and I got the distance record that Eve Jackson returned from Australia. Neil and I went to meet her at her home in Oxfordshire. She is a laconic, almost masculine woman of thirty, offhand about her experiences, but quite willing to share her knowledge. She has a distinct, gritty charm that is all her own. The national media had acknowledged her flight, but not given her the sort of status I thought it deserved, and that other women aviators get as their due. But the aviation world showered her with honours; a Royal Aeroclub Gold Medal; the Sword of Honour from the Guild of Master Pilots and Navigators; and the Hargreaves Trophy, which came with a substantial cash prize which wiped out many of her debts.

The route I planned through Europe was different to Eve's, but from the Middle East onwards, I would overlap her flight. She gave me invaluable hints on where to land, what the capability of the Shadow was, how far I could fly in a day. Neil was more reassured than I was, for although I still had to make the flight – and much faster than the fifteen months she had taken – Neil really wanted to know that all the arrangements he was making were the right ones.

Eve had little experience of publicity, and publicity is what sponsors pay for. She paid for most of her flight out of her own resources, and was fairly scornful of some of the antics needed to generate publicity. Having been a journalist for twenty years, I knew what my colleagues wanted and, as far as possible, gave it to them. Months later, I was to discover that the British microlighting community took the same dim view of this sort of thing as Eve did. On the other hand, it costs a great deal of money to make the flights I want to make, and publicity is a small enough prize to pay to please a sponsor. My sponsor Dalgety and I were locked into an amazing adventure together, and I was happier to have them on my side than the British microlighting community.

Meanwhile, I had to plug away at my flying until it improved. Aside from the record attempts, there were three other flights that autumn, each important for what I learned from them, which was enough for me to be able to set off from London on 2 December with the bare minimum of knowledge necessary to get to Australia.

In the week of the terrible October storm in 1987, I flew from Bristol to the Shadow factory at Leiston in Suffolk so that Mike could be taught how to do a fifty-hour engine service. The flight was characterised by the depressing fact that I couldn't go thirty miles without losing myself, even though I made it in the end. On the way back, I started serious navigation by picking out radio beacons with my VOR, and discovered, to my surprise, how easy they were to use. The last forty miles into Bristol were completed at about 300 feet, in drizzly rain and low cloud, following a canal from Newbury and then jumping to Bristol's radio beacon.

The following Monday – 19 October, the day of the great Stock Market crash – I set off to see my mother in Dublin, my navigation skills only slightly better. Wales was covered by floods, making map reading difficult, so I followed the coastline to Anglesey, where I stayed the night because the Irish Sea was covered in clouds, and my altimeter had stopped working. After a one-day visit to Dublin, I flew back to England, flying for fifty miles at only 700 feet above the Irish Sea and again relying on radio beacons.

Both these flights were done solo, without Peter Davies as guide, and they gave me the confidence I really needed. They also helped convince Neil Hardiman that I could fly an aircraft and navigate as well. But they were still only a prelude to my first (and last) test as an aviator before setting off for Australia.

On 5 November, I set off from Stapleford airfield, just north of London, to fly to Pisa. In the event, I was only about to fly as far as Genoa, but the lessons I learned made all the difference.

Flying from Rheims to Lyons, for example, there was a layer of cloud and mist up to 2,000 feet, and the only way to fly was above it. There, the air was clear and without turbulence, but there were no landmarks by which to navigate. I was left with the choice of jumping from one radio beacon to another, from Rheims, to Troyes, to Dijon and then Lyons, all the time praying my engine would not fail and force me to land in the fog below. But once that was done, a taboo was broken, and I became used to flying without always knowing what was beneath me. I cannot swear I was legal at all times, though. (The law for pilots flying to Visual Flight Rules – that is, microlight pilots and in conventional aviation, relative novices – requires them to be in sight of the ground at all times.)

Another lesson was learned crossing the Alps from Lyons to Nice. Mountain flying can be tricky, and in a microlight, with all the fears about the reliability of a two-stroke engine, not something to contemplate with equanimity. But if I could cross the Alps from Montelimar straight through to Nice, I would cut ninety miles off my journey to Australia, and avoid all the military bases near

Marseilles and Toulon. Again, it was a bottle job, winding myself up to keep heading southeast into the mountains, and constantly scanning the ground for a landing spot. But once done, it was never as frightening again.

Genoa was a nightmare, but not because of the flying. This was a dress rehearsal for the big flight, and Mike Atkinson was shadowing me by scheduled services. He was at Genoa airport to meet me on Sunday at noon. It took twenty-four hours to refuel and get away! Italy had not, and maybe still has not, come to terms with micro-lights, and the bureaucrats descended on me with glee. In all, twenty-six separate pieces of paper had to be signed to release me to fly again. I was required to fly directly out of the country, and it took all Neil's charm and skill in London to get a reassurance that it would not happen on the big flight.

One result, though, was to drive me down the coast of Italy, westward to Nice, and then over the Alps again to the Rhône Valley. Because of the weather forecast of a ceiling of 8,000 feet to the clouds, I went into cloud over the mountains, still climbing in the belief that I would pop out of the top. This did not happen, and for two and a half hours I followed a series of radio beacons across the Alps, totally enveloped by cloud, and without blind-flying instruments. In all my life, even including the Four Frights, I do not believe I have had such a sustained experience of terror.

You cannot see. You do not know if you are the right way up, or upside down. The compass starts spinning, so you try to stop it by putting on opposite rudder. It stops and then spins the other way. You look at your air speed and find you are close to VNE – Velocity Never Exceed! – so you pull back on the stick and the aircraft slows down. But the compass spins again and the aircraft feels as though it is rearing up. Which way is the right way? There is no firm indication, and it goes on for hours.

My life was saved by the VORs, one cradled in my arms, indicating the right course to follow, the other, which normally worked as a radio, tuned into an airfield in the north of the Rhône Valley. So long as I stayed at the ceiling for the aircraft – 10,200 feet – and not too far north, where there were big mountains, I would be fine. Towards the end of the day, I had a period on the very edge of panic, but I knew no one could help me, and so I remained in control.

In fact, it was an airfield at Valence, twenty miles north of my destination of Montelimar, which enabled me to find out where I was. I knew I was following a radio beacon into Montelimar, but not how far away I was. By taking a bearing on Valence off to my right, and drawing both bearings on my map, I knew I was at the point where they crossed. I was less than honest with the controller when I said I was 'having difficulty maintaining Visual Flight Rules'.

'Maintain VFR,' he intoned sternly, 'or make a 180-degree turn and go back where you came from.'

The thought of going back over the mountains in the conditions in which I was flying, made me laugh wildly. The controller confirmed my exact position, clear of mountains and over the Rhône Valley, and I gingerly descended, desperately searching for a view of the ground. When I found the ground, I discovered that I had been spiralling steeply, and it took a while to orientate myself. I then picked my way, 400 feet above the valley floor, to the river, found the little airfield at Montelimar, and landed in lashing rain.

The club's chief flying instructor, a man called Bernard, gave me hangar space for the night, and a lift into town. 'Only an Englishman would fly across the Alps in this weather,' he said.

That night, in an excellent restaurant, with a good meal and a bottle of Château Margaux inside me, I felt the hypnotic detachment that comes from being close to dying. Inside myself, I now felt that I would be able to find the go-for-it spirit I needed to make the Australia flight. It isn't always a sensible feeling, nor a rational one, but I was sure that other pilots before me had been through the same experience and had felt better for it. There were some, of course, who had not survived the experience, but that was how the dice fell.

What else had I learned?

There is a device called a transponder which identifies aircraft on radar for air-traffic controllers. If I had one of these, it could calm their fears about my little aircraft. The Alps experience made me long for blind-flying instruments, but the cockpit was crowded already, and there was little room to add more. I managed to squeeze in a turn-and-bank indicator.

The problems at Genoa also convinced Mike and I to carry a supply of foreign currency for every country we were passing through, as it was often difficult to find moneychangers.

The natural state of mind for a pilot on a flight like mine, according to Francis Chichester, is apprehension. Rereading his book, *The Lonely Sea and the Sky*, I felt a kinship with him across the fifty-seven years separating my flight to Australia from his. It was a comfort to know that he had been frightened too, and had come through. The ghosts of the early aviators become much closer when you go through something akin to their experiences. However, Ross Smith remained the person I felt closest to of all.

Chapter Four
1919: The Greatest Air Race

The more I learned about Ross Smith and the seventeen other men who took part in the event which came to be known as the Greatest Air Race, the more I felt I should link my flight to theirs. No one had any standard by which to judge what I was setting out to do, or what Eve Jackson had done, and the only real yardstick was that race. The 1919 competitors had flown in state-of-the-art aircraft, right at the edge of, and often over, the limits. I would be doing the same in 1987 with a microlight, and the odds were against me beating them.

The original race was started on a whim of Australia's prime minister at the time, Billy Hughes. Hughes was a small, fiery man of Welsh extraction who happened to be in Europe for the great conference of world leaders at Versailles. He saw that aviation was the coming thing, and wanted to encourage Australians to fly.

On his own initiative, but without checking with either his cabinet or the increasingly independent Australian parliament, Hughes offered a £10,000 cash prize from the public purse for the first Australian to fly from England to Australia in thirty days, in a British-built aircraft. There was a big political row about his arbitrary decision, but he had his way.

Eighteen men set off in seven aircraft. Six of them made it to Australia after many adventures. Eight men crashed en route, and though not seriously injured, were unable to continue their flights. Four were killed.

DOUGLAS AND ROSS

Two who died were Captain Roger Douglas, from Charters Towers in Queensland, and Lieutenant Leslie Ross, from Moruya in New

South Wales. They had chosen an Alliance Endeavour for the event, a single-engined machine with enclosed cabin space for both men, specially designed for long-distance flying. It had upholstered seats, cupboards containing quinine for malaria, flasks of tea and coffee, water, earplugs, and a big supply of chewing gum (all the crews were sponsored by Wrigley's).

In a test flight in early November 1919, prior to departure, the Alliance was damaged on landing, but Douglas and Ross were under pressure to set off quickly for Australia because the Smith Brothers had already left. Douglas and Ross prepared to go a day later. Douglas told the press that because of the Alliance's greater speed, he expected to overtake the Smiths the following day. On 13 November, after hours of delay caused by bad weather, they took off from Hounslow at 11.30 am.

They did not survive for long. Douglas made only one entry in his logbook, recording a height of 1,200 feet. Six minutes into the flight, eyewitnesses in Surbiton saw the Alliance emerge from clouds at between 500 and 1,000 feet, go into a spin, straighten out, then spin again and crash into an apple orchard near the cemetery. The 515 gallons of petrol they were carrying saturated the area, but there was no fire. Ross was killed instantly; Douglas died a few minutes later.

The commission of enquiry later blamed the crash on pilot error, for spinning the aircraft at a low altitude which didn't allow enough room to regain control. The enquiry also condemned the practice of enclosing the pilot's cockpit with windows, claiming it reduced vision!

Douglas's strong-minded girlfriend, Mabel Woolley, did not accept the enquiry's findings. She interrupted the coroner a number of times during the inquest. Later she told reporters she had witnessed the bad landing which had occurred earlier in November and which she blamed for the crash, saying that her fiancé had lost confidence and was uneasy about the aircraft.

If she is alive now, she must be nearly ninety years of age. I wish I had found the time before setting off on my own flight to see if I could find her. I regret I never did.

HOWELL AND FRASER

Two others who were killed in the 1919 race were Captain Cedric Howell, one of the greatest of Australia's fighter pilots, and Lieutenant George Fraser, from Coburg, Victoria. Howell, who came from Adelaide, had been highly decorated in the War and had flown the legendary Sopwith Camel to such effect that he had shot down thirty-two German aircraft. Fraser was an air mechanic, and at forty, the oldest competitor in the race (that is, five years younger than I was when I set off).

Flying a single-engined Martinsyde A1, they took off on 4 December, as Ross and Keith Smith were nearing the end of their journey. The Martinsyde was well-equipped, with a range of 1,200 miles. I tried to remember on my own flight to use the quote attributed to Howell – 'ta ta, chaps, we're off' – but it meant nothing to anybody else.

They crossed Europe in four days in dreadful weather, faster than any other competitor. On 9 December, they set off from Taranto in Italy to fly to Athens. Eight hours later, they crashed into the sea just before nightfall, only a hundred miles from their take-off point. Local peasants said they had heard cries for help over the water, but the sea had been too rough to go out. The aircraft was located the following day in twelve feet of water, and the log recovered. Captain Howell's body was washed ashore and later recovered from its Corfu grave to be buried in Australia with full military honours. Lieutenant Fraser was never found.

WILKINS, RENDLE, WILLIAMS AND POTTS

The first airmen to drop out of the race were the four in the Blackburn Kangaroo, known as the 'bomber with a pouch'. The navigator was Captain Hubert Wilkins, of Mount Bryan East in South Australia, later knighted for his aviation exploits in the Arctic. The two pilots were Lieutenant Valdamar Rendle, from Brisbane in Queensland, and Lieutenant Reg Williams, from Wodonga, Victoria. Their mechanic was the exotically named Garnsey H. M. St Clair Potts, from Euroa in Victoria.

The Kangaroo struggled across Europe in bad weather, and on 8 December they left Crete to fly across the Mediterranean to Cairo. Forty miles out to sea, an oil leak developed. Rendle skilfully returned the aircraft to Crete on one engine, but on landing they crashed into a wall protecting a mental hospital. No one was injured, but the aircraft was damaged. The crew were waiting for spare parts when they heard that Ross Smith had made it to Darwin. They lost heart and returned to England by ship.

POULET AND BENOIST

Two Frenchmen, who didn't see why the flight had to be an Australian monopoly, set out before anyone else on 14 October, a month before Ross Smith. Etienne Poulet, the pilot, wanted to commemorate his great friend, Jules Vedrines, a French ace killed on an attempted flight to Australia in April 1919. 'I was Vedrines' friend,' said Poulet. 'He had planned to make the flight. Death prevented Vedrines. I replace him. Voila tout!' He was accompanied by an old friend, mechanic Jean Benoist.

They chose a Caudron C4 biplane, fitted with two 80 hp rotary engines. Their aircraft had a top speed of 94 mph, and cruised at 70 mph, about the same speed as the Dalgety Flyer. As a result, they made slow progress in bad weather. Their route took them through Rome, Albania, Greece, Turkey and Syria, and what was then Mesopotamia and Persia (now Iraq and Iran). They had mechanical problems in Beluchistan, and were plagued by tribesmen who thought they were devils and threw flaming torches at them while they repaired their aircraft. Having flown together with Ross Smith from Akyab to Rangoon, they finally abandoned the flight on 9 December, in Moulmein in Burma, suffering from a broken propeller and a cracked piston.

MATTHEWS AND KAY

Captain George Matthews from South Australia and Sergeant Thomas Kay from Spring Mount, Victoria, nearly made it. They flew a Sopwith Wallaby, a single-engined biplane which had a cruising speed of 107 mph, fast for its day and much faster than the Dalgety Flyer. (When I left London sixty-eight years later, the man who founded the Sopwith Company, Tommy Sopwith, was still alive, due to celebrate his 100th birthday.)

Matthews and Kay left England on 21 October, but were held up by fog in France, and captured in war-torn Bulgaria to be imprisoned as alleged Bolsheviks. They escaped only when their guards were drunk. In Turkey they were stuck in a quagmire, and repaired a leaking water jacket with that valuable standby, hardened chewing gum. They crossed Syria, Iraq and Iran with a troubled engine, damaging their aircraft once in a forced landing in a 40-mph crosswind. On 17 April 1920, trying to reach Bima and less than 2,000 miles from Darwin, they crashed in a banana plantation on the island of Bali. Kay broke his ribs, and the Wallaby was damaged beyond their ability to repair it. They took the wreckage on to Australia by ship.

PARER AND MACKINTOSH

Two pilots who did make it, although they took more than three times as long as I did, were Ray Parer and John Mackintosh. They were the Butch Cassidy and Sundance Kid of aviation, classic examples of the hooligan element inside pilots. Parer came from Melbourne in Victoria, earning his wings in World War I, but had been banned from combat flying because of an alleged weak heart. By the time the War ended, Mackintosh had made just one flight in his pilot training. He learned how to fly on the journey.

Parer and Mackintosh set off on 8 January 1920. Landing in Paris to repair a wheel, they passed some time almost living in the Folies Bergères. Parer later suggested that all the girls had wanted was someone lively to talk to, an extremely unlikely excuse for delaying the flight.

They suffered an engine fire near Pisa, and were bailed out of their high-living spree in Rome by their sponsor, a whiskey distiller called Peter Dawson. On 2 February 1920 they set off for Naples, via Mount Vesuvius in order to take a photograph. As they flew over the smoking crater there was a terrific bang, the engine cut, and they plummeted downwards. Parer ripped skin off the palms of both hands holding himself in the cockpit before the engine started again and they escaped.

Having spluttered all the way across the Mediterranean, they were flying north to Mesopotamia, when they were forced to land in the desert, by the light of the moon. They kept themselves warm in the bitter cold by burning every bush within reach. When it rained they went to sleep in the open cockpits. The following morning they woke to find an Arab standing by the wing. Parer drew some maps in the sand and asked the Arab where they were. They worked out they were only thirty minutes flying from Baghdad.

More Arabs clustered around, and Mackintosh tried to 'impress' them to go away by hurling a can in the air and shooting holes in it with his revolver. The noise doubled the number of spectators. Mackintosh then took a couple of grenades out of the cockpit and beckoned the Arabs to follow him. He led them to a nearby dune, threw the grenades, and he and Parer dropped to the ground. The Arabs were thrown off their feet, and were less than amused. Both pilots legged it for their aircraft, swung the propeller, and got into the air ahead of an angry mob, which Mackintosh did nothing to placate by 'indicating to them an Australian farewell in no uncertain manner'.

Mackintosh continued his diplomatic mission through Persia, delighting in flying low over villages and firing a Very light pistol in red, yellow and green colours. In 1920, just the sight of an aeroplane was enough to terrify remote villages; the lights added an extra dimension. Had they been forced to land, it is doubtful if they would have survived the experience.

In Rangoon a local Chinese millionaire proposed marriage between two of his pretty daughters and Parer and Mackintosh, in an effort to gain entry into the snobbish British clubs in the City. (How those two particular Australians would have been able to help I have never understood.) Ray Parer is said to have declined ('time is too short for a serious romance'), and persuaded Mackintosh to join him in politely refusing the offer.

After crashing and wiping out their undercarriage in Burma, and suffering an engine-seizure over Penang, they crashed again in Surabaya and broke the undercarriage a second time. By this time they were both physically exhausted. They had had little sleep, poor meals, and were depressed and nervous in the tropical weather. Despite this, they made a successful jump to Bima and then across to Timor, the last island before Australia. They spent a day there constructing a raft as a life-saver if they did not make it across 550 miles of the shark-infested Timor Sea. The raft was made from two tyre inner tubes (inflated), two bamboo poles, and wire netting to serve as a 'protection' against sharks. They tied it to the wing and wondered if the aircraft would fly.

On 2 August 1920, the DH9, heavily loaded, was lined up for takeoff. Parer cleared a spluttering engine by removing a piece of perished rubber from the carburettor. They barely managed to clear the trees at the end of the runway, and climbed painfully to their ceiling of 1,000 feet. They had fuel for seven and a half hours flying. After six hours Parer was worried, feeling he should have sighted land long ago. He and Mackintosh were continually seeing mirages, alternatively land or steamships, which vanished when they rubbed their eyes. Then they saw Bathurst Island, and flew on to Darwin. They made a perfect landing and as they rolled to a halt on the runway the engine stopped – out of fuel.

They had been 206 days on their odyssey, and were awarded Air Force Crosses. The more the Australian public heard about the antics the two airmen had got up to, the more they loved them (as I do). My flight to Australia in the Dalgety Flyer was compared to that of Parer and Mackintosh by the curator of the Powerhouse Museum in Sydney, Ian Debenham (though I did not spend any time at all at the Folies Bergères).

John Mackintosh was killed in 1921 when he crashed an aeroplane carrying two passengers. It was said that one of the passengers had been drunk, and had gone berserk and attacked Mackintosh – 'as often happened' in those days.

Ray Parer took part in the 1934 England–Australia air race, and reached Darwin again after a similar series of adventures. He died in a hospital bed at the age of seventy-three in 1967 (when I was twenty-five).

ROSS AND KEITH SMITH, SHIERS AND BENNETT

The 1919 race was won by four men in a Vickers Vimy bomber, and the route they took later became the classic air route from England to Australia. They were Ross Smith and his brother Keith, Jim Bennett and Wally Shiers. It was their ghosts I was chasing in the Dalgety Flyer. But it was Ross Smith who dominated my flight, just as he came to dominate the 1919 race.

Ross Smith was born in Semaphore, South Australia, in 1892, two years after his brother Keith. In 1915, Ross was sent to Gallipoli, where Australia came face to face with modern warfare, and eight thousand young Australians died in the experience. He was there four and a half months, and wrote a graphic private account of his experiences, as an invalid on the way to England. In 1916, he was commissioned and transferred to a machine-gun section with the Australian Light Horse in Egypt. Later that year he transferred to the Australian Flying Corps, first as an observer, later as a pilot, and was promoted to captain. He became personal pilot to Lawrence of Arabia. By the end of the war he had been awarded two Military Crosses and three Distinguished Flying Crosses. If it is all *Boy's Own* stuff – which it is – Ross Smith had lived a very full life by the time he was twenty-six. He had also been very lucky.

His brother Keith, navigator on the Australia flight, had been a flying instructor in the war after unsuccessfully applying to join the Australian Army and paying his own passage to England in order to enlist. The other two crew members were Sergeant Jim Bennett, from St Kilda in Melbourne, and Sergeant Wally Shiers, from Stepney, South Australia. They were both mechanics and had accompanied Ross Smith on an aerial survey he made prior to the Australia flight.

They were backed by the Vickers Aircraft Company, which had provided Alcock and Brown with the aircraft that had been the first to cross the Atlantic earlier in 1919. The Vimy was a twin-engined biplane, huge by the standards of the day, and fitted with Rolls-Royce Eagle Mark 8 engines. There were only four of these engines in existence, and one of those installed in Ross's aircraft had been held as a spare for the Atlantic flight. The Vimy could cruise at 90 mph (20 mph faster than the Dalgety Flyer), with a maximum speed of 110 mph. It carried 516 gallons of petrol, and could stay in the air more than fourteen hours. (The Dalgety Flyer carried twenty-eight gallons, and could stay in the air nine hours.)

Ross Smith's approach to the flight was professional. He made his crew do physical exercises daily to be fit for the ordeal. Everywhere in the aircraft, spares were stowed, including bully beef, Army dog biscuits (about the size of a bathroom tile and, it was said, almost as hard), Bourneville chocolate, Bovril, and Wrigley's chewing gum. They were obsessed with cutting weight, and resolved to leave England with only the clothes they stood up in, plus shaving gear and a toothbrush. Their registration mark was G-EAOU – 'God 'Elp All Of Us'.

They left on 12 November from Hounslow. The directors of Vickers turned up, and they and the crew were photographed standing in front of the aircraft before departure. I saw that photograph just before I left, blown up giant size on the BBC *Blue Peter* programme. It was like any other official photograph, self-conscious and posed. But Ross Smith is on his own in the middle of the loose group, small, tough, almost arrogant. I thought that the others were lucky to have him.

Despite appalling weather, they took off just after nine o'clock in the morning, carrying away the equipment of a persistent press photographer who stood at the end of the runway. Skies were clear over the Channel, but they ran into cloud over France and climbed to 9,000 feet to try and see where they were going. The ground was not visible, and they flew dead reckoning above the cloud. It was cold and their sandwiches froze solid. After hours of blind flying,

Ross wrote in his diary: 'This sort of flying is a rotten game. The cold is hell, and I am silly for ever having embarked on the flight.' He later said that this was the most difficult stage of the whole flight, but they landed safely in Lyons that night.

The next day they skirted the Alps and reached Pisa in Italy, where they were bogged down all the following day. It rained so heavily that the airfield was flooded. They were only able to get off on 15 December because Bennett sat on the tail to keep the nose from dipping into the mud, and then scrambled on board as the Vimy gathered speed, helped by a rope around his waist held by Shiers. That day they had the first of two emergency landings to repair an oil gauge. Landings out were much more common in those days, and caused far less comment than they do today. They flew on to Rome, averaging only 50 mph in a strong headwind.

The flight through to Taranto was the roughest of the trip, and they flew on to Crete in low cloud and rain. For most of the route they followed, the Smiths landed at RAF camps. These were the days of the British Mandate, one of the later phases of Empire building, and after World War One there were British bases everywhere. This made the politics of the flight, by contrast with today, very easy indeed.

On 18 November, the seventh day out of London, in more low cloud and rain, they set off across the Cretan mountains and over the Mediterranean to Africa. They made landfall at Mersa Matruh and flew directly to Cairo. It was here the famous chewing gum incident occurred, when Shiers discovered a broken manifold pipe and no replacement could be found for two weeks. The flight could have ended there as far as the thirty-day limit went, but Shiers set the whole crew to chewing gum. He pasted the gum around the cracked pipe and wrapped tape and glue over it. Ross test-flew the repair and found it worked. Wrigley's must have been pleased with the publicity. It was the sort of repair of which my engineer, Mike Atkinson, would have been proud.

Ross was worried about the delays to his flight, especially at Pisa, and wanted to catch Poulet and Benoist in India. Instead of resting as planned in Cairo on 19 November, he flew on to Damascus, crossing battlefields where he had fought as a machine gunner, and through a thunderstorm that soaked them to the skin. On the following morning they found the Vimy, which weighed six and a half tons, sinking in the mud, and only just got away from Damascus. Heading for Baghdad, they landed shortly before dark at an Indian cavalry camp at Ramadie. The Indian troopers proved invaluable: fifty of them held the Vimy down half the night when a storm blew up. It was noon before the broken cables and damage were repaired.

When they reached Karachi, they were delighted to find that the Frenchmen were in Delhi, only one stage ahead, but in Delhi on 25 November, they found Poulet and Benoist had left and were struggling through to Calcutta. By this time, Ross knew he could catch them whenever he wanted, and coolly called another rest day. Sixteen days after leaving London they arrived at Allahabad, finding that Poulet had been there and gone, and Ross was still looking for the Frenchmen when he set off for Calcutta on 28 November. When he got there he found a huge crowd waiting at the only possible landing field, the racecourse. It was a tight landing, and luckily no racing was in progress. Poulet had left that morning.

The 29th November 1919 was a Saturday and there was racing at Rangoon, which could not possibly be cancelled to allow one of the 'Flying Gharries' to land. So Ross Smith was forced to go from Calcutta to Rangoon in two stages, via Akyab in Burma. He nearly didn't make it. The aircraft was ten feet off the ground at Calcutta when a hawk flew into the port propeller. The Vimy shuddered, but though the big bird ended up as so much meat and feathers, the propeller was not shattered and the aircraft continued to fly. One of the hawk's wings remained jammed in the bracing wires through to Burma.

At Akyab, on the coast of Burma, the Australians at last caught up with Poulet and Benoist. The six of them had a party, discussing each other's flight, and resolved to fly on for a while together. Ross must have known the Frenchmen could not stay with him for long. On 30 November, the Caudron left an hour ahead of Ross (the Australians were suffering from the previous night's party, and had to catch up with maintenance) but Ross's much faster machine was still the first to reach Rangoon. It was also the first ever aeroplane to land there. Poulet took two hours longer, but made it in time to have dinner with the governor, Sir Reginald Craddock.

Both Poulet and Ross Smith were nervous about the flight over the Thai mountains to Bangkok, covering terrain as inhospitable as any in the world. They resolved to fly together again. Both crews were up just before daybreak, but the Frenchmen had trouble starting one engine. As it was hot and very humid, the Australians wanted to get into the air, so Ross took off early. Again, he nearly did not make it.

There were three factors working against an easy takeoff: the small racecourse, the huge size of the Vimy, and the heavy load of fuel. Ross felt he had just enough speed to clear the fence at the far end, but from the ground Poulet thought the Vimy was going to hit a tree. The aircraft wheels just brushed through the branches, however, and flew on. One foot lower, said Poulet to those watching, and it would have crashed.

The Thai mountain range, east of Moulmein, was covered in cloud. Ross believed the mountains to be 7,000 feet high, and took a chance and climbed the Vimy to its ceiling, 11,000 feet. They were fighting a 20-mph headwind and were soon enveloped by cloud. Visibility was so bad at times that Shiers and Bennett in the back cockpit could not see the Smith brothers in the front. They had little confidence in their maps. Their plan was to fly at 11,000 feet until they estimated they were through the mountains, and then descend through cloud to find out if they were right. If they were wrong it would all be over very quickly.

They flew blind for an hour before descending. What a feeling of profound relief it must have been (I came to know it so well myself later) when they broke through cloud at 4,000 feet, and found themselves in the valley north of Bangkok. They landed there without further incident. (This was the day that put paid to Poulet and Benoist's chances.)

On 2 December, Ross left Bangkok for Singora, following the east coast of Malaysia. The weather was fine at first, but later they ran into a tropical rainstorm. The rain lashed against their faces and made it impossible to wear goggles. Ross and Keith took turns to fly.

One poked his head up and held the wheel for as long as he could endure the tearing rain, normally about five minutes, then the other took over. They flew in this way for three hours.

They left the storm eighty miles from Singora, but when they reached their 'landing field' found that whoever had constructed it had no idea what an aircraft required. Trees had been cut down, but stumps were left, some as high as eighteen inches. They had not enough fuel to go on to Singapore, so Ross chose a narrow track to land on in a crosswind, and put the Vimy down safely, breaking only the tailskid.

Instead of the 500 gallons of fuel they were expecting to buy in Singora, there was only 500 litres. Telegrams were sent for extra fuel to be dispatched by rail. There was a tropical rainstorm overnight, ten inches of rain fell, and the four weary Australians had to hang on to the Vimy to stop it being blown away.

Next day Ross and his bedraggled crew and hundreds of Malays began uprooting trees to make a decent runway, which they completed by noon. The tailskid was repaired. Now all they needed was fuel, which arrived late, and with rain still falling it was considered unsafe to put it in the aircraft. Refuelling was normally done by Keith handing Ross a four-gallon can, and Ross pouring it slowly through chamois leather into the tanks.

On 4 December, Ross spent his twenty-seventh birthday pouring fifty cans of petrol into the Vimy. Then he told his crew to get on board and they lined up for takeoff. There were rainshowers, which left deep puddles down the 'runway'. Fifty yards into the takeoff run the Vimy hit a puddle and lost momentum. The aircraft went through three more puddles, and with seventy yards left had still not reached flying speed. But Ross kept the throttle open and the aircraft staggered off the ground, brushed through the branches of trees, and flew on.

They went via Kuala Lumpur down to Singapore, and landed on yet another racecourse, the smallest they had encountered so far. Jim Bennett did his tail-balancing act once more, this time hanging on to the plane to slow it down before it hit the fence at the far end. Singapore was another rest day, to prepare for island-hopping 2,500 miles to Darwin, and they jettisoned everything they could (mainly photographic equipment) to make it easier to get away from the tiny racecourse, which they did successfully.

They were met in Bandoeng by representatives of the Dutch Air Force. Ross was anxious to find out if his recommendations to establish airfields at Bima and Timor had been carried out. They had. The Australians, worn out from the nearly nonstop flying, set off on 7 December for Surabaya in Eastern Java. When they landed, however, the Vimy began to sink below the surface. They were bogged down, and could not get out! Thousands of Indonesians pushed and pulled the Vimy to try and free it, and it was so mauled that there were serious fears for its safety if it flew again.

By nightfall they had been trying for nine hours to free the Vimy. Morale dropped to its lowest point on the whole flight. Then Keith Smith suggested borrowing bamboo mats and making a runway of them. All night the word went out, and thousands of natives turned up with mats out of their houses. They spent the morning laying the 'runway'. At the first attempt, hundreds of mats blew away in the slipstream and the Vimy failed to get off. The mats were nailed to the ground, making a path 300 yards long. Ross had another attempt at takeoff, and shortly before noon on 8 December, pulled the aircraft into the air. They reached Bima, 350 miles away, after an uneventful flight, and landed between the two mountains that characterise that island. The next stage of the journey – from Bima to Timor – was also without incident. Ross landed at Atambua, now part of East Timor, and they spent the rest of the day preparing for what came to be called 'The White-knuckle Route', across the sea to Darwin.

On 10 December there was a dense haze covering the sea at sunrise. The four tired men were tense, but reassured themselves. 'After all,' said Ross, 'Alcock and Brown flew 2,000 miles in a Vimy, so why should we worry about 500?' But they did. It was Darwin – or the Timor Sea with all its sharks. There was a faint chance they would land by HMAS *Sydney*, a cruiser on patrol halfway across, stationed there to rescue those in the Great Race. But it was a risky flight, the more so in that winds between Timor and Australia are notoriously unpredictable and can blow through 360 degrees in one day. A flight like theirs needed luck.

They set off across the islandless sea to follow a compass course for 550 miles. On time and on course, they came across HMAS *Sydney*, and flew low over the decks while the sailors cheered. Several hours later, Ross sighted Bathurst, and they were able to see from twenty miles out the white marker on the Darwin aerodrome. It was called Fanny Bay, opposite the local prison. At 3.40 pm local time, twenty-seven days and twenty hours after leaving London, they touched down, their fuel tanks dry. 'We almost fell into Darwin,' said Wally Shiers later.

They won the £10,000 for the Darwin flight, but all their accumulated luck ran out during the journey to Sydney. They broke a propeller in the outback, and blew up an engine at Charleville in Queensland, causing a delay of six weeks. Their aircraft became known as 'The Flying Chicken Coop' from all the wire binding it together. They took ninety-six days to fly from London to Sydney, as opposed to the twenty-eight days from London to Darwin. But they were fêted wherever they went.

Ross and Keith were knighted for their exploits; Shiers and Bennett were given commissions and Air Force Crosses. Sir Keith Smith died in 1955, having received many honours, after a career working for Vickers. Wally Shiers lived until 1968, and there is a sound recording of his experiences, the transcript of which I have read, but which I would love to hear.

Ross, however, died young, as did Bennett. On 13 April 1922, not yet thirty years of age, Sir Ross Smith was due to test-fly a Vickers Viking amphibian aircraft, in which he planned to make the first round-the-world flight. His mechanic was Jim Bennett. It was foggy in London, which delayed the train carrying Sir Keith Smith to the Brooklands aerodrome where the flight was planned. Keith arrived in time to see his brother and his friend take off. The Viking climbed to 1,000 feet, went into a spin, half recovered, and then crashed. Ross was killed instantly. Bennett died of terrible injuries.

The enquiry blamed Ross for lack of experience on amphibians, and exonerated the aircraft. The other great Vimy pioneer, Sir John Alcock, was also killed test-flying a Vickers Viking.

Chapter Five
Last Days

By the beginning of December 1987, I had done all the flying training possible before leaving for Australia. If I was not experienced enough by then, I could learn on the flight itself, or suffer for it.

Meanwhile, my family prepared to do without me for at least three months, and Fiona warded off dozens of queries asking how she put up with my adventures. 'Someone asked me if I was going to sit by the fire knitting and worrying,' she told me indignantly.

She was forty-one when I set out for Australia, still slim, still able to get into the hotpants she wore twenty years ago, but with some grey in her curly black hair. She is not physically strong; when her energy runs out it does so from one minute to the next, and she has to take to her bed. But when she has it her energy is enormous. She has a very sharp intelligence and a number of skills: management, organisation, computing, and marketing. I spent a year teaching her radio journalism, which she loved so much she never even submitted any expenses. Now, however, with a full-time career in marketing, and one that challenges mine as principal breadwinner, she cannot get involved in the organisation of wheezes in the way she used to. But if she was worried by the Australia trip, she never burdened me with it.

My son Jamie was twelve when I set off on the flight. His experiences of my flying had never been fortunate. In 1977, as a small child, he had been carried to the front of the hill at Mere in Wiltshire, just as I cartwheeled my hang-glider in a spectacular-looking accident across a competition target, looking for a bull's-eye. I was not injured in the landing, but if I had succeeded in hitting the spot cleanly, I could have been British Open Champion. Jamie also saw the film of 'the fall' a year later on television. He has never really liked flying, although he comes up sometimes in my microlight because I am his dad and he thinks he should.

He is obsessive, as I am. His obsession at the time was Dungeons and Dragons, which he lived, breathed and slept. I don't think he gave a lot of thought to the Australia flight, but every now and again it impinged on his mind. Once, when he was having morning coffee with Fiona in our bedroom whilst I was away flying somewhere, he asked, 'Mum, I know this isn't going to happen, but if Dad doesn't come back, you won't take to drink, will you?'

Tracey, my daughter, was nine when I set off. She likes flying and is the perfect passenger. She was also much more attuned to the danger. A journalist asked Tracey one day what she felt about the Australia flight. She thought a moment before replying: 'I wish Daddy wouldn't do it, but I know he has to.'

I spent the last week before departure with Fiona and the children in Bristol, laying out maps of the route and writing flight plan notes. My study had been turned into an office, and was overflowing with equipment. Neil was on the phone for most of the week. Sometimes he would wander into the dining room where I was poring over maps to discuss a problem: what if there were more bureaucrats like those in Genoa? Who was the best person in Britain to help with a problem, if Barry Davidson at the Aeronautical Information Services was unavailable? What was our position for communications between Mike and myself if Neil and Patti were out of touch?

We had maps covering the whole route, but they were far too big for the Flyer's cockpit. Laying them out on the floor, I glued them together in order, pencilled in my expected route, and then cut them into strips. Some were as long as five feet, showing terrain a hundred miles either side of the planned flight.

The ideal route was a straight line, but I sketched out a series of jumps, looking for natural or man-made features I could follow. Often, a straight route would cut across a curving coastline, for example, and I knew I would follow the coast. As it had done for Eve Jackson, IFR for me meant I Follow Roads and not Instrument Flight Rules. (Sometimes during the journey flight I was to become so tired I actually followed the bends in the roads rather than cutting across them.)

Studying the terrain and looking for landmarks I would recognise easily, I was still not confident about my skills as a navigator, having been lost enough times in England on small cross-country trips. Flying across half the world, I had to be sure of where I was going. If I drifted too far to the north crossing Saudi Arabia, I would end up in Iraq, which would not be wise. If I steered too far to the west, jumping the mouth of the Persian Gulf from Muscat to Pakistan could mean ending up in Iran, which would be even less wise. Too far to the east, of course, and I would still be at sea when I ran out of petrol.

With four days to go, I had to have another full set of injections: typhoid, diphtheria, cholera, the lot. The first batch had been in London a month earlier, and had not incapacitated me. Mike, on the other hand, had had all his injections in one go, and had been confined to bed for three days in a terrible state. I teased him about his 'weakness' right up to my second batch of injections, but half an hour after I had them I started shivering uncontrollably, and lay under a blanket for hours, ill and miserable. It took me a couple of days to recover fully.

During the last week in Bristol, weather conditions were perfect for a flight through Europe. Every day the wind blew from the northwest, not just across Britain but across much of Europe as well. Had I been working to the same rules as Ross Smith, that is, choosing my own time to go, I would have gone on one of those days. But modern-day televisions, particularly the outside broadcast that BBC *Breakfast Time* was contemplating, needs to be planned exactly, and I was committed to leaving on 2 December whatever the weather.

Two days before departure, I went up to London, met Mike, and spent a day dashing all over the place to make last-minute arrangements. We picked up our cash float from Barclays in Shoreditch High Street, and realised, to our horror, that we had ordered too much cash! Thousands of dollars in small denominations, from one-dollar to twenty-dollar bills, took up an amazing amount of room. Mike and I were both worried that just by opening our bags we would invite a mugging. We took about $1,500 each, and sent the rest back.

The takeoff site was in Victoria Dock, a derelict part of the Docklands in East London, since used by Jean-Michel Jarre for his gigantic pop concert. I had carried out my original recce one evening and was not absolutely certain it was OK, so I went to see it again in daylight. The distance between the cranes on Victoria Dock looked adequate for takeoff, and we watched workmen erecting what was to become the hospitality tent. As long as the wind was either east or west, I would have an into-wind takeoff.

The forecast for 2 December, daily becoming more accurate, was very depressing: a strong to gale-force easterly, the worst possible wind. Beyond hoping I would have a good takeoff, I did not brood about it.

On the last night there was a party in our Bethnal Green home. Mike returned from the ICOM agents, where he had been having the HF radio checked, and left the Flyer on the docks, after draining off half the petrol. The sitting room was full of equipment and sleeping bags. Judy Leden turned up, and she and I went over to the Greyhound pub opposite to say goodbye to the landlord.

Peter Davies arrived, and Neil Hardiman, and then Fiona and the children, then Neil's parents and friends, and Patti Hewstone's boyfriend, David, and Tony Spalding. I floated through in an atmosphere of unreality. It did not seem possible that I was actually about to attempt the flight. Looking around, I thought about how I did not want to let down any of those present.

Accustomed, until recently, to getting out of bed at 3 am, I was first up the next morning, and once shaved, I woke up the others. Neil, Mike, Peter and I packed the Jaguar outside, and set out in darkness, looking at the wind in the trees and the yellow lights against the cold black sky. We stopped on the way to Docklands to buy four litres of two-stroke oil, and a pile of Mars Bars. (The chocolate lasted through to the Middle East.) It was blustery at the docks, with a freezing wind, and people were beginning to move inside the hospitality tent, silhouetted against the dawn. The other three assembled the Flyer from her caravan, while I pottered around, pulling out bits of luggage and talking inconsequentially to people.

BBC's *Breakfast Time* had a live outside-broadcast unit there, with Francis Wilson the weatherman – TV weathermen are often expected to stand out in the cold and talk about weather – and Francis did his 6.55 spot sitting in the Flyer. My interview was scheduled for about 7.20. More people arrived. The interviews began. There were five television crews in all, including three Australian stations. The press photographers had their usual spats with TV crews over who had priority, and Simon Newlyn refereed.

Faces floated in front of me, as in a dream. From Dalgety, Tony Spalding, Terry Pryce and Sir Peter Carey came to say good luck and goodbye. They must have been full of tension, looking at the little aircraft and the man they had backed to fly it across half the world. Fiona arrived, with Jamie and Tracey looking a bit bemused. In one interview I saw the face of Steve, landlord of the Greyhound, who, despite a late night, had still got out of bed to see me off. Mike, Peter and Neil took charge of the Flyer, checked the fuel, and walked her down the docks to where I would start the takeoff run.

A BBC producer said they wanted live pictures, and would I take off just after the 8.30 news? A car would flash its lights as a signal. Mike saw that the car was in a gap he had deliberately made so that if I muffed the takeoff I would have somewhere to land out. He had a good swear, but there was nothing he could do. Meanwhile, I answered lots more questions in a sort of professional daze, with whole parts of my mind a long way away.

Judy Leden gave me a big hug, and a card with the Ten Commandments she believed should govern the flight. The card itself is now smeared from having been in the Persian Gulf but it is still possible to make out what Judy wrote:

1. Thou shalt honour thine engine and be sensitive unto its needs.
2. Thou shalt not become so dedicated to thy sponsor that thou losest perspective.
3. Thou shalt pay heed at all time unto the weather.
4. If thine engine should fail, thou shalt not panic, for a muddled head will cause an accident.
5. Thou shalt look to thy safety first – if thou shouldst become rent in twain, thou impresseth no one.

6. Thou shalt pause at least twice a day to enjoy thyself and think, 'verily this is a wonderful wheeze!'
7. Thou shalt not lose thy head with bureaucratic idiots.
8. If thou shouldst not make thy thirty-day deadline, thou shalt relax and still enjoy the rest of the flight.
9. Thou shalt have confidence in thyself and thine ability, for verily I say unto you, you can do it.
10. Thou shalt remember at all times of stress that we are thinking of you.

Close to departure time, I went over to see Fiona, who was being interviewed by ITN. The formal interview stopped, we kissed goodbye, I hugged the children and stomped off down the docks. The Flyer was lined up, ready to go, the engine having been run to warm it. Overhead, the wind increased in strength, coming from the east and still a headwind.

In the cockpit, my lap was filled with equipment: a spare radio, two stills cameras, the ITN video, maps, radio reference book, ruler, protractor, chewing gum and chocolate bars. I turned the VHF radio into the frequency of London Stolport, only a mile away and from which I had been banned from takeoff because I was not a Dash-7 airliner. ATC replied, and then made a strange request.

'Can anyone hear us?' they asked.

'No, just me,' I replied.

'Good. We have to inform you that your flight contravenes Rule Five of the Rules of the Air.'

Rule Five states that if an aircraft flies over a built-up area it must at all times fly so that it is within safe flying distance of a landing field if the engine cuts. I knew I had to conform to Rule Five, I always had, and it was much easier in a microlight than in other aircraft. But why were they informing me at that time, right before a very public takeoff?

'I have to advise you, sir,' I replied, 'that I believe I will obey Rule Five at all points of the flight, because my aircraft is capable of landing virtually anywhere.'

The voice in my ear repeated his message, and I came to understand that all they required was a formal acknowledgement of their message. If I flew away safely, well and good. But if I did not, then Stolport ATC would be able to say they had warned me of the dangers before I took off.

Mike came to the cockpit to see if everything was OK. He was still fuming about the cars blocking my escape route. We had a brief conversation, started the engine, and checked that the Flyer had been packed completely. She had twelve gallons of fuel on board, and the passenger compartment was crammed to the brim with luggage and equipment.

Then the lights flashed. I waved everyone out of the way, revved the engine, closed the canopy and locked it, and went for it!

The Flyer did not run exactly true, but I got the wheels off just above stalling speed, skidded left, and went through the gap in a staggering climb. The nose took a long time getting up, and the crane by the hospitality tent, where the BBC had a camera, seemed close enough to come through the canopy. There were high-tension cables on my left, which worried me, but I climbed in a slow circle, putting the nose down once when I saw the airspeed reduced to less than 45 knots. She whizzed downwind, and crawled back into the wind again, and I tried to waggle my wings to signal all was fine.

Those below thought I was going very slowly. The Stolport came into view and the whole of East London, grey and overcast. The wind threw the aircraft around. Scrabbling through all the stuff on my lap to get my map in place, I headed eastward, downriver.

I'm off, I thought; I'm off, I'm off.

Chapter Six
Europe

Given the right ferry times, you could drive from London to Le Touquet faster than I flew it. It took three and a half hours to cover a distance of less than a hundred miles. My average speed was 30 mph over the ground, though I thrashed the Flyer, pushing her through the air at 80 mph. Across Kent, the strong headwind was bumpy, with low cloud and mist. At Dover, I took a few pictures with the ITN camera; the coastline to the west, some ships, and a shot of me chewing gum. There was a radio beacon just north of the port of Dover, and I followed a radio beam out to sea and said goodbye to the last British air-traffic controller.

Mike had left twelve gallons of fuel in the Flyer, which should have been more than enough to get to France. But I was pushing the engine, which I soon started calling the Gobbler, and I grew alarmed at how quickly the fuel was disappearing. The French coast appeared in a slight mist, and as I fought my way south there were just two gallons left in the bottom tanks. I was relieved to get to Le Touquet, where Nikki Turner from Shandwick arrived by private aircraft to pick up the ITN film and take it back to England.

It took little more than an hour to go through customs and immigration and refuel, and I struggled on southwards, via Abbeville and the Somme and the city of Amiens, scene of much of the bloodiest fighting in World War One. Amiens were where I should have spent the night, but there was still light left in the winter's day, so I flew on to a small airfield called Mondidier. No one was there, but a call on the radio was responded to, and five minutes later a small French aircraft swooped overhead and landed. The pilot, an instructor, was based at Beauvais, to the southwest of where I was. (Beauvais was where the British airship, the R101, crashed in October 1930, on its maiden trip to India.) It was at right angles to any course I needed to steer for Australia, but the Frenchman said I could get fuel there. Just to stay with human company – always difficult to break with at the beginning of a big journey – I took off to follow him to Beauvais. It was 4.30 in the afternoon, and I ran a terrible risk of it growing dark before I arrived.

After a few minutes all I could see were his lights. How he saw me I don't know. Microlights were not expected to fly in the dark and I had no lights. Terrified of losing him, having no idea where to land, I swore away inside my sweaty cockpit, bitterly regretting that I had left Mondidier, and thrashing the Flyer to stay up. But after what seemed a very long time I saw a strong light in the distance, and followed the Frenchman in to land at Beauvais, where I was made very welcome at the local aeroclub. They arranged a hotel for the night, but locked the Flyer in a hangar, and I did not make arrangements to pick up the key.

When, virtuously, I arrived at the airfield just after dawn, I found I could not get into the hangar. It was very frustrating, and I stomped around in the freezing cold for two hours, shouting earthy Anglo-Saxon swearwords at the top of my voice to relieve my feelings. The French pilots were embarrassed when they arrived at ten o'clock, each thinking the other had made arrangements to open the hangar. It took another half-hour to refuel and get into the air, on course for Lyons. Meanwhile, the ghost of Ross Smith had jumped to Lyons in one day, and was now on its way to Pisa.

Heading east, I flew around the heavily controlled Paris airspace, following VOR beacons. France is full of these navigation aids, and you can go virtually anywhere by tuning into a beacon and getting a position fix. After flying forty miles in an hour and a quarter, I turned south, by Romilly-sur-Seine, Troyes and into the high country of the Forêt de Châtillon. The wind had changed from a strong easterly to a strong southeasterly, always a headwind, and I spent five and a half hours reaching Dijon and the Rhône Valley. It was like bashing my head against the wind, and I suffered great periods of angry frustration at not being able to go any faster. Landing at Chalon, south of Dijon, I was still short of Lyons, where Mike was waiting for me. A blanket of low cloud coming up from the south prevented me from flying any further. If I stayed above it I would not have anywhere to land, and going beneath would mean flying below 500 feet.

Mike drove from Lyons and checked the engine over. We booked into a little hotel across the road from the airfield, and I went to bed, deeply depressed.

The third day out of London dawned fine and misty, but the wind still came from the south. Where was the famous mistral wind, I kept asking Mike, which was supposed to blow from the north in the winter? By 9.30 I had fuelled up and cleared customs. I took off, full of a nameless apprehension, and set off south. It was possibly the slowest flight I have ever done.

That day, I covered 125 miles in five and a half hours. As if this was not depressing enough, there were only two gallons of petrol left when I landed sixty miles south of Lyons, at Valence. I had done 558 miles for the British and European Distance Record in September in seven and a half hours, on less than sixteen gallons. Now I was using twenty-six gallons for only five and a half hours, and a quarter of the distance! The problem, I discovered later, was that I was flying too fast, and thrashing the engine to try and make up time. To increase my time in the air I had to learn to calm down and go more slowly, otherwise I would not be able to fly some of the long legs I had planned for later in the journey.

The air-traffic controllers at Valence found me a hangar, and were full of commiserations the following day when I arrived and looked at the weather: low cloud, rain, and mist, especially to the south, the way I wanted to go. Ross Smith's ghost was setting off from Pisa that day, as I was all too well aware, and due to make Rome. If I was to catch him, I had to fly, whatever the weather.

My first attempt at flying was at 10.30 am. Keeping below the 500-foot cloudbase, my plan was to stay low through the narrow part of the Rhône Valley at Montelimar, a notorious weather bottleneck where all the cloud was piled up thickly. Hopefully I could break through south of there, at Avignon, and take the coastal route to Italy via Marseilles, Toulon and Nice. But as I headed south, twisting and turning with the river, and with the hills closing up on either side of me, I was driven lower and lower by the clouds. At about 300 feet the clouds wrapped themselves around me, and I experienced that gut-wrenching fear that comes when you do not know which way up you are. It wasn't possible to continue without a real risk of smashing into a mountain, so, carefully watching the compass and the turn-and-bank indicator (I had no artificial horizon), I turned north slowly. The cloud thinned out and I saw the ground again. I called Valence and asked for a QDM – a bearing to return to their airfield – and landed safely after only thirty minutes in the air.

The words of Richard Meredith-Hardy, who had flown from London to Cape Town in six months, kept returning: 'It is possible to make Australia in thirty days, but you have got to *go for it*.' Brooding darkly in the control tower and worrying about killing myself was not 'going for it', I reasoned, and I talked myself into another flight. This time I would go high, to see whether the clouds formed layers, and whether I could fly between one layer and another. It would not be legal, because I had no instruments to be able to fly blind. But I could follow radio beacons with my VOR, and would be able to jump from one beacon to another, even if I could not see the ground, as long as I knew I was the right way up.

At noon I took off again, and climbed in circles over the airfield. Every now and again, I lost sight of it, and almost cut the power and returned, but I talked out loud to myself and pressed on climbing. At 5,000 feet, the airfield disappeared, and when I looked around there was cloud everywhere. But it looked as though it was layered, so I headed south once more, following the VOR beacon to Monteli-mar. There was a slow and gradual change in the bearing I was taking to the beacon, but I was so wound up that I didn't realise its significance. The aircraft was drifting to the west, right across the Rhône Valley and into the high mountains!

The wind continued to blow from the south, causing me to make slow progress over the ground. I kept watching my VOR, waiting for it to indicate that I had flown over the beacon. Nothing happened, except that I continued to drift to the west. Then the cloud, which had been layered, closed around me.

In cloud a pilot gets disorientated without the right instruments, and the training to use them. You can't tell what's happening to you. You are surrounded by a fog, and any way could be up – or down. You race through the air at 70 mph, but can only see ten feet ahead. The compass spins, and you put on opposite rudder to stop it. It slows and stops, and then starts spinning the other way. You take off rudder, but the compass swings faster. You look at your speed – much too high! – and find you are descending at more than a thousand feet a minute. So, you pull back the throttle, feel the aircraft climb, look at the compass again, and it is really spinning this time. Bang on the rudder, and the same process starts again.

Sweating in the confined cockpit space, half mesmerised by the swirling white nothingness on the other side of the canopy, I descended from 5,000 feet to 2,000 feet. There was little rational thought behind the descent, except that I hoped to break through clouds. Eventually I did, and to my horror found that I was in a valley surrounded by mountains. By a lucky chance, I had flown over the mountains, but hit none of them. I saw the huge River Rhône over to my right – to the *east* – and shakily headed that way, threading around low mountain ridges. When I reached the river I made one more half-hearted attempt to fly south again, but when the cloud threatened to enclose me I bottled out and headed back to Valence airfield. I had been an hour and a half in the air, and would not repeat the experience for anything.

All that afternoon I sat in the control tower and looked at the cloud and rain. A young Frenchman, Christian Canu, invited me to stay the night with his family. It was obviously out of pity for the thoroughly miserable Englishman who spent hours staring out of the window and sighing. Ross Smith's ghost had made it to Rome, and I knew he would fly on the following day to the foot of Italy. It looked as though I was beaten before the race had even begun. Yet I could not think of any way I could have gone faster. It did not make me any happier to hear that the weather forecast for the following day was for more low cloud and rain. When I telephoned Mike Atkinson in Milan he was patiently bored, but tried to cheer me up.

The fifth day, 6 December, dawned misty, and Christian drove me to the airport where I listlessly checked over the Flyer. It was a Sunday, and we were the only two people there. Christian was duty air-traffic controller, and went to the tower to see me off. Then the mist started to clear and it looked as though the forecasters had got it wrong. Though I was not familiar with mountain weather, it had all the signs of a calm blue day.

There were two choices of route, either down the valley to Marseilles and around the coast, or turn left at Montelimar and go over the French Alps. The second route was much more dangerous than the first, but ninety miles shorter. If I took the second route successfully, I might be able to make that day's goal – Forli in eastern Italy – and get back into the race with the ghost of Ross Smith.

By nine o'clock I was heading south, climbing steadily. There was a distinct chill in the air and I was dressed for cold-weather flying. When I reached Montelimar and looked left at the Alps, there was cloud in the valleys, but the peaks were clear. Go for it, I thought, and turned and headed into the mountains. Looking at the ground from 9,000 feet I found the wind was behind me. My airspeed was now 70 mph, with revs below 5,500, but I was covering the ground at 83 mph. It became very cold, though, and the airspeed indicator froze so that it was only possible to judge airspeed by looking at the rev counter. However, in less than three hours I was on the ground again, at the little field of Albenga in Italy.

Italian bureaucrats had become a personal nightmare, because of the experience Mike and I went through in Genoa on the practice run. But Albenga, by contrast to Genoa further up the coast, was wonderful, and it took only an hour to clear customs and immigration, and to refuel. Clouds were piling up to the east above Genoa, and I was warned that I could lose sight of the ground if I continued, but it remained a beautiful day. Twenty-four hours after fighting for my life in the mountains, I set off from Albenga along the coast to Genoa, climbing steadily.

Occasional glimpses of Genoa below kept me dubiously legal, but when I turned north to follow a beacon over the mountains, the cloud cleared and I could see a hundred miles of frozen earth all around. The deep pall of gloom that had fallen on me at Beauvais lifted. I began to cheer up, and when I called England on the HF radio I was full of the fact that at last I was completing a day's flight on schedule.

Through Portishead radio, there was a bizarre radio linkup with Neil Hardiman. They connected me to Neil, who had a Vodaphone and was walking up Oxford Street at the time. I called him to tell Mike Atkinson to take a taxi from Milan to Forli, but we spent much of the transmission giggling at the incongruity of him being out Christmas shopping and pulling a phone from his pocket to have words with me, 1500 miles away, over the Italian Alps.

Following motorways and railway lines along the north side of the mountains, I reached Forli just as they turned on the landing lights. Ross Smith's ghost had reached Taranto, at the bottom of Italy, now only a day's flying away from me. If I cut out any rest days and pushed on, I could catch him, despite his faster aircraft. When Mike arrived not long after me, we had a joyous pizza near the hotel, and decided we had been through a bad experience and things would now improve.

Going south from Forli on 7 December, I wanted to make Brindisi at the heel of Italy in one day's flying. I had to plead for special clearance because of fog, but was given it. Mike said the takeoff was very painful, with the heavily over-loaded Flyer staggering into the sky, looking as if she would fall at any moment. To avoid jet airliners landing nearby, I had to fly low through mountains to the coast, nervously noting the lack of landing places among the red-roofed villas and ploughed terraces beneath me.

There was no following wind, but no headwind either, and I ticked off towns and villages on Italy's east coast. Once, near Foggia, I was routed inland by air-traffic controllers, and again made to fly low over towns to avoid jet aircraft. Three jet fighters streaked across my path, but everyone seemed to know what they were doing, and after nearly six hours' flying I landed at Brindisi military airfield, once the landing field for the prewar Imperial Airways service. The hotel I stayed in that night was the most miserable I have ever been in – no one smiled, there was no food in the restaurant, no one was happy to see me, and there was only one other guest – but I was happy at my progress. Ross Smith was a day ahead of me, but only a day; I could still catch him as long as I kept going.

On 8 December the weather forecast was poor, but I left Brindisi at nine o'clock and flew down the coast. I had trouble with cloud before reaching the heel of Italy – if I climbed, I soon lost touch with the ground; going low left me little chance of finding a cop-out field if the engine stopped – but I made it safely to the end of Italy, and turned out to sea. It was 100 miles of water, my first long sea crossing, and the area where, one day short of sixty-eight years ago, Howell and Fraser had drowned. It took three hours to cross to Kirkira airport at Corfu.

A handsome and formidable Greek lady called Ranta Macris saw me through the customs formalities. Fuel was slow to arrive and I fretted about it (Ross Smith was on his way from Crete to Egypt!), but I was flying again, still heading south, just after noon. It was bumpy in the air, and so bloody slow! Six hours' flying, and only 240 miles covered. The staff on the island of Kefallinia kept the airport open for me, an hour after the official close-down, while they followed by radio my long and painful progress. Kefallinia had no Avgas, but I had seventeen gallons remaining from Kirkira which should last me through to Crete. I did not take my five-gallon mixing can with me into town to refuel. It was to prove a bad mistake.

The first week of the flight had been a slow ordeal, but nothing had gone wrong with the Flyer itself. I had gone as far as it was possible to go safely, in the winter hours between sunup and sundown. But I was gradually falling behind Ross Smith, with little prospect of being able to catch him. Calling London, I could feel that they did not want to put pressure on me to go faster. On the other hand, there was also a certain impatience. Having sold Dalgety the idea that I could match Ross Smith's time, it was reasonable for them to ask – whatever the excuses I came up with about the weather – why I was not doing so. The race with Smith's ghost was looking tattier and tattier. All I could do was persevere and hope the weather would change, and my luck with it.

On 9 December conditions did change, and so did my luck. The weather got worse, and you must make up your own mind about my luck.

The sympathetic Kefallinia air-traffic controllers worked more overtime to get me away safely at dawn. Cloudbase was 500 feet, and it was raining. VOR radio beacons linked the next few islands together, and despite being afraid of the rain because my visibility under the darkened canopy was so poor, I took off. Navigation was only possible with the hand-held VOR. Looking for radio bearings to fly, I stayed just below cloud level and flew over the sea, peering into the gloom, watching for islands. Whenever an island appeared I virtually felt my way around it until it lay behind me and I could carry on south looking for the next one.

After two hours the cloud lifted, but the wind increased from the south. I thrashed around the eastern tip of Greece, and then set off on the long sea crossing to Crete. The journey seemed to go on forever, and I began to worry seriously about fuel consumption. An island called Kythira appeared on my left, and stayed there for hours, hardly moving. Whatever height I chose, from 3,000 feet to down below 1,000 feet, it made no difference to the slow progress.

When there were just seven gallons left in the bottom tank, I knew I could not make it to Crete. The map showed an airfield on Kythira, but no fuel. I tried calling Kythira ATC on the radio for half an hour, without reply. The fuel situation was critical by then, so I decided to land on the island, and fill the tanks with 4-star car fuel.

Turning downwind, I raced across the island and soon reached the airfield. It was half tarmac, half dirt, with a lot of earthmovers and one small building in the middle. Off to my right, the windsock was horizontal, indicating more than twenty knots. The air felt very turbulent, and I inched forward, losing height to bring the Flyer down safely on the tarmac runway.

Looking right and left for human life, I started to taxi forwards. No one appeared. As I turned slightly left I felt the right wing lift. Then the left wing banged on the ground, and the Flyer started to slew around. I tried to turn her back into wind, but she wouldn't go. The nose wheel, always the weakest point on the Shadow, collapsed under the pressure, then the cockpit nose hit the ground, and with a series of terrible grinding crunches, she was tipped upside down.

I fell out of the cockpit as the Flyer was driven upside down along the runway in a wind gusting to 30 mph. Bits of the aircraft broke and snapped around me. In five seconds, she was turned from a beautiful little aircraft into a battered piece of wreckage. No one appeared. I swore very loudly.

Chapter Seven
Captain Cook, Linda, Somersault
and The Bodger

Kythira is south of the west coast of Greece, northwest of Crete, and not one of those Greek islands you would choose for a holiday. About 3,500 people live there. They make a living by growing and selling olives, processing olive oil, and from fishing and agriculture. The island seems to have exported more people, especially to Australia, than actually live there, though some have returned to Kythira even after thirty years abroad. It is an island of poor soil, renowned for its violent winds. The one aircraft a day that comes from Athens often does not set off, or turns back halfway, because of bad weather.

Five years before I arrived, the Greek Government decided to build an aerodrome on the island. One tarmac runway was laid out and a dirt strip was cleared on the north side of the island. But it became too expensive to complete the job, so work stopped. The earthmovers and bulldozers were shut down, and there they have remained, totally idle. An independent survey of the cost of completing the job, I was told, came to less than twenty per cent of the official government price, so someone, even lots of someones, may have been lining their pockets.

But the half-completed airfield on Kythira is supposed to be manned through the working day, even though there is normally only one aircraft due each day at 1.45 pm. The airfield staff were somewhere else when I landed, and for the following week all sorts of excuses were made to explain their absence.

People arrived at the wreck of the Dalgety Flyer five minutes after I crawled from the cockpit. One of them accepted my stills camera and took some photographs. The airport manager turned up, said his name was Bill, and then started shouting. He wanted to know why I had landed there. I said I was running short of fuel, and an

airport on mainland Greece had suggested calling Kythira on his
frequency. He said he had not picked up my radio request. This was
not surprising because he had no facilities to hear calls not coming
through on schedule. Later, I discovered that he had been practising
what he was going to say to the official inquiry.

The Flyer remained upside down, moving and crunching in the
strong wind. Thinking I might be able to right her again, I asked for
help to turn her tail into wind, but we only succeeded in enlarging
the holes in the top of the wing. Then I dismantled the wings, and
was nearly blown away putting them into a truck. We rolled the
body upright, and she swayed in the wind, the integrity of the
monocoque destroyed, and the wing section over the cockpit
loose.

The truck drove the wings half a mile to a spartan, two-roomed
building, centrepiece of the unbuilt airfield, while the rest of us
pushed the body of the Flyer there. All the time, Bill complained that
I should not have landed there without his permission, even though
he had not been there to give it.

Tying the aerial of the ICOM HF radio to an old set of aircraft
steps, and insulating it with one of the Flyer's spare inner tubes, I
rigged up and called Portishead, and was linked by telephone with
Fiona.

'I've been turned upside down on a Greek island called Kythira,' I
told her. 'I'm OK but the Flyer is badly damaged. I think it can be
repaired. Don't worry if you read all sorts of lurid accounts in the
newspapers. We'll sort this out as soon as I can get hold of Michael.'

Getting the message through to Mike waiting for me in Crete was
complicated, but eventually achieved via Patti Hewstone. Being in a
state of shock, I did not reveal the full extent of the damage to Patti.
She in turn was quite blasé in explaining to Michael what repairs he
would need to do when he finally reached me after having flown
back to Athens to catch the Kythira flight.

Meanwhile, the now separate pieces of the Dalgety Flyer were
stowed in the two rooms, or lashed to the ground, while Bill
continued to whinge, asking impossible questions about how I was
going to repair her. One of the other Greeks gave me a lift to what he
called 'a good hotel, the best on the island'. It was twenty kilometres

away, and run by the local mayor, a man called Johnny. From there, I phoned Dalgety's HQ on a very bad line and gave Patti my phone number, and then sat in the hotel's main room for the rest of the night, answering the phone calls that came through. When I was not talking on the phone I played solitaire.

I was desolated. The crunching noise the Flyer had made as she turned over kept going through my mind, and I replayed my actions to keep the aircraft upright. The solitaire diverted my mind, which bounced from one thought to another, recoiling when it became too painful. There were plenty of painful thoughts.

That night I slept in a cold-water room with no sheets. At about three o'clock in the morning, I woke with a start and knew that I needed David Cook on the island. David had designed and built the Flyer. While I trusted Mike, the aircraft was so seriously damaged that whatever Mike did, I needed the nod from David before I could fly her again.

Later that morning I woke again, phoned London, and asked them to send out David. Patti was irritated and inclined to argue – 'Why do you need David when we're already sending you Mike?' – but it was my decision, and my life in the aircraft. There was a contingency fund in my budget, and it was this money which would be used to bring out David. Patti's opinion was an irritation to me. David Cook telephoned later on a dreadful line and said he was willing to come out, but it was to be two more days before he arrived in Kythira.

Before Mike arrived that afternoon, I wrote a note assessing the damage. The wing section of the Flyer's body had three big holes in it, each perhaps nine inches across. All eight spars were broken; on the left side in three separate places, on the right side in two. The top of the wing moved like heavy jelly when pushed, and all pretence of a wing shape was lost. The bottom of the wooden leading edge was separated from the spars.

Underneath, there were four main aluminium tubes which normally strengthened the aircraft, and linked the fuselage with the wing. The bolts which attached the tubes to the body had pulled out, taking bits of the fibrelam monocoque with them. The arch above the pilot's head was split in two, and the nose cone was like jelly, having received the full weight of myself and my aircraft. But the main damage to the front of the Flyer was to the nose wheel, which had broken off. The structure holding the wheel was ripped and split.

At the back, the tail was bent in four places where it had taken the aircraft's weight when she was upside down. I thought the aluminium tubing would straighten, like hang-glider uprights used to do, but when Mike stood on them that evening to test their strength they all broke. The elevator, which controls the pitch of the aircraft, was broken in two places into a V-shape. Both wings, now separated from the body, had holes in the wooden top leading edge, and the tips were savagely holed where I had banged first one side and then the other before being turned upside down.

All through the long hours of that morning and early afternoon I waited for Mike to arrive, still playing solitaire to pass the time and to turn off my mind. I must have played a hundred games, but none came out. Otherwise I walked urgently, first one way and then the other, willing the time to pass. The weather was the main source of anxiety, in case it was too strong for the Dornier shuttle to land. But the aircraft arrived on time, and Mike, stocky, tough, and indomitable, got out. First I photographed him, then I hugged him (or it may have been the other way around). He pulled his tools, luggage and Sweetie Pie, the spare engine, from the Dornier, and I walked him to the pieces of the Flyer.

'Will she fly again?' I asked.

He looked at the pieces, laughed, and scratched his head. He just kept laughing. This is a bad sign with Mike, meaning he can't see a way to complete a job. He scratched his head and walked around the pieces, laughing every now and again, a short nervous laugh. Waiting for a reassuring comment, I trailed along anxiously. The wind blew and it was very cold. A few Greek islanders watched and talked among themselves.

Months later, Mike said that he could not see any way that December afternoon to get the Flyer into the air again without a major repair job at the factory. (When David Cook turned up two days later, *he* said it would cost a minimum of £5,000, and a month's hard work to repair.) But after a while Mike looked at the individual jobs and thought, well, I can repair the hole in the wing by doing this, and I can fix the nose wheel by doing that. In this way he began to repair the Flyer in his mind, and then he set to work. We used one of the two rooms as a workshop, with Mike as the master, and me as his gofer.

We worked all afternoon, breaking as much as mending, trying to ascertain the full extent of the damage. Michael cut off the front of the nose cone, and cut pieces out of the skin to get at the main monocoque underneath. The sanding down was my job, while Mike removed the nose wheel and used the spare fibrelam he carried with him to begin building a new, reinforced housing for the wheel leg. He stopped work when it was too dark to see, and we took a taxi back to the delights of Johnny's hotel.

That evening we were eating dinner, interrupted by my jumping up to answer phone calls from London, when a beautiful girl walked in. Mike and I watched her talk to some of the Greek customers who were busy composing and writing messages in the Birthday Book, and then she came up to us to ask what had happened. We were surprised, on that bleak island, to discover that she was English.

Her name was Linda d'Antal; she was twenty-five years old, and had lived in Kythira for the last five years. She had long black curly hair, brown eyes, a sunny smile, and had just finished another hard day's work picking olives for her handsome Greek boyfriend Michalis. She asked if she could see the aircraft the following day, and offered us a lift to the airfield. All that day she stayed with us, running errands for glue, tools and food.

'Anything's better than picking olives,' she said.

We needed transport and someone who spoke Greek, so I hired her at $20 a day, good money for the island. She became unofficial photographer for the week we were there, an indelible part of our memories of Kythira.

The biggest problem with the aircraft, after Mike had worked out how to fix the nose wheel, was restoring the integrity of the wing roots and fixing the aluminium tubes linking the monocoque to the wing. Mike was preoccupied with working out ideas, and communication was reduced to grunts and shrugs. The day after he arrived, for example, Linda and I watched him as he wandered around the windswept airfield, picking up pieces of driftwood, and hurling them into puddles.

'What is he doing?' we asked each other.

We could hear him muttering about fixing the wing, but throwing bits of wood about was a mystery to us. Then he asked me to mix a pound of araldite glue, and laid the newly cleaned pieces of driftwood along the top of the wing root. Other bits of wood were loosely roped to the bottom of the wing. Then, taking the araldite and an old knife, he reached inside and began filling the cracked spars, quickly slapping the glue into place. Some of our spanners were used to twist the rope in what Mike said were Spanish windlasses, tightening the top and bottom pieces of driftwood together. This splinted the wing, as though it was a broken leg. I couldn't believe it when I saw the cracks in the broken spars tighten up, and when the splints were removed the following day the wing root was whole again.

We spent the evening of 11 December scouring Johnny's small village for bits of tubing to try and fix the tail. We were offered vacuum cleaner tubes and pieces of old cast iron. Nothing quite fitted. If necessary, we would have to cut them to fit, but it was still possible that David Cook would have enough bits in his repair kit to cover the broken aluminium.

The islanders were very kind to us, and wanted to get me flying again. They were particularly excited by the Birthday Book. One man we went to see about spare tubing cut us a number of pieces of cast iron, and as a matter of course we asked him to sign the book. He looked at his clothing and shook his head.

'I am not dressed well enough,' he said. 'Let my son, who is better dressed, do it.'

We laughed and said no, no, we wanted his signature, but he was adamant that his clothes were not fitting for such an honour as writing a birthday greeting to the Australian nation, and nothing we said or did could persuade him.

Our host, Johnny, was eccentric in a Greek way. He was a powerful man in the village, and ran his hotel as though he was father to a very large family subject to his whims. Sometimes he took it into his head not to feed us, even if we wanted food. Other times, he put a huge pile of food in front of us and did ...ot charge for it. Johnny did not at first approve of Mike's enormous thirst for tea. Mike drinks fifteen to twenty cups a day, each with three sugars, and gets very ratty without his cuppa. Every evening, Mike would arrive at the hotel and ask for 'chai'. Johnny would not make it the first night, whatever we said. But soon he decided that Mike was a good chap, and after that would rush, unbidden, into the kitchen every evening on our return to make tea.

When we asked Johnny to sign the Birthday Book, he spent a long time thinking about what he was going to say. We saw him making countless drafts and consulting with the elders of the village. After two days, he asked formally for the book, put on a pair of half-spectacles, and slowly wrote out his message. What did he say? I cannot tell you, because like all the other carefully composed messages from Kythira, it is all Greek to me. But as Melbourne is the third largest Greek-speaking city in the world, maybe that is appropriate.

For two days the weather changed and mild northerlies blew over the island. When I could spare a moment, I looked wistfully at the sky, and hoped it would stay that way for when – or if – I could fly again.

David Cook arrived on the afternoon of 12 December, on the scheduled aeroplane, and carrying his repair kit. He must have been used to looking at half-finished aircraft in his factory, but when he saw the Flyer he became very quiet. I hung on to his every word, but Mike just watched him out of the corner of his eye and continued to make the repairs he had been working on, including fibreglassing the top of the wing root.

David wrote out his own assessment of the damage, and made a few small changes to Mike's work. They bickered amiably; Mike thought his repairs would work, while David was obsessed about the weight of the extra materials Mike was using for the repairs. Neither Mike nor I gave a toss about the weight, just so long as the Flyer got into the air again. David had been living with ideas for cutting weight on his aircraft for years (to qualify as a microlight the CFM Shadow had to weigh less than 150 kilogrammes), and when making Shadows, he paid £1 for every suggestion that saved an ounce.

As a result of their argument, we took the fibreglass from the top wing and rebuilt the leading edge with the thin strips of beech plywood which David had brought with him. These they glued and riveted to the wing. It looked so makeshift that Linda went off to buy a pot of white paint to paint over it. In the process, we lost the Dalgety Flyer logo over the pilot's head, and it remained missing from Kythira all the way through to Abu Dhabi, when Dalgety sent me another one. That logo was Dalgety's principle return for their sponsorship, though I did not realise it at the time.

David and I had known each other for years, going back to the days when I founded and ran the National Hang-gliding League, and he was a lone voice in the wilderness crying for competitions for his type of glider. He did not at first approve of the League, believing that it excluded him, but I invited him to one competition and told him he was welcome to enter so long as he qualified like anyone else. He was so charmed by the atmosphere at the competition that he changed his view completely. But we had never worked together, and I did not know him well.

A self-taught aeronautical engineer, David had recently been made an honorary fellow of the Institute of Aeronautical Engineers, of which he was justly proud. Like many self-taught men, he had a strong personality, and felt that whoever bought them and whatever they were used for, the seventy aircraft he had made remained his children. When, in England, we had removed all the CFM Shadow logos from the Dalgety Flyer because we wanted to concentrate media attention on Dalgety, David saw this as a deep slight, and we had one tense evening 'debating' this point.

David's approach to work was eccentric. He kept up a constant low monologue, a stream of quotes from films and television series he had seen, interjected with extravagant praise for his own work: 'Just look at that brilliant job . . . Oh, David, you are a genius, sheer genius . . . Of all the gin joints in all the world . . . Oh, that is so good . . . I know nuzzing [Mañuel in *Fawlty Towers*] . . . David Cook, this is total brilliance . . . I know nuzzinnnggg . . .' We all fell about laughing as he completed the sleeving repairs on the tailplane. He told us his call sign when flying was Captain Cook, and we decided we should be known as Captain Cook, Linda, Somersault (me) and The Bodger (Mike).

David showed us where the original glassfibre nosecone was joined to the monocoque, and we pulled it off. Mike spent an afternoon getting his hands covered with glassfibre resin as he put the cone back together again. When he finished, it didn't look pretty, and it was full of scars, but we thought these added to her character and did not paint over them.

On the morning of 14 December, five days after I had been flipped upside down, I woke up and looked out of the window with more anxiety than usual. The wind howled through the trees, shaking them violently. I knew I was going to have to fly again soon, and I dearly wanted good weather for when I did. That first flight was something I lived, nightly, a hundred times. Would she stay in the air? I expected to get airborne and head across 140 miles of sea to Crete that afternoon. But as I mooched around miserably, Mike and David said firmly that I would not be flying that day; there was still too much to do.

All day, the Flyer was put back together. Patches were glued on to the wings and then painted by Linda. Mike used fibreglass to fill in the holes in the wing tips. The nose cone was slipped back on to the aircraft, glued into place, and the canopy riveted back on. She began to look like an aircraft again, a very battered aircraft, but one still capable of flight.

David said he was going to test her before I flew away. Secretly I was relieved, and did not argue. We went over to see the airport manager, by now known to all as Whingeing Bill, and told him we thought we would fly again soon. Whingeing Bill had lived in dread of the Greek accident investigator who had turned up from Athens, but who had lost professional interest when he discovered I had been flying a microlight. Writing reports on microlights did not fall within his brief. On the other hand, he was fascinated by how the Shadow was built, took lots of photographs, and he and David spent hours talking about the theory of flight. By the time he left the island they had become friends.

During the official investigation I had helped Whingeing Bill by skating over his absence from the radio when I had called on 9 December. Now that the investigator had gone, Bill wanted us off as quickly as possible and was calculating my parking charges by the hour. Though I was terrified about my first flight, I was relieved at the thought of leaving. One of the attractions of making the flight to Australia in the first place had been to get away from the Whingeing Bills of this world, of whom there are too many.

The wind dropped in the evening to about 15 mph. We wheeled the patched-up Flyer across to the tarmac runway, and prepared her for flight. Using the ITN camera, I interviewed David Cook, who was chirpy, if a little tense. Linda lined up her car next to the runway, and when David began his takeoff run, we tore down the runway, filming him. David kept below 500 feet during the whole flight, but threw the aircraft around. He only had five gallons of fuel on board, a very light load, and the Flyer responded easily to everything he did. Tomorrow, I would find out how she would respond to twenty-eight gallons on board, plus myself and all my equipment.

In the dark evening, while a cold wind blew and David and Linda chatted in the shelter of our workshop, Mike and I changed engines on the Flyer. She had two engines, one of which Mike carried in a handbag and swopped with the working engine every fifty flying hours. Sweetie Pie had been the engine I used to make the British and European Distance Record of 558 miles only three months earlier. The Gobbler was the second engine and had driven the aircraft from England. Mike said I slandered The Gobbler, rightly blaming its thirstiness on my using too many revs. Anything higher than 5,500 revs gobbled fuel, whatever engine was used. But The Gobbler was now due for a service, so by the light of a six-volt bulb hung from the wing, we took it off and substituted Sweetie Pie.

Even though it was late, there was a small celebration that evening. My first test flight would be over 140 miles of water, and I felt slightly detached. It was easier to cope by turning off parts of my brain and not allowing some thoughts to develop. But in the night you cannot do that and I woke up a number of times before dawn.

On 15 December the weather was blustery, with a violent southwesterly wind and low cloud, the same conditions that had

flipped me upside down six days earlier. My stomach was very tight
and I could not eat breakfast. There was a dull ache just under my
ribcage, a familiar part of my life of late, but worse than usual that
morning. I drank a cup of tea and brooded as clouds scudded
quickly by the window. Neither Mike nor David said much, and I
do not think there were any willing volunteers to take my place in
the Flyer's cockpit. Linda was late picking us up. The thermostat on
her car had broken, causing overheating problems. We got to the
airfield at 9.30 am.

There were a few last preparations to make to the Flyer. She
needed refuelling, and Mike wanted to look over his repair work.
All the glued joints were checked for stress cracks; none were found.
Mike pottered around the aircraft, while David talked to Linda.
Alone in the control tower, Whingeing Bill was adding up my
landing charges, and I walked over to see him. There was a
substantial bill for having landed there, and he said he had no choice
but to ask for it given that the accident inspector had arrived. Every
hour was charged for. Curious to see what he would do, I said we
would be delayed for an hour. Sure enough, he added an hour to the
bill.

He asked me to write out a statement absolving him of any
responsibility for the flight I was about to make. After a con-
temptuous silence, I thought why not? If she fell to pieces when I
flew away I would not be around to argue the toss. It was my
decision whether or not to fly, and it never really occurred to me not
to go. He was just covering his ass; it was one of the reasons he was
called Whingeing Bill.

Back at the aircraft, Mike had stopped pottering and was strip-
ping down the spare engine. The Flyer stood on its own, battered
but whole, everything in place. Mike said nothing, but worked with
great concentration on the spare engine. It took a few minutes to
sink in. There was nothing left to do but to put in my luggage, set up
the radios, and fly. Mike didn't say anything, not wanting to put me
under pressure. He was as wound up as I was. If the Flyer fell to
pieces in the sky, it was his reputation as well as my life.

We packed the Flyer, and pushed her across the gravel and mud
to the tarmac airstrip. Whingeing Bill answered my call on the radio

and I told him I was going to take off. He wanted to argue with me again about the exact wording of the disclaimer I had written him, but I wasn't interested. In the cockpit, I strapped up and scattered all the equipment around me: spare radio, two stills cameras, maps, flight sheets, protractor, ruler, pens, chewing gum and chocolate bars, tape recorder and flight calculator. Mike took the ITN camera because it was not mine and, frankly, if anything was going to happen to me, it would be better to have the pictures taken from the outside; inside the tiny cockpit my mind would be on other things. In any case, there was a good chance it could get wet.

Looking strained and tense, Mike pull-started the engine and we ran it up. At 11.45 am I shook hands with David and Mike, and waved to Linda. They all stepped back, and I closed the canopy to make last-minute preflight checks. All OK. Look ahead, watch the windsock, no reason to delay any longer, bang the throttle, *go for it.*

The Flyer lumbered down the runway and staggered into the air. She pitched and rolled but I gained height going over the end of the runway. The wind threw me around and she felt very heavy; the elevator was still broken in a slight V-shape, and was difficult to use. After a minute I let go of the control stick to adjust my radio and the Flyer went into a steep dive. Watching from the runway, Mike went grey with fright, but I thought she would recover, and sure enough she did. My last contact with Whingeing Bill was to say that everything was OK, and then I changed frequency and told Mike I was fine. He replied weakly, because his radio was not that good. Staying below the cloud, and feeling vulnerable, I set off across the sea for Crete, 130 miles away.

Mike and David jumped into Linda's car and tore across the island to a port on the north coast. There was an airline strike that day, and the only way they could get to mainland Greece was by boat. They caught one at two o'clock in the afternoon and spent fourteen hours calling at every little town before reaching Athens. The taxis were on strike in Athens but Mike actually got one to work for him and they made it to the airport. David's return ticket had run out of time so Mike bought him another one (thank God for Dalgety money and my contingency fund). David went back to

England and told the press that the Dalgety Flyer was now the Flying Bandage. One headline read 'Hero in a Flying Bandage'. Mike mooched about all day, and in the evening caught a plane to Cairo.

Chapter Eight
Kythira to a Jordanian Road

Every move I made in the cockpit had to be worked out very deliberately because I was so frightened. I hated being frightened, and was angry that it was affecting me so much, but I could not help it. Visibility was very poor, with a mist over the sea and hanging from the clouds, and there was no option but to follow a compass course to Crete.

The first landmark was a small island called Andikythira which came up on time, but after passing that, I flew for a very long time without seeing anything. Thoroughly alarmed, I wondered whether to head south, run into Crete, and then bumble along the north coast to the airport at Iraklion. Then I thought that perhaps I hadn't flown far enough east to be north of the island; if so, flying south, I could miss it altogether in the mist, and find myself heading out for Africa without enough fuel to arrive there. Becoming detached from reality, I continued following my compass, and devoutly wished I was somewhere else.

After an hour and a half in the air I tuned one of my ICOM VHF radios into the VOR frequency for Suda Bay, the military base where Ross Smith had landed in 1919, and where Hubert Wilkins and the Kangaroo had crashed. The bearing I took showed that I was east of Suda Bay, and therefore on course. To my delight and relief the beacon at Iraklion also showed a bearing on my VOR, and once I had turned south it was not long before Crete loomed out of the mist. My uncle Christie had been evacuated from the island in 1941 when it was invaded by German airborne troops, and he still had nightmares about his experiences there.

At Iraklion airport there was a strong crosswind. With visions of my last crosswind landing at Kythira crowding into my mind, I brought the Flyer in like a pantomime fairy and dropped her on to the runway, breathing a big sigh of relief. The local air-traffic controller congratulated me on the landing, saying it had gusted to a 30-knots crosswind as I came in, way above the safety limits.

In the best hotel I could find on the island I spent three-quarters of an hour sitting under the shower. The six days at Kythira had included only one shower, and it was bliss to sit under hot water. It was also a relief to pick up the phone and talk to London without the whistles and crackles of a typical Kythira phone line. But I got Patti on the other end and not Neil; she was not a flyer so she was entirely unaware of the terror I had been through, and I was brusque and matter of fact with my account. I told her that the weather forecast was not brilliant for the 400-mile jump across the Mediterranean, but if it was possible I would have a go.

That evening I ate a thin, tatty hamburger and went to bed full of anger and frustration. Ross Smith, I thought, was by now in India and I no longer had a chance of beating him to Darwin. Of the other 1919 competitors, four were already dead, four were due to crash leaving Crete for Egypt, and six were ahead of me in distance, if not in speed.

At dawn on 16 December, I filed my flight plan at Iraklion, giving Cairo as my destination, with Alexandria as an alternative. The forecast wind was southerly and light, still a headwind which could leave me over water if I ran out of fuel, but I was filled with a sort of reckless bravado; even if the margins of safety were small, I was going for it. At eight o'clock, my stomach grumbling hollowly from tension, I took off and headed east along the north coast of Crete, climbing all the time.

My route took me to the east end of the long island, where I turned right and headed straight for Alexandria on a compass course. Egypt would appear more quickly if I headed due south, as Richard Meredith-Hardy had done, but if I deviated to the right I would land in Libya, and that I did not want. Alexandria had a VOR which would guide me in; as long as I headed in its general direction, I would find it.

It was a calm day, with banks of clouds from east to west, pushing north. My best altitude to fly, I decided, was 5,000 feet, much higher than I normally flew. Going over the sea in a single-engined aircraft is frightening enough, but in a two-stroke engined microlight it has the capacity to numb you for hours. At 400 miles, this was the longest sea crossing I had ever done, and was perhaps the longest ever sea crossing in a microlight. But it would lift the Dalgety Flyer out of Europe where it had been jinxed by headwinds, and take it to the first really foreign country.

On a long flight over the sea you fall into a dozy state of mind. There is nothing to look at, in Francis Chichester's phrase, but the lonely sea and the sky. You check the compass and constantly monitor the engine and exhaust temperatures, and you watch the fuel gauges. But this becomes automatic. The major part of your mind goes somewhere else. Part of the time I imagined arriving in Sydney, other times I imagined scenes out of my past, trying to play them in a different way. Two ships appeared on the whole flight, and I deviated to fly over them, but they took no notice. I saw no aircraft.

After five and a half hours in the air, I was able to talk to Alexandria on the radio, and asked for permission to land and refuel. It was granted cheerfully. The coast of Egypt kept appearing out of the mist, but it was an illusion and turned out to be a different type of cloud to that surrounding me. When I did see land, the city of Alexandria was right below me, and I found the airfield immediately and landed. In the one and a quarter hours I spent on the ground I discovered that Alexandria deserved its reputation as a den of thieves and robbers, and the only den bigger was Cairo.

Clearing customs and immigration seemed straightforward enough, and so was buying five gallons of fuel, but in less than half an hour it was like walking through honey. Everyone was on the take: the airport police, customs officers, immigration, the bank manager changing money, the man who fetched petrol, the fire crew, and finally a big fat policeman who stood in front of the Flyer as I was about to take off to Cairo and demanded thirty Egyptian pounds.

'What for this time?' I shouted in exasperation.

'It is required,' he said.

There was no time to argue the toss. There was an hour of daylight left and more than ninety miles to Cairo, and they all knew that. He got his money, as did everyone else, and they must have thought it was a holiday. But I laughed and laughed as I took off; I had crossed the Mediterranean safely, and if the Egyptians robbed me in Alexandria, what else did I expect of Egyptians?

On a compass course to Cairo, flying over flat, irrigated fields linked to the Nile by thin canals, I sang raucously, and looked for the landmarks which I had marked on the map so many weeks earlier. But I was still short of Cairo when the sun disappeared below the horizon. The air-traffic controllers had me on their radar, which reassured me, though they started vectoring me as if I was a jet airliner and needed a ten-mile approach to the runway. Later, in other countries during the flight, I asked to be directed straight to the airfield, but in Cairo I just obeyed instructions. To my horror I was still in the air when it grew seriously dark, and I could not see my unlighted instruments in the gloom.

Cairo is a busy airport, and a great many jet airliners use it. The airwaves were filled with the voices of captains of Jumbo 747s being directed to the runway, but I could not see anything, even though I knew they were somewhere out there in the same air. Close to despair, I followed every direction given by the ATC, but lost a great deal of confidence when I was told to turn left on to a certain course when I knew I should be turning right.

Which way to go?

The exasperated voice of a British pilot broke in on the strained conversation I was having with air-traffic control, and told me to turn right to see the airport. Sure enough, in the distance, I saw runway lights. Keeping my eyes glued to these, and fearful even of blinking, I struggled to cover the distance as quickly as possible, announced 'final to land' on the radio, and slipped out of the sky over the runway, looking frantically right and left to maintain perspective. It was another pantomime fairy landing, perhaps a little less heavy than in Iraklion, but nothing fell off. Mike and David's repairs were being severely tested.

A television crew interviewed me after I had taxied in, and the reporter became the only Egyptian name in Australia's Birthday Book. It took three hours to get away from the airport, and I could feel every person I talked to measuring me up, and calculating just how they could fleece me out of money. Spending only $10 gave me a certain satisfaction, but they were biding their time for the following day. Using the airport phones, I let London know I was safely across the Mediterranean, and that I had completed more than eight hours' flying that day.

Mike arrived at the airport hotel after I went to sleep, having left the spare engine and his tools with customs. We talked at dawn the next day, 17 December, had a quick breakfast, and then tried to get to the Dalgety Flyer. It took four hours to be able even to touch the aircraft, and cost an amazing $140. This money we paid to a fat Egyptian who called himself a handling agent, and without whom we were unable to move. Even with his help it was after ten o'clock by the time I was united with my aircraft. Refuelling took another hour and a half, and I resolved to get as far away from Egypt as it was possible to go, and never return.

When I requested permission from air-traffic control to taxi for takeoff to Amman in Jordan, I was told that my flight plan showed an earlier takeoff time, and I would have to start all over again. The delays had been caused by the airport itself! I bellowed down the radio, and after a short silence, I was allowed to leave. It was another misty day as I set off east for Suez.

During the interminable negotiations with Cairo air-traffic control, I had asked to cross direct from Suez to Aqaba in Jordan, rather than go around the Sinai Peninsula. The speed of my aircraft meant that I would never make Amman in one flight if I was diverted. This was accepted by ATC when I was on the ground, but when I actually reached Suez I made the mistake of talking to Cairo on the radio. My original flight plan was no longer approved, and I was required to divert around the Peninsula. I refused. The air-traffic controller became very excited. What about my permissions to go direct? I asked. He said if I did not do what I was told, I would have to return to Cairo. It was a fateful decision to obey him and divert, and if I had not the whole flight would have been different.

It took nearly six hours to fly to Aqaba, less than 200 miles direct from Cairo, but 370 miles the way I was forced to go. It was a thrash all the way down the Gulf of Suez to the Red Sea, following the coast and being banged around by thermals. As ever, I was flying into wind, but when I turned the corner at Ras Nusrâni and headed north, I really started to motor. There was a bad moment, thirty miles short of Aqaba, when the engine suddenly lost power and I looked frantically around to see where I could land. On the right was Saudi Arabia, on the left Egypt, and I did not want to land in either. The engine's power returned after I had chosen a sandbank on Egyptian soil and turned towards it, and I shakily continued flying north again.

Aqaba is an Arab port, and the only outlet to the Indian Ocean the kingdom of Jordan has. It is also a holiday resort earning valuable foreign currency, mainly from German and Scandinavian tourists. But it lives right next door to the Israeli port and holiday resort of Eilat, and the two countries are divided by a firm but invisible line. Pilots must approach Aqaba from the southeast, outside Israeli airspace, which I remembered to do, but I nearly blew the whole flight by setting up the normal left-hand circuit over the airport and going dangerously close to Israel.

It was not just the Jordanians who were upset. The previous month, six Israelis had been killed after an attack by two kamikaze Arabs flying powered hang-gliders. Unknown to me then, this was probably the trigger for the Intifada, the Palestinian uprising against the Israeli occupation which had just begun. If I *had* infringed Israeli airspace in the Dalgety Flyer it could easily have been shoot first, ask questions afterwards. But I landed safely just before darkness, and was greeted delightedly by a civilised bunch of people who seemed very competent and helpful. A petrol bowser turned up quickly, I asked for petrol to refuel, and it was delivered straight into my mixing tank with two-stroke oil and then into the Flyer. That evening I went to bed unhappy at failing to make it to Amman, but sure that I would get away the following day. I was mistaken.

At Aqaba airport at dawn on 18 December, I was presented with two bills. They added up to an amazing US$900. The airport authorities wanted 'landing fees' of $200, and Royal Jordanian Airlines 'handling fees' of $700. Landing fees are normally calculated by aircraft weight, and because the Dalgety Flyer is so light, I have paid as little as $1. There is a minimum to cover the cost of paperwork, and it is reasonable to charge around $10, so I was

The Vickers Vimy used by Ross Smith and his crew in the Great 1919 Air Race.

Mike Atkinson, Neil Hardiman and Brian Milton.

Above left: With Fiona, Jamie and Tracey just before takeoff, 2 December 1987.

Above right: The Docklands takeoff.

Below: The cockpit of the Dalgety Flyer: note how cramped it is.

Above: Upside down in Kythira.

Below left: The Flyer in splints.

Below right: Mike Atkinson and David Cook repairing the Flyer in Kythira.

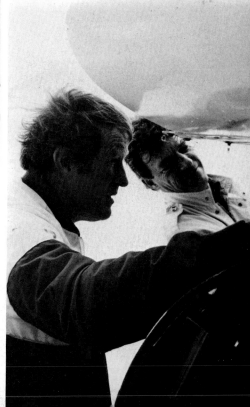

Above left: With King Hussein in Jordan. You can't see it, but he has his arm around my shoulders.

Above right: Mending a tyre in Saudi Arabia, after landing in a sandstorm.

Below: Desert landing among rocks in Saudi Arabia.

Above: Rescuing the Flyer from the Persian Gulf on Christmas Day, while the Iranians were attacking two tankers just to the north.

Below left: Rescuing instruments from the Flyer, on board NMS401.

Below right: Abu Dhabi docks, Boxing Day.

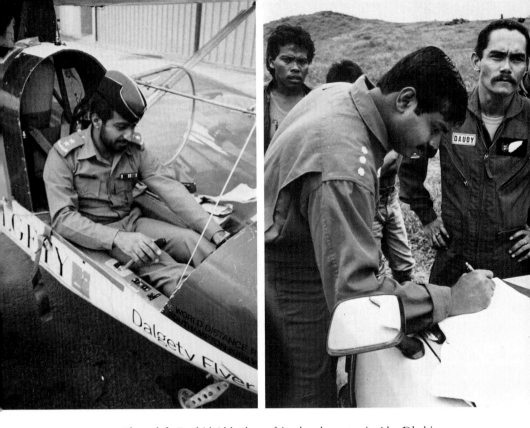

Above left: Rachid Abbad, my friend and mentor in Abu Dhabi.

Above right: Captain Revi Chandran and Chiefy Daudy signing the Birthday Book – before almost killing me!

Below: Landing out in Malaysia on a mud track, 14 January. Two hours later the road behind was used as a runway.

Above: Pull-starting in Bima, 19 January.

Left: Arrival in Darwin, 21 January.

Below: With Alice Mae Mackinnon signing the Birthday Book in Charleville, 25 January. She met Ross Smith in 1920, when she was eleven years old.

Above: Australia Day in Brisbane.

Left: The arrival in Sydney, 29 January.

Below: With Terry Pryce, the Dalgety Chief Executive, in Sydney, 29 January.

staggered at the Aqaba charge. As for the handling fees, the airline had done nothing to earn any fee at all, never mind this astonishing bill.

'Sorry. We understand why you are upset, but that is the law,' I was told by a man called Sami Saaed. 'Of course, if you have a friend at the Palace . . .'

As far as I knew, I did not have a friend at the Palace, and had to fight the charges on my own. In London Patti weighed in, pulling strings at the British Embassy, and by early afternoon the landing charges were dropped. But the handling fee remained, though reduced to about $300, and I signed a credit agreement to pay them. One solution suggested to me had been to fly to Amman to see if I could get any help, but Mr Saaed said the same fees would also be charged there. Late in the day, thanks to Patti's hard work on the telephone, I was invited to Amman to see Dr Mutadi, an adviser to King Hussein. Dr Mutadi also said that I would not have to pay $900 in Amman, or haggle down a price. Still, that night I went to bed despondent, though I had more cause to be despondent than I knew.

The atmosphere at Aqaba next day was strained, but if I had been fleeced, as I felt I had, it was by gentlemen compared to the barefaced crookedness of Egypt. The engine did not sound quite right when I started up, but it ran reasonably well for ten minutes, with the occasional cough. Just after 7.30 am I took off, and it soon became obvious that there was something seriously wrong. I could not go back to Aqaba and face another demand for $900. Instead, flanked on my right by scree-covered mountains, I climbed slowly, heading north and staying to the right of a road leading up to the Dead Sea. To the left of that road, in the wide valley leading from the Dead Sea to the Red Sea, lay Israel. Out of curiosity, I noted where the Israeli airfields were, but for most of the two hours I spent in the air, I worried about the engine.

It began to misfire seriously as I approached the Dead Sea. My plan had been to fly north until the mountains to the east dropped to below 6,000 feet, then cross them and pick up the road to Amman. At about 9.15 am, flying at 5,000 feet and near to where I wanted to cross, I was in touch with air-traffic control, but increasingly unhappy. The controller urged me to cross the mountains as there were airfields on the other side. I declined, saying that I wanted to circle to try to clear the engine and prevent it dying on me. I circled for two minutes, waiting, and then, to a fearful silence, the engine stopped . . .

Chapter Nine
King Hussein

In the silence my heart thumped very loudly, and for a few moments I went a long way away. It was as though the engine stopping had nothing to do with me, and I was looking down at the Dead Sea and the Wadi-el-Araba through the thick end of a telescope. ATC buzzed in my radio. When I returned from wherever I had been, I told them my engine had stopped, but that I was confident of landing on a road below me. The town of Safi was just to the north and west of me.

As I descended slowly, ATC faded on my radio. As an experiment, I pulled the start cord, and the engine fired again. It sounded very sick, though there was some power available. Losing height and looking at the road, I circled slowly, trying to judge the traffic. There was one long straight stretch where the telephone poles moved away from the road and there was room for the Flyer's wings. That, I thought, is where I am going to land.

There was enough power to slow the descent and enable me to cruise north and south along the road to pick a clear patch. At about 500 feet below sea level I found one, and almost threw the aircraft out of the sky. Turning left and right for the final run-in, the engine stopped again. Committed. No way out. Over the telegraph wires we went, and then skidding along the road, but we landed safely. A car came out of a side road and then turned back again hastily, but I stopped long before reaching it. With my heart still thumping loudly, and my blood rushing through me, I pushed the Flyer to a parking spot a hundred yards up the road, and then sat down to wait.

The Jordanian army turned up first, starting with a sergeant who asked questions in Arabic, to which I had no reply. He went away. Then a lieutenant arrived and became very aggressive, but still in

Arabic. He pointed to the border and shouted 'Israel!' I showed him my British passport and said 'no', but he shouted 'Israel!' again. In my paperwork I found my flight plan, filed that morning at Aqaba in the Hashemite Kingdom of Jordan. It was printed in both Arabic and English, and after reading it he calmed down a bit.

For the next few hours there was a procession of officers who examined the Flyer, and questioned me about what I was doing on the road. A strange air of detachment settled on me. When I could find someone who spoke a form of English, I asked that Amman be telephoned, and that a Mr Mike Atkinson take a taxi to where I was, but none of these messages got through.

Half an hour after I came down, two huge helicopters burst out of the mountains in the east. One was white with red crosses on it, the other green and camouflaged. They looked as if they wanted a fight as they hurtled towards me. The white helicopter circled once when I waved at it, and then left in apparent disgust. The other helicopter landed, and some doctors emerged.

'We heard you were seriously injured after crashing your aeroplane,' one said, which must have been the origin of the 'Crashed in Jordan' story that circulated in England the following day.

'No, no, I'm fine, but I can't get the engine to start,' I said. 'I'm hoping my friend, a mechanic called Mike Atkinson, will turn up soon and tell me what's wrong.'

We talked for a few minutes. They looked the Flyer over and grinned at each other. The engine would not go, no matter what I did or how many times I cleaned the carburettor. If they were going back to Amman, would they tell Mike to grab a cab and hurry? They waved a cheerful goodbye, took off and headed for the mountains.

To show willing, I fiddled with the engine occasionally, but with little faith. It was an easy matter to strip the carburettor and clean the jets. But although I pulled the starter until I was exhausted, nothing happened. Dozens of locals stared from across the road in that intent way Arabs have, and soldiers who had been detailed to guard me drove them away. Any car that slowed down was shooed on. Then it started to rain. I sat in the cockpit, shut the canopy and dozed.

Hours later, a soldier knocked on the canopy and pointed north, smiling. There was the big camouflaged helicopter heading back towards us. It circled once and landed about a hundred yards away, and I was delighted to see Mike staggering across the field with a big bag full of tools and spare parts. The helicopter that had landed earlier in the day had, I was told, gone straight to Amman, 100 miles away, and sent out soldiers to search the airport until Mike was found. He joined a number of cheerful and sharp accident investigators and engineers in the helicopter, and was flown to get me. The kindness and efficiency of the Jordanian Air Force was astonishing, but as it happened, this was only the half of it.

Mike stripped the Flyer's carburettor, and he and a tough Jordanian engineer went through the whole fuel system. Still the engine would not start. They checked the electrics and found a spark, but the engine remained dead. Then they drained off the fuel and Mike tried to set a cupful on fire with his lighter.

'This isn't petrol,' he said. 'This is jet fuel.'

We checked the receipt I had been given and there it was, A1 jet fuel! I knew I had asked for petrol in Aqaba, but I had been given jet fuel, which is rather like paraffin. In Europe, jet fuel is a different colour to Avgas, but this colour coding did not apply in Jordan. Mixed with oil in the mixing can and in the evening light, it had not looked any different to petrol.

Mike drained away all the bad fuel, and the helicopter flew off to find petrol at a potash plant twenty miles away. It returned less than an hour before darkness, dropped us the petrol and flew away to Amman with all the engineers and experts back on board, minus Mike. No one wanted to stay the night so close to the Israeli border. But Mike and I flushed out the system, and put in clean two-stroke fuel. It was fully dark by the time we got the engine going again.

A large man called Nasser Al-Sadour, manager of the potash plant, had arrived with the petrol and watched our attempts to get the engine going again. He spoke excellent English and told us that soldiers had been assigned to guard the aircraft all night. We were welcome, he said, to stay the night at his industrial plant. A house had already been assigned to us.

We accepted his invitation gratefully and a car took us all to the plant where we were shown our house and then fed royally. The potash plant was the usual dirty industrial complex sited next to the Dead Sea, but nearby was an estate for workers and management. The house we were allocated was one of a hundred similar houses, white with a roof balcony and Arab in style, although with all the plumbing and electricity of a European house. We were taken by car everywhere, including to the local club, where there was an all-male social life. Another car was arranged to take us back to the Flyer at dawn, and that same car would then drive Mike the 100 miles to Amman. This was the first of a number of occasions when I was lucky enough to enjoy the legendary hospitality of the Arabs.

All Jordanians asked me about my attitude to Israel. Every night Israel was roundly condemned on television. This was, I thought, normal for Arab TV, but when I saw the Western media later, I realised that the disturbances were bigger and more important than I had thought. Had I been to Israel? Did I intend going there? A lot of Arabs said they had once lived in territory now occupied by Israel, and still thought of Palestine as their home. But there was none of the drive-them-into-the-sea threats you often hear hardline Israelis claim the Arabs make, and which are used to justify the occupation of the West Bank. I was as diplomatic as I needed to be with my answers. It was not my job to strike attitudes. The Flyer had to go again, and I had a date in Australia.

Mike and I left at dawn on 20 December and were driven at great speed back to the aircraft. The soldiers had had a weary night of it, and we found some dirty T-shirts – all we had – to give them as a thank-you present. They called their local commander while we prepared the Flyer, and when we were ready, soldiers cleared the main road for a kilometre. I taxied to one end of the cleared space, turned and opened the throttle, and took off. It was, as road takeoffs are, quite exciting. I had to steer a very narrow track to reach takeoff speed, and one mistake would put me into the rough ground on either side. The problem was compounded by the fact that the valley I was leaving was 1,200 feet below sea level, and the air felt heavier than usual. I took a long time getting into the air.

For fifteen minutes I climbed steadily and looked at the mountains. My nerves were on edge, listening for any missed beat in the engine, but it worked perfectly. At cloudbase, I looked east and saw a hundred feet of clear air between cloud and mountains. Many of the peaks were covered, but, full of tension, I threaded my way along a road due east, twice turning around and heading west again because I was not sure I could stay out of cloud. Being caught by cloud in mountains is one of my personal nightmares.

The wind was blowing from the west, but on the other side of the mountains it came from the south. The ground seemed to be going by very fast, perhaps 80 mph, but in fact I was doing only half that speed. The gap between cloud and mountain widened once I passed the peaks, and I was soon into rugged open desert, flying over occasional flocks of sheep. In the distance there was a north–south road, and once I reached it, I headed north.

The country over which I flew was now story-book desert, sand as far as the eye could see, with mountains in the distance, and one thin straight road stretching to the horizon. It took an hour and a half to reach Amman Marka airport, close by the city of Amman itself. After a routine landing I was directed to a very smart building, passing two brilliantly shiny Lockheed jet airliners.

An Air Force officer came out to the Flyer and guided me into an office. Five or six wing commanders were standing smartly to attention, and there was a lot of saluting. In the middle was a smallish man wearing a beret and chain-smoking. He had a moustache, crinkly eyes full of humour, and he looked as tough as old boots. He introduced himself as Ihsan Shurdom, Commander of the Royal Jordanian Air Force, and he had been waiting for my arrival for the past twenty-four hours. By the strangest chance, we had been together at RAF College Cranwell back in 1961, when he was a senior cadet with 81 Entry, while I was a junior cadet with 85 Entry. It was a fine irony that having at one time both been in the same position as junior air-force cadets, he was now commander of his country's air force, while I was a journalist in a battered little aeroplane struggling to get to Australia.

Ihsan said that Crown Prince Abdullah, son and heir of the King, was coming to look at the Dalgety Flyer. Tea was brought, and two deep gashes on my left hand were treated medically. The Flyer was wheeled into the Royal hangar, next to the Lockheeds, which belonged to King Hussein himself and were being prepared to take him to Moscow the following day. Ihsan smoked and talked, and occasionally answered the phone. Mike arrived grinning and said it had been a hair-raising drive across the mountains. He joined a bunch of mechanics huddled around the Flyer and trying to get the HF radio to work. The HF had not worked since crossing the Mediterranean; the radio itself was fine, but we later discovered a broken wire leading to the remote controls.

Ihsan answered one call, put the phone down and smiled. 'The King wants to see you,' he said. 'Come on, I will drive you to the Palace.'

King Hussein was the only ruler in any of the countries I passed through for whom I heard spontaneous declarations of loyalty. He had been on the throne thirty-five years (he had been on the throne when, as a young man, Mike had been sent to Jordan with 2 Para in 1958) and had survived a number of assassination attempts.

Hussein was a real king, not just a tribal chief lucky enough to be appointed by the British when they ruled the Middle East. He was a direct descendent of the prophet Mohammed, through the prophet's only daughter Fatima. This gave him immense prestige within the Arab world, even among the Iranian Shiites, who otherwise hated him. Before leaving England, I had read a few books on Islam, and as I sat in Ihsan's big Mercedes car I thought about this, so abstracted that I forgot the Dalgety Birthday Book.

We went through the Palace gates and walked down a corridor to have coffee with the chief of protocol, who was, said Ihsan, the grandson of the Arab chief Auda Abu Tayi (played by Anthony Quinn in the film, *Lawrence of Arabia*). I asked Ihsan if he would carry my cameras when I met the King and take some photographs. After fifteen minutes we were shown back into the corridor, a door opened into another room, and the King smiled and offered his hand.

We talked a while about the flight and the Dalgety Flyer, and when we stood up he noticed Ihsan taking photographs. He stood next to me, smiling at the camera, and put his arm around my shoulder. I was overwhelmed, and could understand all those tense bodies outside in the corridor, poised to leap in to protect the King with their lives. Ihsan took a couple of snaps. The King gave me a watch, and a second one for Mike. The Arabic inscription said that they were the King's watches.

He showed me out into the corridor to meet his brother, Prince Hassan, and his eldest son, Crown Prince Abdullah. The Crown Prince was a pilot, like his father, and wanted to own a microlight, but the King would not allow him. I said I thought my aircraft was one of the toughest microlights in the world and the Prince replied that perhaps my visit and my flight would convince his father. Ihsan laughed at this, and the pair of them, Prince and Air Force Commander, looked like two younger brothers trying to persuade a stern but much-loved elder brother to change his mind. I left the Palace in a daze.

King Hussein became patron to the Dalgety Flyer, which was to save the whole flight a few days later in the Persian Gulf. Royal Jordanian Airlines was deputed to see me through the Middle East, which gave Mike official airside credentials and eased my path a great deal.

That night it bucketed with rain. As official guests of the King, Mike and I were taken to the Amman Plaza hotel, one of the plushest hotels I have ever stayed in. We had adjoining rooms, and delighted in running from one end of our rooms to the other. After a deep, hot bath, we rummaged through the small, tatty pile of clothing we carried with us, then went downstairs for a superb French meal and a good bottle of wine. We thought we were lucky people, and of course we were. There was nowhere else in the world either of us wanted to be that night.

Chapter Ten
Crossing the Great Saudi Desert

There is only one way for a low-flying aircraft to cross the Saudi Desert, and that is to follow the great oil pipeline linking Dhahran on the Persian Gulf with the Mediterranean. The desert is a thousand miles across, inhospitable in the extreme, and prone to sudden sandstorms. When Ross Smith and the other pioneers made the crossing, they carried letters from prominent Arabs in case they came down among hostile tribes. They also took a route further north, via Baghdad and through Iran, for political reasons impossible during my flight. My plan was to do the crossing in two giant hops, from Amman to Al Qaysumah in Saudi one day, and from Al Qaysumah to Abu Dhabi the next.

To do that I needed a following wind, one of the prevailing northwesterlies supposed to blow in December. But I had another headwind when I set off from Amman on 21 December. Amman's airport is located in mountains 2,500 feet high, and my takeoff was laborious. With a full load I could climb at only 100 feet a minute. I clattered around the valley in which Amman is set, trying to gain height, and there was a short period when I thought I was going to hit one of the high buildings near the airport. It took ten minutes of hard work to reach 3,500 feet, just enough height to scrape over the top of the mountain ridges, and head east into the desert.

Three hours into the flight, which had been uneventful until then, I had a bearing on Turayf and was working up the nerve to leave the road I was following when the engine suddenly lost power. The aircraft went into a steep dive, and I looked frantically for somewhere to land, my heart pounding loud enough to hear. But after thirty seconds the engine regained power, so I climbed back to a thousand feet above the ground and continued to hug the road.

Twenty minutes later it happened again: lost power, steep dive, pounding heart, recovery, stagger on. Another five minutes and it happened again, followed by a gap of fifteen minutes, then ten, then thirty minutes. The more it happened, the less frightened I became. You can only take so much of one particular type of fear. There was still tension, but never again that day the pure terror of the first loss of power. Obviously there were different types of fear. I felt I was becoming an expert on the subject.

At Turayf, I turned east-southeast again, and was actually over the airfield when I had another loss of power. But I didn't want to land because Neil Hardiman had secured permission for me to land only at certain airfields in Saudi Arabia, and Turayf was not one of them. There were dreadful stories about the paperwork and bureaucracy that would ensnare a pilot who landed in the wrong Saudi Arabian airfield. So when my engine power came back, I flew reluctantly away.

The pipeline stretched into the distance, seeming to go on forever, and I stayed to the right of it, constantly looking for landing places. Nothing improved in the engine's performance. One moment it would be running sweetly, the next choking on less than half-power. By the time I reached 'Ar'ar, 300 miles from Amman, I knew I was not going to get to Al Qaysumah that day, and I was concerned about landing in the desert when darkness came.

Feeling miserable, I circled over 'Ar'ar, calling the tower on its frequency. Eventually I was answered, learned there was no con-flicting traffic, landed, and taxied in. One of the officials greeted me cheerfully and escorted me to the airport manager. I was armed with a letter written by the Saudi Embassy, plus the Dalgety Flyer book, and was prepared for a fight if I was grounded and imprisoned for landing at the wrong place. But to my amazement the manager read the Embassy letter and welcomed me warmly. After fifteen minutes' polite conversation in English, which he spoke well, he summoned an Englishman, Tom Lyon, who worked there. I told Tom about the carburettor problems, and he found a hangar for the Flyer. It was the same hangar that Eve Jackson had used, and the first of many traces of her journey a year earlier.

The manager invited me to a lunch being given for visiting VIPs. It turned out that I was the only European there, and easily the most shabbily dressed. We went to his house, took off our shoes (my socks were clean, thank God), and entered a room full of cushions. In the middle was the roasted carcass of a whole sheep, surrounded by rice and vegetables. Everyone sat down cross-legged on a cushion to eat, and I was invited to do the same.

'Use your right hand,' someone kindly told me.

It's good manners in Arab feasts to root around inside a carcass, find a choice piece of meat, and offer it to a visitor. There were half a dozen offerings that I smiled over and accepted, but none were the eyes of the sheep. It was awkward to eat Arab fashion, mixing different foods in one hand and emptying it into my mouth, and I can't have been good at it, for I was soon given a plate and a fork to relieve my embarrassment. The food was excellent, and we drank lemonade or mineral water. When the meal was over, we got up to wash our hands (in my case stiff-legged from loss of circulation), the carcass was turned over, and a second sitting arrived. The newcomers included, I believed, the women who had cooked the sheep.

The manager, in an expansive mood, drove me to the airport where a television crew was waiting. We were then interviewed at great length. First, the reporter placed the airport manager in front of the Dalgety Flyer and asked a question. The manager replied with a torrent of words for five minutes. What was he talking about? About the Flyer. What did he know about her? As far as I could tell nothing beyond what he had read in the Embassy letter. That must have been what he told his television audience, with embellishments.

The reporter then turned to me, standing next to the airport fire chief. He asked the fire chief a question in Arabic. The fire chief beamed, took away his microphone, thanked the reporter in Arabic, then turned to me and greeted me lengthily in English, ending with a question: 'What do you think of 'Ar'ar?'

Most of the two hours I had spent in 'Ar'ar I had been rooting around inside the carcass of a dead sheep. What could I reply?

But I rose to the occasion and dwelt at some length on the beauty of 'Ar'ar from the air, and how pleased I was to be there, plus lots of truthful compliments about Arab hospitality. The fire chief thanked me in English, turned to the reporter and, in Arabic, replied floridly and at length to the reporter's question. It had been his moment of fame, he told me gratefully later, and he wasn't going to let it go without making a meal of it. The reporter snatched his microphone, snapped another question, and the whole process began again.

All this time the cameraman, an Egyptian who really fancied himself, was running his camera and taking shots of anything that interested him. He seemed to have no connection with the reporter, focussing the camera on the Flyer's scars, for example, whilst I was talking about Arab hospitality, and it was difficult not to burst out laughing. But it gave me a fame of sorts in Saudi, and when the story appeared in a news programme two days later, my journey was made easier. It seemed as though every Arab had seen the programme and knew what I was doing, and as a result helped me.

After the TV crew left I took the Flyer's carburettor to pieces, and soon found out what was wrong. At the bottom of the float chamber was a tiny pin, hardly big enough to see. It had fallen from a plunger which feeds fuel into the main jet, and also attaches a lever to the floats. Without the pin, the plunger became separated from the lever and could get stuck in the jet. The pin itself had been distorted after fiddling with the carburettor on the road in Jordan. It was an easy job to straighten it and attach the plunger to the lever again so that it would not come off.

There were problems finding two-stroke oil in 'Ar'ar. This was the first of a number of occasions when SAE30 grade was used as a substitute, once from a tin left behind by Eve Jackson. Petrol was very cheap and easily available, but (I now know) it was very low grade, probably sixty-five octane. Unknown to me, 'Ar'ar was noted for the bad quality of its gasoline. Because the Rotax engine needed at least eighty octane to run cleanly this was to cause me a day of problems. But when I went off to stay the night as a guest of Tom Lyon with six expats who worked at 'Ar'ar, I still thought I might make Al Qaysumah the following day, and be in Muscat for Christmas.

The expats worked in construction. Much of the actual physical work was done by Thai labourers who were overseen by Englishmen, but the decisions were made by Arabs who appeared not to know very much about the nuts and bolts of a job. The Englishmen had a deep contempt for the Arabs, thinking them hypocritical.

'When the Saudis are abroad they drink and chase women and smoke, everything they ban us from doing in their country,' said one Englishman. 'Then they come back here and they are Holy Joes. Yet they boast about the number of European women they have had.'

All that was keeping the Brits in Saudi was the money, and proposed changes to the taxation laws could drive them away. It was a spartan existence. They drank alcohol-free beer, and cupboards and chests of drawers throughout the house were crammed with thousands of well-thumbed books.

Dozens of videos, the other main form of entertainment, lined the floor. Tom told a story about the Arab censorship of a scene from an American movie where a woman appeared in a bikini. On Arab TV screens a hand appeared, holding a board which covered the woman's body. Wherever the woman went on the screen, the hand and the board shakily followed her. Once the hand came down, presumably to see if she was still wearing a bikini, found she had taken the top off, and shot back up again. But I was struck by the pervasive American culture in so many programmes on Arab television.

The next morning, 22 December, I took off from 'Ar'ar with a full twenty-eight-gallon load, and was nearly killed.

Thirty seconds after leaving the runway the engine failed. It was in the middle of a left turn to head east, and when the engine lost power I had a sudden, vivid picture of crashing and burning to death. To gain airspeed, I put the nose down and turned back towards the runway, with the engine running in a strangled, powerless way. The Flyer crabbed through the air, sideslipping and skidding into wind while I fought to land on tarmac instead of rough ground.

The airspeed fell to below forty-five knots, dangerously close to falling out of the sky. As on previous such occasions, I landed like a hang-glider pilot, almost stepping her out of the air sideways, and finally swooping over the tarmac and putting the wheels on the ground. Back at the apron, I spent a shaky half-hour cleaning out the carburettor.

Still not happy, I took off again at nine o'clock. It was the beginning of a day marked on my map with HFs – Heart Failures. Later in the day, as I became more sophisticated, I detected a difference between HF and BHF – Big Heart Failures. An ordinary heart failure was losing height, but not more than 500 feet. A big heart failure was when the engine lost power, I dived at the desert, and was lining up for a landing fifty feet above the ground when the engine regained power. In all, I experienced fifteen losses of power that day.

The weather was misty, with (of course) a headwind, hot on the ground but quite cool at 2,000 feet. After only three heart failures, I noticed that visibility was falling. The horizon became fuzzy and the road below seemed to get shorter and shorter. As usual, I had stomach cramps as I tried to comprehend what was happening, and talked aloud to myself as a warning that I was in trouble.

'Sandstorm! C'mon, decide what to do. Go lower, that's it, get closer to the road – wait! Are there any aerials coming up? I could hit one! Where's the map? Passed one ten miles back, another one in ten miles. Can't see the ground! Get lower!'

The road was beginning to disappear in fine whirling sand as I circled to lose height. There were occasional glimpses of the ground, but nowhere suitable to land. On either side of the road was sand, but I could not be sure how flat it was, and whether there were hidden ridges or rocks. Then I saw a track at right angles to the road, and almost facing into wind. The track led to a small power station a quarter of a mile north of the pipeline.

That was my landing spot, I decided, and flew around the power station once to make certain there were no hidden wires or tall chimneys. I came in low over the power station gates and put down bumpily on the track. When I got out, the front tyre was punctured. As I removed the wheel, two Arabs silently appeared.

Mike had some of the tools needed to repair the tyre, but one Arab drove me off to a nearby shanty village which had repair facilities. The other Arab stayed by the aircraft, and I worried about things getting stolen, but it did not happen, there or anywhere else in Arab countries. A villainous-looking young man took out the tyre and fixed the puncture by setting a patch on fire to make a tight seal, which I had never seen done before. He lost the tyre valve and we had to make another one from bits and pieces. In all, more than an hour was spent on the job, but during that time they discovered why I was making a flight to Australia. When I attempted to pay for the repairs they refused the money, but took a number of photographs of each other, standing proudly next to the Dalgety Flyer.

By 11 am I had replaced the front wheel, and taken off again to fly east. The town of Rafhā, in the middle of the desert, was passed about half an hour later, and I began to hope that, despite the engine failures, I could reach Al Qaysumah that evening. There were two more sandstorms which were not as bad as the first one (or maybe I was less worried by them), and I flew through them. But close to four o'clock in the afternoon I had another engine failure passing over the town of Shoba, and as I skidded all over the sky, losing height, I felt that power would not come back.

The desert surrounding Shoba was full of rocks and boulders as far as the eye could see, particularly unsuitable for a landing. There was a road on the outskirts of town, where I tried to put the Flyer down. The engine was roaring and dying, and on the faintest chance that it would regain power, I did not turn it off to try gliding in. Sinking lower and lower, I flew south, away from the town, certain that the undercarriage would be wiped off in the landing.

During the last few moments before hitting the ground I shouted to myself, 'Hold her up! Keep the nose up! Pull it! Pull it!' and then the back wheels were down, and I put the nose on the ground, shouting 'Brakes! Brakes!' We stopped without that awful lurch I had been dreading and which would have meant a broken undercarriage. (Eve Jackson had suffered two broken undercarriages.) But when I stepped out and walked around I found the Flyer was, by some miracle, undamaged.

For a couple of minutes I was alone, but then streaming over the desert came hundreds of Arabs, many on foot, others hanging on to cars. They soon surrounded me, men and boys, touching the aircraft in a childlike way, and greeting each other with hugs. They smiled at me, but none of them spoke English.

The letter from the Saudi Embassy in London had proved to be a powerful juju at 'Ar'ar, so I hauled it out of my bag and watched it circulate around several men in the crowd, each apparently more highly ranked in their social system than the last. They gave me the letter back and gestured towards the town. Youngsters gathered to push the aircraft, and I closed the canopy and turned the Flyer so that she was tailfirst to the town. We walked about a kilometre, and then the Flyer was installed in front of the police station.

I had a chance to look more closely at Shoba than at any other Arab town. It was built, naturally enough, on either side of the oil pipeline and road which dominated it. There were hardly any 'streets' as such, just flat desert between little clumps of buildings. Most of the houses were enclosed by courtyard walls, which hugged the buildings closely and made them far more private than English homes. There was a clear distinction between young children running around on the streets, who could be of either sex, and grown-ups, who were almost all men.

Dr Ahmad Tainuni, a Palestinian doctor who spoke English, was produced. He explained to the town elders what I was doing, and about the Birthday Book. There was a conference of headmen, during which Ahmad asked me to stay the night with his family. I accepted, which caused him great delight, the more so as each of the headmen made similar invitations, and I had to turn them down. We drank sweet tea, for which I was acquiring a taste. The town headman said he could put the Flyer on a truck and drive it to Qaysumah, 150 kilometres away. However much trouble it was, I said, I would rather fly there. A guard was assigned to the aircraft, and I went off to Ahmad's place.

His wife and twelve-year-old daughter welcomed me to the house, which is very unusual in Arab homes. The house was approached through a door, rounded on top, which led into a small yard enclosed on one side by the wall and on the other by the house itself. Inside the house, all the living accommodation was on one level, with whitewashed walls and hanging carpets and icons. There was a spartan air to everything; it was not poverty, just that nothing was ostentatious. The toilets, which I always feared, were of the old French type, a hole in the ground with two concrete pedestals on either side.

Ahmad had four children, delightful creatures, full of curiosity.

He had been educated in the West, met his wife at university, and planned for his daughter to go there. But he was also sensitive to traditional Arab views on the role of women. When the children clamoured to see the aircraft later in the evening, we all piled into his car. His wife and daughter suddenly appeared in the back, and I was shocked when I saw they were dressed so that only their eyes showed. We drove to the Flyer and the children tumbled out and were photographed sitting in the cockpit, but Ahmad's wife and daughter stayed hidden in the car. They could only watch from afar, and question the children about it afterwards.

Ahmad shrugged when I asked if they weren't disappointed. There was nothing he could say. The laws of Islam are exact about the deportment of women, and desert Arabs think town Arabs corrupt and decadent in not obeying them to the letter. But I thought about his daughter growing up, going to college, wearing Western clothes and tasting the world before marrying and becoming the obedient servant the *Koran* told her to be. Ahmad said most Arab women were happy with their lot, and anyway indirectly they exercised a great deal of power which Westerners could not see.

That evening I sat under a dark starry sky and tried to contact airliners 40,000 feet above me on the emergency 121.5 frequency. No one in London knew where I was, and I wanted to pass on a message that I was safe. The town of Shoba had 2,000 inhabitants, but no phone. No airliner answered my calls, but I never saw any lights in the sky and it may have been because there was no one within range. I did not try for long, but I felt very lonely.

Shoba was next to the pipeline, on the great trans-Arabian road, over which traffic roars twenty-four hours a day. Police cleared the road the next morning for the two minutes I needed to line up and get airborne. At 7.30 am I was in the air, and at 7.35 am nearly back on the ground again, when the engine lost power on the other side of town. A car shot off into the desert after the driver saw me shape up to land on the main road, but finally power came back and I flew on to Al Qaysumah.

By now I was certain that the petrol I had been given in 'Ar'ar was the cause of my two dozen engine failures, and when I landed at Al Qaysumah, I drained all the fuel away. It took the rest of the day to find suitable oil for the two-stroke mixture, and in any case, there was a strong headwind blowing that made it doubtful that I would get to Dhahran before the early winter night.

The young fire chief in Al Qaysumah, Mohammad Saleh Sulymani, invited me to stay the night at his house. He had learned how to be a fire officer in Newcastle-upon-Tyne and despite being married to an Arab girl for five years had fond memories of the English girls he had met there.

'Ooh, those Newcastle girls,' he sighed, happily telling stories about his training. He opened my eyes for the first time to the notion that Newcastle-upon-Tyne is one of England's centres of sensuality.

Mohammed told me the weather had been so bad the previous day when I had run into three sandstorms that airliners had been grounded. A Saudi Boeing 737 had been due in Al Qaysumah from Riyadh but circling the landing field, the pilot had decided conditions were too bad to land and had returned to Riyadh. I had been four and a half hours in the air in a microlight.

During the evening at Mohammed's I saw his wife once, but you wouldn't describe the experience as actually meeting her. He had invited friends, all men of course, around for dinner. It was laid out Arab style, so we sat cross-legged on the floor. The food consisted of a number of dishes, including lentils, spiced vegetables and meats. We each took handfuls from the separate plates, eating without knife and fork. When more food was needed Mohammed left the room, closing the door behind him. We could hear him talking, and a woman's voice replying, but when he appeared again with more food there was no one behind him.

At one point in the evening, greatly daring, his wife walked past an open doorway. We both saw each other for the time it took to pass from one side of the doorway to the other, perhaps a second. I can only describe her as a handsome young Arab woman. What, I wondered, would Mohammed's particular girlfriend in Newcastle think about an Arab marriage?

With good fuel and sufficient oil I thought I could make it to the coast and the big airfield at Dhahran without trouble. The fuel cost me nothing. The desert Arabs saw me as a guest and would not allow me to spend money. On Christmas Eve, I arrived at the airfield at 7 am, and was delighted to find that, for once, there was a following wind which would help me on my way. Fifteen minutes later I was in the air.

At the coast a thickening mist made my familiar fears return. But despite the mist I covered 275 miles in three and a quarter hours, at an average of 85 mph. Mike Atkinson was at Dhahran airport to meet me, carrying credentials from Royal Jordanian Airlines as an official airline engineer.

There was no petrol bowser easily available, but I put in an extra five gallons of fuel from my mixing tank, which brought my total to twenty-two gallons, easily enough for the 340-mile flight across the Persian Gulf to Abu Dhabi. The radio began playing up, and we discovered a broken wire in a connecting box which was probably responsible for the HF radio not working. Connections to the VHF were poor, and after they were repaired there was not enough daylight left to fly to Abu Dhabi. We spent Christmas Eve, alcohol-free, in Saudi, and planned to spend Christmas Day in Abu Dhabi with a celebratory beer.

Chapter Eleven
Christmas Day 1987

On Christmas Day the wind at Dhahran changed direction from the previous day, swinging more to the south, which was a worry. But it was a light wind, and I had easily enough fuel to cross the Persian Gulf. The war between Iran and Iraq was at its bitterest during this period, and I was crossing a war zone. Air-traffic control wanted to route me north of Bahrain, and then southeast, 300 miles in all, across the most heavily policed stretch of water in the world. My destination was the small emirate of Abu Dhabi.

Eve Jackson had told me in England that Abu Dhabi was an oasis of Europeans in an Arab world, and she had been greatly helped by an outfit called Emirates Air Service. Mike and I decided we would celebrate Christmas by taking a half-day off while he changed the engine. It was the only 'holiday' we planned during the entire flight.

Equipment was packed into the back of the Flyer, including my small travelling bag and the five-gallon mixing tank, empty of course. There were three fuel tanks on the Flyer: the standard five-gallon tank at the back, a seven-gallon slipper tank underneath, and a sixteen-gallon main tank in the passenger compartment. Both the back tank and the main tank fed into the slipper tank, which in turn supplied the engine. The main tank was not tied down, and perhaps something we did with the luggage moved it. The effect, as I discovered less than four hours after takeoff, was to kink the fuel pipe and cut off half my fuel.

Takeoff was at 7.15 am. Crossing the coast, the engine lost power again, but as it felt just like her morning cough rather than anything more serious, I managed to refrain from telling ATC. After about fifteen seconds, power came back again, and I flew out to sea thinking that it was probably water in the fuel system.

For three hours the flight was uneventful. The air-traffic controllers were either British or American, and Bahrain ATC stayed in touch until I was out of radio range. There were warships from many nations stationed in the Persian Gulf, and following a compass course, I looked to see if I could find any. The Americans had put out a NOTAM – a warning – not to fly too near their ships, and to stay tuned to the emergency frequency to pick up their messages. When the flight was being planned I had hoped to find a US aircraft carrier and get permission to land on it to pick up the captain's signature for the Birthday Book. But I saw no warships, only tankers, and passed too far to the north to see any islands.

It was about 10.15 am when I noticed that the fuel gauge on the five-gallon back tank was reading empty. Switching to the seven-gallon slipper tank, I saw that it was reading less than half full. This realisation did not, as might be expected, strike me with terror, because I had distrusted my fuel gauges ever since Kythira and knew that there was a lot more fuel on board than the gauges showed. But when Abu Dhabi came into radio range – I heard them calling for me, which was comforting – I told them I might have a problem. They had me on their radar, and told me I was fifty miles out.

Talking to and reassuring myself, I flew on. If the gauges were right, there was nothing I could do about it. I just hoped they were wrong.

But they weren't.

Forty miles from Abu Dhabi airport, at just after eleven o'clock, the engine stopped.

There was a big tanker heading north below me, and I looked down in the stillness from 2,000 feet.

My heart pounded like a drum and I could hear the air rushing past the cockpit.

'Hello Abu Dhabi, this is the Dalgety Flyer,' I radioed in a shaky voice. 'My engine has stopped. I am going in.'

ATC calmly started vectoring aircraft towards me, as if it was the most normal thing in the world. For the first thousand feet I was very frightened.

David Cook and I had talked, one night in Kythira, about the possibility of going into the sea. It had been a purely academic discussion because – ha ha – it would never happen to me. At the time David had said it was necessary to wear shoulder straps as well as a lap strap, otherwise when the aircraft hit the water, the pilot would be thrown forward and smash his face against the instrument panel. I had argued, however, that it was better to go in with a lap strap only, so that if the aircraft was turned upside down I would be able to bash the canopy open, undo the lap strap and dive away. Shoulder straps could mean death.

When the engine stopped I was wearing only a lap strap. I tried half-heartedly to get into the shoulder straps, but it was too difficult in the confined space, so I gave up and thought about how to fly her on to the water.

My life jacket was the one I had used trying to cross the English Channel by hang-glider ten years earlier. Then I had made the mistake of blowing it up before I hit the water, which was a mistake because I had been nearly trapped underneath the wing, and had found myself unable to dive because of the lifejacket's buoyancy. Now I made the same mistake in the Dalgety Flyer. It must have been nervousness.

At about a thousand feet, still a couple of minutes away from getting wet, I became fatalistic. Inch'Allah, I said, the Will of God.

It was not that I believed this in the Muslim sense, but what was happening – was happening. There was no alternative but to make the best of it. I turned the Flyer into wind and watched the tanker. It gave no indication, then or at any time later, that I had been seen. The sea was very calm, and I was relieved in a detached sort of way, at the possibility of a flat landing. A small piece of me was also relieved that now the flight was over, I would not have to put up with being afraid for very much longer. There was no possibility in my mind that the aircraft would fly again; I just wanted to get out of her safely.

At 500 feet I radioed, 'What a way to spend Christmas!' but I think I was too low to be heard, and anyway ATC were calmly sending aircraft my way and probably had no time for frivolities. Close to the water I tried putting my spare radio in the back, in the vain hope that it would not get wet. I pulled the flaps down. David Cook had said I should not use them because of the torque they would create on the damaged wings – but, what the hell! She flew very slowly over the surface of the sea and I held her off and held her off, and then she went in.

The canopy sprang in at me and I tasted a mouthful of salt water. Then water poured off me and I could see again, and the canopy was gone. The sea lapped around my waist as I sat in the cockpit. My cameras had gone straight to the bottom of the Gulf; bits of paper floated around in the cockpit. I undid my lap strap, stood up in the cockpit and looked around. The tanker cruised northwards as if nothing had happened. About half a mile away an Arab dhow was sailing south, towards me.

Money, I thought, I must get my credit cards and money out of the back, where they were in a travelling bag, which I pulled out and put on top of the wing. Then I got hold of the dinghy, but decided it would be melodramatic to blow it up immediately, as I was in no danger of sinking. Uninflated, I put it too on the wing.

The empty five-gallon mixing tank was jammed by water pressure in the roof of the wing, and I left it there. A plastic bag floated on the water – Dalgety's Australian Birthday Book! Without it, I felt my whole flight was worthless. I dived for it, and brought it back to line up on the top of the wing. The seat cushion floated away, and I watched it go, uncaring.

After five minutes, a twin-engined aircraft flew overhead and started circling. The pilot waved and I waved back. The Arab dhow had stopped in the water and turned. I watched it fearfully, not wanting them to rescue me, because of semi-formed fears that they might claim the Flyer as salvage. They stood off 300 yards away and watched. After a while I looked at the Flyer itself.

She isn't damaged, I thought. The wings are in place and nothing appears to be broken. The instruments were awash, and the beautiful ICOM HF and VHF sets were ruined, and probably the engine too. But Mike had a spare engine, and if he put it on, why should she not fly again?

Twenty minutes after I hit the water I heard a helicopter, and a Bell 212 came out of the south and circled low over me. The pilot, a Canadian called Bill Kipke, took his aircraft down until it hovered just six inches above the Flyer's wing. The observer, Calum Fryer, also a Canadian, reached down and took hold of the luggage I handed him. Both men were based at an oil rig called Zakum West. Calum lowered a rescue harness, which I grasped and climbed into the helicopter. I felt very weak.

'Can you take my aircraft too?' I shouted. 'She's very light.'

'No,' he shouted back. 'It's too dangerous for helicopters to carry aircraft.'

We circled the Flyer, which lay flat in the water. Though I was rescued I felt numb. The dhow had turned away from my aircraft, but was not leaving. Bill Kipke opened the throttles and as we climbed, the Flyer and the dhow became smaller and smaller. I clutched the Birthday Book to my wet jacket and thought about very little.

They flew me to the oil rig, where I had a cup of tea and talked to the air-traffic controller. A phone was made available, and I called London and gave Tony Spalding the details of going into the water. Fiona was only half awake when I phoned her with my latest story, but I told her I was going to try to get the Flyer out of the water and make her fly again. It was very early on Christmas morning in London, and Tony phoned Simon Newlyn at Shandwick Public Relations, who immediately started to phone media contacts.

On Zakum West, I could hear from another phone the tinny sounds of aviation authorities trying frantically to find out what had gone wrong, and to get their teeth into me. But I did not want to speak to them; I was more and more convinced that we could rescue the Flyer, if only I could discover how.

Bill and Calum had Christmas dinner while I was on the phone. Afterwards they helicoptered me to Abu Dhabi, landing at an air-force base called Bateen on the coast, next to the city itself. My wet luggage, soggy maps and jacket were dumped on a trolley, and I trailed, irritated and distracted, into the control room. It was a little while before I noticed a young Arab, dressed all in white from head to toe, like Lawrence of Arabia. He was quiet, with a gentle smile, and all the others in the room deferred to him, despite his youth.

'My name is First Lieutenant Rachid Abbad,' he told me, 'and you are under the patronage of Sheik Mohammed Ben Zayed.'

Who was Sheik Mohammed Ben Zayed? I had never heard of

him, and did not actually understand what Rachid was saying. My grief at losing the aircraft filled me to distraction, along with the faint hope of rescuing her. It was Mike I needed.

Rachid explained that Sheik Mohammed was the Armed Forces Minister for Abu Dhabi, and he was at that time hawking in Pakistan. Learning that I was under the patronage of King Hussein, the Sheik had said that I should be given whatever I wanted to allow the flight to continue, and had appointed Rachid as his agent. Whatever I wanted!

'Can you find me Mike Atkinson?' I said, with little hope that he would even know what I was talking about.

'No problem,' he said.

It was a comment I had heard before on my flight, and it usually meant exactly the opposite. But Rachid showed me out to a gleaming new Mercedes 300, we drove a few hundred yards and, there was Mike!

He had seen me off in Dhahran that morning, and caught a scheduled flight to Abu Dhabi. When he arrived he was met by a Royal Jordanian Airlines agent, who told him the Flyer had crashed into the sea, but that I was safe. Mike took a taxi to Bateen, only to find that the Abu Dhabi Air Force guard would not let him beyond the boundary gate. He put the spare engine – 'The Gobbler' – on the ground and was walking around in frantic circles, wondering whether to go to Australia immediately, to join his wife before his ticket was cancelled, or whether to fly straight back to England.

'There's no damage to her, aside from the fact that she's wet,' I called out to Mike as I got out of Rachid's car. 'If we get her out safely and put that spare engine in, there's no reason why she shouldn't fly again.'

The only other pilot I knew who had ditched his aircraft and then retrieved and rebuilt it to fly again, was Francis Chichester in 1930. He flew a Gypsy Moth between New Zealand and Australia, and his aircraft sank overnight at Lord Howe Island when the floats sprang a leak. It had taken Chichester three months to rebuild his machine. His book, *The Lonely Sea and the Sky*, had been an inspiration to me, and from it I learned that most aircraft which go into the sea are damaged as much by retrieval as by hitting the water.

Mike jumped into Rachid's car and we went back to the operations room.

'What else would you like?' Rachid asked gently.

'Can you tell the two ships going out to the Flyer not to touch her, but to wait until we get out there?' I said.

'And can you get us a helicopter?' added Mike.

'No problem,' he said again, but it was a problem for a while. Rachid had amazing powers for a young lieutenant. There was a rumour going around the European community that he was the son of a sultan, but he would not confirm this for me. He mustered a major who was a helicopter pilot, but who was also reluctant to fly us. The major, who was Egyptian, thought we wanted him to lift the Flyer out of the water and was afraid that if she was damaged we would sue him. We assured him we did not want him to lift the Flyer.

'Just take us there, throw us in and leave us if you like,' said Mike. 'The ships can rescue the aircraft.'

'Ah,' said the major. 'If that is all, then no problem.'

While we were conducting these delicate negotiations, the four phones inside the operations room rang constantly. Mike was trying to use one to contact the ships on the way to the aircraft by radiotelephone, but every time we picked up the phone an English voice would say, 'This is *The Times*/ITN/BBC/*The Guardian* . . . Can I speak to Brian Milton?' Christmas Day is traditionally a bad day for stories, and on all the newspapers and television stations the duty journalists in London and Bristol were on skeleton staff and half asleep. Then Simon Newlyn broke the story that the Dalgety Flyer was in the sea, but that we proposed to take her out and fly again. It was a lovely Christmas Day story, with just the right amount of madness to it, and the phones started to jump.

During a slack period waiting for the helicopter, I did an interview with *The Times* which made the front page the following day. But as more demands came in for interviews, we ran out of time. Mike got through to the ships and half-sent his message but we were not sure that they would wait for us, and we wanted to get away quickly. Trailing half-finished interviews, we left the operations room and were taken by the major and Rachid to a huge Puma helicopter. Mike had the ITN camera, but it was gently but firmly taken from us while we were on the military base. Rachid joined us in the helicopter, which took off and turned out to sea.

At about this time the Iranians were attacking two tankers to the north of where the Flyer was lying in the water. Seven people were dying or dead.

The helicopter had a full search-and-rescue crew on board, who smiled at us through all their equipment. Mike and I wore trousers and Dalgety T-shirts, leaving shoes and socks on board with Rachid. Mike had a handful of tools, including a hacksaw blade and an old screwdriver. He had been thinking about how to lift the Flyer out of the water, but did not tell me his plans. The pilot followed a bearing, guided by the beam of a VOR, and strained to catch the first glimpse of the Flyer.

When we found her, forty miles out, she was lying nose up and deep in the water. The leading edges of the wings and my cockpit were clear of the sea, but the rest was submerged. About fifty yards away was a flat ship with two cranes, and behind that was a tug. A small rubber dinghy had put out from the ship, and was slowly circling the Flyer.

'Don't get too close!' I shouted to the major, worried that his downwash would destroy it. Rachid looked as if he was enjoying himself. At the open hatchway I watched the water grow closer with Mike repeatedly telling me not to jump. He said the only person able to judge when to go was a jumpmaster, and without one I would probably jump when the helicopter was too high, and knock myself unconscious. I waited. Mike said later that I had looked very apprehensive. Neither of us thought at that time about sharks in the Gulf.

Finally the jumpmaster put his thumbs up, and, 200 yards away from the Flyer and fifteen feet off the water, I jumped. The sea was warm. When I surfaced, Mike jumped after me. We started swimming, and watched the helicopter make a dramatic turn (news of the Iranian tanker attack was coming through and they were needed) and fly away towards Abu Dhabi. Mike swam with a slow, dignified breaststroke, while I surged ahead of him, or trod water, laughing madly. Jumping from a helicopter into the sea is something

I have seen numerous times on television, and I had always wanted to do it myself. Mike grinned as he made his stately progress towards the Flyer.

It was for both of us the best moment of the whole trip.

The dinghy pulled towards us. In the bow, improbably, was an Englishman. Introductions were made from the water.

'Hello, I'm Brian Milton,' I said between mouthfuls of sea water, 'and this is my friend Mike Atkinson.'

'My name's Charlie Rogerson,' he replied, 'and I'm a diver on that ship.' Charlie came from Manchester.

He said he had not touched the Flyer, for which we thanked him, and he towed us both to the aircraft. Her tail was deep in the water. Taking off my life jacket, I swam down, attached it to the tail, and inflated it. The tail slowly rose to the surface. Mike asked Charlie for the towing rope and attached it to the Flyer's nosewheel. Charlie towed us slowly to the ship and laid us alongside.

'Charlie!' I called out. 'Please get a camera and take whatever photographs you can of us taking the Flyer out of the water.'

Leaving the dinghy, Charlie went off for a camera. Mike climbed into the Flyer's cockpit and started cutting, bashing and karate chopping a big hole in the top of the wing. I clung on to the right strut and watched in horror. Bits and pieces of the precious wing rebuilt in Kythira were thrown away, and when the hole was fifteen inches square, he started to thread a rope under the intersection point between fuselage and wing. This was, he decided, the only place to lift the aircraft, and whatever damage was done could be repaired later. When he had difficulty threading the rope through, he tore the radio aerial out of the cockpit roof and bent it to make a hook.

'Will that work again?' I asked dubiously.

Mike grunted and continued pushing, and at last threaded the rope through and made a loop. He called for a crane, a hook descended, and the Flyer was pulled a couple of feet out of the water. We dived to dismantle the wings, first the right wing and then the left. That meant diving to undo the linkages between the cockpit and aerilons and flaps, then the struts linked to the bottom of the cabin, and then the two big pins that hold the wing on. We stuffed all the bolts and pins into our soggy pockets. The wings floated easily and we pushed them around to the crew's waiting hands. Fifty hands reached down to lift each wing gently on to the deck. The crane lifted the body of the Flyer and deposited her dripping on the deck. Mike and I climbed out of the water.

The NMS401 was an oil rig support vessel, flat shaped, with two cranes and a central superstructure. Her crew, mostly from the Philippines, had been in the Persian Gulf for a month, and had run out of beer. Until I hit the water, they were due to spend two more beerless months at sea before returning to their base in Abu Dhabi. It was Christmas Day, and when they pulled the Flyer out of the water, they were going to get a bonus they had never expected: they were going to dock immediately at Abu Dhabi!

Mike looked the bits and pieces over carefully, feeling the wings in particular. Everything was repairable except the wings. In the six hours she had been in the water, the waves had moved the elevator so much that the Morse cable which controlled it was broken. That was the only structural damage.

'You're right, she will fly again,' said Mike.

We were shown to a cabin and a shower, and given clean, dry clothes. It was Christmas, and we had forgotten this in the struggle to get the Flyer out of the water. Anyway, we had thought that being in the Persian Gulf, no one would be celebrating Christmas. But the captain of the ship was a Lebanese Christian called Ibrahim Youssef Makhoul (known as Michel), and he and Charlie were sitting down to a big turkey dinner with Christmas pudding to follow. Mike and I joined them, and in the heat of the Persian Gulf we had the most extraordinary Christmas dinner we have ever had.

Afterwards, with the moon soft and yellow, and the sea calm and dappled in the moonlight, we steamed towards Abu Dhabi. The big deck lights were turned on, and Mike filled a fifty-gallon drum with diesel fuel and began throwing in engine parts from Sweetie Pie. I hosed down the wings and fuselage with fresh water, a process we continued for the next five days in order to remove all the corrosive salt from the airframe. We lifted out the radios and instruments and sprayed them with WD40, but they were beyond hope.

Dismantling the fuel system and taking out the tanks, I wanted to know what had gone wrong. There should have been twenty-two gallons on board at the start of the flight, but I was deeply fearful that I had miscalculated, and had been out of petrol when the engine stopped. We discovered that both the five-gallon standard tank and the seven-gallon slipper tank were full of sea water, but when we emptied the main sixteen-gallon tank we found it was half-full of fuel!

'There you are,' said Mike. 'You were in the air four hours, and the two empty tanks hold twelve gallons. At three gallons an hour that accounts for those tanks. There must have been a blockage to stop fuel coming from the main tank.'

We made a careful examination of the main tank, but could find no obvious source for the blockage. It could only have been a kinked pipe caused by movement of the tank on the back seat.

By the time we docked at eleven o'clock in the evening we had completed the strip-down, and there was Rachid to meet us in his beautiful Mercedes.

'Leave the aircraft on board tonight,' he said, 'and I will make arrangements tomorrow to get it taken to the airfield.'

We were driven to pick up our luggage and then on to the four-star Airport Hotel where we checked in. We had a meal in the restaurant and some much needed beer, and then unpacked. I took all my money, more than a thousand dollars in $20, $10 and $1 bills, separated each note and laid them out to dry. There was £2,500 worth of travellers' cheques, also laid out separately to dry. Mike peeled all the wet maps apart, some of which were very tatty, and laid those out. When we had finished, the room looked like a counterfeiter's paradise.

I was jumpy with energy and adrenaline. It was two o'clock before I went to bed, on the best Christmas Day of my life.

Chapter Twelve
Abu Dhabi

On Boxing Day morning, Mike and I lifted the Flyer off the NMS 401 and on to a truck provided by Rachid. From the port it was a two-hour drive through the town to the international airport; each of us held a wing to limit damage, with the body of the Flyer roped to the floor between us. Rachid escorted us in his Mercedes, talking constantly to friends on his car phone. I filmed everything on the ITN Sony 8 camera: removing the aircraft, transporting it, all the repair jobs done over the next week.

One repair we could have done without was caused at the airport itself by an overzealous guard closing a metal gate too early and trapping the aircraft's tail. As a result part of the tail snapped, as well as the filler pipe on the five-gallon tank. The guard caused more structural damage than six hours in the Persian Gulf had done. It took a day of Mike's time to repair that damage alone.

We were guests of Emirates Air Service, which was manned by Canadians and Englishmen who serviced aircraft for an airline of that name and for anyone else in the area. Eve Jackson had kept her aircraft in the Emirates' hangar when she was in Abu Dhabi. Mike settled down to replace Sweetie Pie with The Gobbler, cleaning and oiling the gearbox and exhaust system, for which we had no spares. I carried on the dogsbody role I had perfected on Kythira, hosing down wings and body for hours and running errands for Mike. But all we could do was clean things and wait, and the key figure in getting the Flyer going again was Neil Hardiman back in England. He had to find spare parts during the Christmas holiday and get them to us quickly. This was his finest hour.

The news that we had gone into the Persian Gulf had been greeted in different ways at home. Simon Newlyn of Shandwick PR and his merry bunch of pirates, Oliver Daniaud and Nikki Turner, broke open the champagne on Christmas Day because they had placed a story in the ITN news bulletin. Neil Hardiman had come upon Terry Pryce, Dalgety's chief executive, alone in his office on Christmas Eve, surrounded by maps and route charts covering my flight. Terry must have been deeply depressed on Christmas morning, but he said nothing to me about it. Tony Spalding always believed the best stories of the flight were how we got out of what went wrong rather than perfect flights. He was probably curious to see what we would do now.

But Neil was heartbroken. He had worked so long, and for so much of the time alone, to get the flight going that the prospect of it ending really hurt. He was phoned with the news of my flight into the Gulf by Tony Spalding at nine o'clock in the morning on Christmas Day. Neil said there was nothing he could do, and he would leave it to the PR boys. He thought I had no chance at all of getting the aircraft to fly again, and when he put the phone down he was close to tears. He went downstairs with his portable phone to make coffee, and all day the phone never stopped ringing. His Christmas was ruined.

That evening I phoned him, full of the joys of life, and said we were still in the game. He frankly did not believe me, and maintained the cautious attitude he had been forced to adopt surrounded by mad optimists. He asked for a full list of spares, and the next day went to Bristol to see Fiona and pick up my Jaguar.

When Neil phoned the Shadow factory, they laughed as soon as they heard his voice. He told David Cook that the Flyer was out of the water, but asked whether when she flew again she would fall out of the sky because of the effect of salt water on the glued joints. David checked with the glue manufacturers and some boating friends and decided the glue would hold.

'Not indefinitely though,' he said. 'It should be OK to get to Australia, but in two or three years' time there will be significant deterioration.' He told Neil we should worry more about the effects of corrosion on the aluminium tubing.

On Boxing Day evening Neil drove to my house in Bethnal Green, collecting Judy Leden on the way. Judy, a fiercely independent woman who reacts strongly against 'office girl' jobs, spent the next two days as secretary, typist and cook to Neil as he tried to meet tight deadlines for shipping spares out to us.

We agreed a final list that evening: an instrument set, including vario, altimeter, temperature gauges, a rev counter and a fuel gauge. I opted not to replace the original compass because it was a sealed unit, unaffected by the salt water. I forgot to ask for an airspeed indicator. Neil sent one later, and it was installed in Karachi. Neil also agreed to get a new canopy, a cable to work the elevator, a headset and cushion, and most importantly, an ICOM A-20 radio/ VOR. I could not see myself crossing the Persian Gulf to Pakistan without a VOR to guide me. If I went to the left of Pakistan by only ten miles I would end up in Iran!

Neil had to find all this equipment in one day, in the middle of the Christmas holiday period. It was like putting together a gigantic jigsaw puzzle. David Cook was the obvious contact for the instruments. He had a number in stock, but some poor Shadow owner in New Zealand got his aircraft late because they raided it for instruments.

Finding the ICOM was more difficult. Peter Davies, my instructor and an ICOM agent, was in the USA buying gyrocopters. ICOM itself was closed. Neil and Judy went into a brainstorming session by the phone and Judy remembered her next-door neighbour in Camberley had set up a business in avionics. His name was Tom Malony and his company was called Transair. Judy tried ringing him at home but he was away for Christmas. Eventually he returned, and picked up the phone.

'Have you got any ICOM A-20's?' Judy asked.

Tom said he had one left.

'Can we have it? And will you bring it to Heathrow Airport at six o'clock this evening because we have got to go to Suffolk to pick up instruments and have no time to go by you – can you do that?' asked Judy.

One advantage of being a news story is that everyone knew what the Dalgety Flyer was, and how the aircraft had landed in the Persian Gulf.

'No problem,' Tom said, and was as good as his word. He even gave them a discount.

Abu Dhabi

Neil and Judy leapt into the Jaguar and tore up to Suffolk, Judy sitting in the passenger seat and hating the whole experience. Neil dictated a letter to her while driving, 'adjusting' the prices so that I would pay the least possible customs duty. Judy grabbed a typewriter at David's factory while Neil and David roamed around selecting spare parts they thought might be needed. They packed everything carefully and then drove as fast as they dared to London airport, where Tom was waiting with the ICOM. All the spares were packed into the connecting Gulf Air flight in time, and cleared customs the following afternoon.

Judy cooked an exhausted Neil a meal that evening and said later in a letter to me: 'If it wasn't for you and this flight I would never have done all those awful jobs.'

In Abu Dhabi, Rachid turned up at Emirates every day in his big shiny car and asked if we needed help. One evening he brought a friend, a captain in the Abu Dhabi Air Force called Hussain Almoalla, one of the ten microlight pilots in the emirate. Microlight pilots in the United Arab Emirates were restricted to within two miles of takeoff and were allowed to fly at only a small number of sites. Hussain thought that my flight would open the eyes of the Abu Dhabi authorities to the possibilities of microlights, and that this would help him and his friends to negotiate less restrictive flying rules.

Rachid and Hussain took Mike and me out on the town. They showed us the seafront which the emirate's ruler had changed twice because he was not satisfied with the way it looked. Each time he had decided he didn't like the buildings, he had extended the seafront by reclaiming more land, and another set of buildings had gone up. He was said to be happy – and with reason, we thought – at how it looks now.

Rachid took us on to an Arab restaurant made from the former private yacht of the Sultan. The boat, which was built from the most expensive woods, had been lifted out of the water and carried to its new site. All the customers were Arab with the exception of Mike and me, but the four of us talked flying. At that time I had no airspeed indicator, and proposed to fly on without one.

'I have an ASI which is not totally accurate, but it might do you,' said Hussain.

Not only did he have one, but it was in his car outside, and he fetched it at once and gave it to me. It was the right size to fit into my cockpit, and if it was inaccurate it was consistently so and gave me some idea of my flying speed. What were the odds, I wondered, against meeting Hussain, and his having the only instrument I needed hanging around his car? I was very grateful for his present.

Rachid said, as we parted that night, that I should not concern myself with the hotel bill. The Abu Dhabi Government would pick it up. During my stay of five nights and Mike's stay of seven, the little Arab emirate did everything to enable me to fly on again to Australia. It was not that I was without funds, but I appreciated their kindness.

Repairs on the Flyer were shared with David Wood, one of the chief engineers of Emirates Air Service, and licensed to check out work on the most complicated of modern aircraft. He picked us up in his car every morning from our hotel to take us to work, and when his normal job finished in the afternoon he joined Mike on major repairs. The hole in the top of the wing needed covering, and the patches at the end of both wings were tatty. It was odd and very moving to see so well-qualified a man lying on the ground with a big file, smoothing the lumps of car filler we had put in the wing tips to get a better flying shape.

Emirates Air 'did a Rachid' about my bills, and charged us nothing for an invaluable service, which included putting up with the string of journalists and telephone calls that came in daily from British and a small number of Australian journals.

One night I was called at the hotel by a radio station in Darwin. Mike and I had worked for twelve hours and we were exhausted. Our only goal was to get the aircraft to fly again. It was as though we were blinkered. The Darwin station asked all sorts of questions about what was going on, before I realised to whom I was talking.

'Are you really there?' I asked. 'Does Darwin exist? How far away are you?'

On the afternoon of 30 December, five days after the Flyer went into the water, Mike said she was ready to fly again. The linkage between my earphones and the radios was still very poor, and never worked well again, but the rest of the aircraft was repaired. At 3.20 in the afternoon I taxied out to the runway and lined up to take off.

My old friend Fear had returned, but once more I was able to stuff him into a small corner of my mind and get on with flying. The Flyer leapt skittishly all over the sky in a ten-minute test flight, being only lightly loaded. With a full load, I thought as I taxied in, she will be different, but I will head straight out for Muscat tomorrow and that will do for a test.

The Bicentenary celebrations were on 26 January, only twenty-seven days away, and I had begun to despair of getting to Australia, never mind Sydney, in time. If I failed, the whole flight was pointless. I was already twenty-eight days out of London, and twenty-eight days after leaving London, Ross Smith had been celebrating his arrival in Darwin. Mike Atkinson and I spent evenings discussing how to get more speed out of the Dalgety Flyer and avoid the incidents which had twice nearly stopped me altogether. Mike thought the wing struts, being round in profile, were a major cause of drag. He made a set of fairings out of clear plastic to streamline them.

'If you hold a hang-glider control bar out of the window of a moving car,' he said, 'it's nearly torn out of your hands. But you can hold a faired one in the same wind with only one hand. It stands to reason that fairings will help.'

On New Year's Eve, I checked out of the airport hotel and David Wood drove us to the airfield. Mike and I agreed to meet in Karachi, but he was going to stay in Abu Dhabi until I had jumped the mouth of the Persian Gulf, before catching his own flight. I said goodbye to everyone at Emirates, and to Rachid and Hussain who came to see me off. At 8.20 am, I took off and headed east into the Omani desert towards Muscat.

Three minutes later, at 1,000 feet, the aircraft started juddering violently. It felt as though a wing was being torn off.

Airframe failure, I thought; this is how I am going to die.

I pulled back speed and turned slowly towards the airfield, wondering if she would hold together long enough for me to get her down without falling out of the sky in pieces. The juddering stopped. I looked left and right, expecting to see something broken from the wing. One of Mike's new fairings had blown away.

I landed cautiously and taxied to where Mike was standing.

'What's wrong?' he asked.

'Look at the wing struts.'

Mike looked at one, and then the other.

'Sorry,' he said.

'Ah well,' I said, 'we'll never get anywhere if we don't experiment.'

Mike took off the wing fairings, and I flew away.

Chapter Thirteen
Muscat, Pakistan and India

For the next thirty days I did not stop flying. The longest day in the air was ten and a half hours, the shortest just half an hour. Having been down on Kythira and the Persian Gulf, I was filled with impatience to get to Australia; I could not afford any more delays.

To get to Muscat on the Indian Ocean I had to cross 250 miles of the Omani Desert. In the summer it is incredibly hot, but for me it was just misty, with cloud around the mountains. I was scared of everything: of climbing too high, of getting close to cloud, of any turbulence. During the three-and-a-quarter-hour flight I imagined the aircraft falling to pieces a thousand times, and every foot of the fall to the desert below. But the Flyer made it to Muscat without incident. After five hours of argument and the intervention of the British Air Attaché, Tony Ogilvy, I was able to get out of the airport and into a hotel. There I spent the worst New Year's Eve of my life, alone in a big hotel in another country, cut off from friends and family.

There was an old *Daily Mail* in my room, and I remember reading a column written by Lynda Lee Potter attributing a New Year's quotation to the millionaire adventurer, Richard Branson: 'If you watch people dancing to pop music on television, and turn down the sound, they all look mad – but that's because you can't hear the music.' That was a night I wished I couldn't hear the music.

From Muscat to Gwadar in Pakistan was another 250 miles, across the troubled waters of the mouth of the Persian Gulf. Eve Jackson waited six weeks at Muscat before she was happy with conditions to make the crossing; I did not have that luxury. The weather forecast was discouraging, but I still set off on New Year's day.

And I failed.

For two hours I dodged through cloud, sometimes over, sometimes under, sometimes around. There were only a few ships, and those were close to the southern shore of Oman. I followed a compass course of sixty-four degrees, anxiously watching to pick up Gwadar on my VOR. Then I ran up against a wall of rain cloud. Flying in rain in a Shadow is like driving a car at dusk in rain, with no windscreen wipers. I tried climbing over the cloud, but at 6,500 feet it became a thick carpet, and though I tried to penetrate up through it, I lost my nerve after a few minutes and dived down into clear air. Then I circled down to below a thousand feet, looking for a way through the rain. The closer I got, the darker it became, and again I bottled out. There was a gap to the north, and I flew that way, but that brought me closer to Iran. After ten minutes I could see there was no way through to the east, and I turned around and took a miserable two hours to fly back to Muscat.

On 2 January, in conditions that were only slightly better, I had another go. About 120 miles out I ran into a similar wall of cloud, but this time it was not so thick and I was able to dive underneath it and burst out the other side. It was a far from enjoyable experience. After four and a quarter hours in the air I reached land and, recognising the coast, flew into the dry, desert airfield at Gwadar.

That night I was the guest of the young airport manager, Tariq Rizvi, and slept on a sofa in the airport lounge. Tariq was a city boy from Karachi, doing his stint in the provinces but longing for the bright lights. He had spent some time in England, and was obsessed by the thought that I should not be ripped off in Pakistan. He went everywhere with me, making certain that I was charged the correct price for petrol and oil.

'If anyone cheats you, Brian, you must tell me and I will go and smash his face in!'

He said there was too much corruption in Pakistan and his countrymen had a poor reputation abroad. But he and his friends were embarked on a deliberate campaign to restore Pakistan's good name. I was touched by the intensity of his vision for Pakistan, and moved by the way he seemed to be in a lonely fight against the odds.

When I went to sleep that night I was also relieved that I had made it across so much water without incident. Gwadar had no phone, so

I was cut off from London. A passing airliner captain on the way into Pakistan told me by radio that Mike had flown to Karachi, and was waiting for me there.

Carrying a full load of fuel, I left Gwadar just before 9 am on 3 January, and spent most of the day hugging the coast. It was hot and dry, and the roughest country I had passed over, a whitish-grey dust covering great barren plains and mountains. My fuel gauge no longer worked after the Persian Gulf, and after four hours I became worried about fuel consumption. Logic told me I had at least seven hours' worth available, but logic had failed me in the Gulf. Mentally choosing a thousand landing places in case the engine stopped, I scanned every yard of beach and ground I passed over, but The Gobbler ran sweetly.

After six and a quarter hours, and with – I later discovered – only two gallons of fuel left, I reached Karachi, only to be given the runaround by ATC. They were accustomed to sending big aircraft on various courses in order to ensure a six-mile straight-in approach to the runway. Using this technique on me, they sent me all over the place, although I had only one-tenth of the speed of the airliners. As in Cairo there was a certain loss of confidence when the chap guiding me suddenly said he had lost contact, and where was I?

'I am coming straight to the airfield on your beacon,' I snarled, 'and I will circle off the main glide path until you have room to admit me.'

Karachi was the first place I came across the fuel fiddles common to the Far East. Mike had taken care of the fuelling while I went to a hotel to check my route for the next day. A mechanic arrived on a motorbike, asking for US$150 to pay Mike. I bummed a lift to the airport to find out why 115 litres of petrol was so expensive. I was presented with a bill for 140 litres.

'The Flyer has a capacity of only 125 litres,' I said acidly, now entering into a state of rattiness which came at the end of each day and was only dispelled by two beers.

They insisted I had used 140 litres. We showed them the twenty-five-litre mixing tank we carried, where oil and petrol were turned into two-stroke fuel before being poured into the Flyer's tanks. They admitted that we had mixed just over four and a half tanks, but insisted that our tank was bigger than twenty-five litres. In the end I agreed to pay them for 125 litres, and to pay in American dollars, even though I was being cheated. It was their little fiddle. We came upon petrol meters later which had been altered to read as much as twenty per cent too high. Perhaps more conventional aircraft pilots take on so much fuel they do not notice.

Mike and I dined that night with John Kerapiet and his wife Mona. John, who was chairman of the authority administering all private aviation in Pakistan, could have passed for an English county gentleman in the way he spoke, and the things he believed in. Mona would have been at home in a Surrey drawing room. They fed us mild Pakistani food, over-concerned that our European stomachs would not be able to cope with hot curries, and talked of their plans to emigrate to Australia. John told stories of the Indian–Pakistani War in 1971, how there was a bond between opposing pilots: 'Don't call us enemies, Brian, we were . . . adversaries.' When an Indian pilot was shot down and ejected from his aircraft, the Pakistani pilots would rush to find him before their own army treated the Indian badly. They would bring him back to their mess, giving him drinks and talking about flying as though they had more in common with flying men of opposing countries than with their own countrymen.

At the time I was reading a book called *Winged Victory* by a man called Yeates who had flown Sopwith Camels in World War One. This I read from cover to cover, and then started again, and when I finished a second time, started a third. There was, in the daily grind of my flight and the doubt each morning whether I would be alive that night, a great deal in common with the life of an early fighter pilot. But John's story reminded me of flying and fighting in the early part of the Great War, when a romantic aura surrounded pilots, and there was a certain chivalry, which was only touched on by Yeates. Yeates did not adhere to this chivalry, but acknowledged cynically that it had been there. The Pakistani Air Force described by John seemed like a shadow of the Royal Flying Corps, of what the Corps purported to be rather than what it was.

(The odd thing was, when I arrived in India I heard exactly the same stories from Indian pilots, but the other way around. They had rescued their shot-down Pakistani adversaries from retribution by Indian soldiers. They were so similar, and in British India they shared the same history, and yet they had been adversaries since the British left in 1947.)

On 4 January, John Kerapiet personally saw me through customs and other formalities. Before I left England, I had heard Pakistan was 'absolute hell' for bureaucratic formalities, and I needed his help. Despite John's very senior position we spent nearly three hours trying to gather all the signatures to let me out of the country.

The route through to India was very inhospitable, over the infamous Rann of Kachchh, over marsh and desert, miles of wasted land covered with stagnant pools of seawater and poor, tatty villages. It was only my watch that told me when I had left Pakistan and arrived in India. A VOR beacon guided me out of Karachi, and six and a half hours later another VOR guided me into Ahmadabad. It was a long, weary flight, and my temper was not improved on landing by finding out that I was in a dry state, and there was no beer to mellow me.

There was a second shock at Ahmadabad. Neil Hardiman had told me while I was in Abu Dhabi that the Indian Government had changed my route, but I had not appreciated the consequences. My first route had taken me almost straight across the subcontinent: Ahmadabad to Nagpur to Jamshedpur to Calcutta. In Bristol my maps had been cut and glued for that route, and I was happy enough with it. Now I found that I was expected to go north of Nagpur to Bhopal, then almost directly north to Varanasi, before turning east again, down the Ganges to Calcutta. The problem was that I had no maps for the new route. And none seemed to be available.

Bhopal, which I knew as the city where thousands of Indians had died in a release of poison gas a few years earlier, was just about on the maps I had. But from there to Calcutta by the new route I had no maps. Other pilots I talked to flew from beacon to beacon, and did not use topographical maps any more. Because I flew a microlight, my style of flying was old-fashioned – a look-out-the-window style – and I wanted a map where I could follow rivers, roads or railway lines, dodge past mountains and mark towns. Which is not the way flying is done these days.

In none of the shops I was directed to in Ahmadabad could I find any maps. There was a brief period when I thought I should argue with Indian ATC and get clearance for my old route. But then it struck me that I was incredibly lucky to get clearance at all, and Neil had worked very hard to get it. If we started all over again wrestling with the paper octopus of Indian bureaucracy, it might be days before a clearance came through. Eve had been held up for weeks in India. Even if I had no maps, I was cleared to fly, so fly I must.

The trip to Bhopal was marked by two losses of engine power, both occurring as I taxied to the runway at Ahmadabad. Each time I returned to the tarmac and cleaned out the carburettor. After the second time ATC demanded a written report guaranteeing the safety and airworthiness of my aircraft before leaving again. With bad grace, I gave this guarantee, though I was not sure myself whether or not the engine would stop again. It was a misty day and conditions were not really suitable for flight. The haze, I found, went up to 5,000 feet, and it was very close to fog. Aircraft were being grounded in some of the airfields I flew over.

To begin with, the VOR beacon at Ahmadabad guided me on my flight, but I was soon lost. All I had to do was to get within fifty miles of Bhopal, which also had a VOR, and I could follow the beacon in, but for three hours I was not at all sure where I was. When I came across a railway line I followed it north until I came to a big town, which, by the shape of its roads and railways, I recognised. It was thirty miles north of where I should have been. From there it was easy to set a new course and punt off for Bhopal, where I landed after five and a half hours.

India, to an Englishman, is an echo of his own past, and even though I spent only four days there, I liked it. At Bhopal, for example, next to the new ATC tower, there was an old building, rotting and nearly windowless. It was obviously the former RAF mess and ATC tower, built during the Raj. My footsteps echoed on the broken concrete as I walked through it and read the faded lettering on walls: 'ALL PILOTS REPORT HERE'. With only a little imagination I could hear the Hawker biplanes landing there in the late 1930s.

The Indians seemed at ease with their past as the greatest of the

British dominions. All the hours of paperwork I had to fill in were familiar, the style of the lettering, the phrases, the smell of the paper, and the formal, loving way officials handled them. I could sense the slow, even rhythm of the Indian Civil Service that moulded and held together British India. However impatient I was with bureaucrats, I felt that the sheer inertia of the ICS – the nit-picking concern of every civil servant to do his job by the book – was the strongest bond holding India together. It's difficult to have a revolution if you have to fill in a hundred forms in triplicate just to organise a demonstration. Without the bureaucrats, the hundreds of different races in India would fall apart.

In the evenings in Ahmadabad and Bhopal, I used the tatty trishaws instead of taxis to get to my hotel. My flights may have been nerve-racking and uncomfortable, but this was alleviated by the sheer excitement of cramming myself and my luggage in the back of these small two-stroke tricycles, and tearing at great speed through town. No one stopped for traffic lights – were there any? – and everyone used his horn. Cows wandered into the middle of the traffic, which flowed around them without resentment. All the time, car horns blew an unsteady chorus of beep-beep-beep, one driver telling another he too was on the road. The horn noises mixed with revving engines, shouts and animal noises. As for the smells, they came wafting in through the open sides of the trishaw; curry, decay, excrement, sweat, in a continuous affirmation of life. I hung on tight in the trishaw and revelled in it. Almost as good as a beer.

Again in Bhopal, I tried for a map, calling at the improbably named Lyall's bookshop. Many of the shops and hotels in India have retained the names of their original European owners, even though they have been owned for generations by Indians. Lyall's was the best bookshop in Bhopal, but the only map I could find was a road atlas for India. It showed that my next destination – Varanasi – was on the great River Ganges. If I steered north, I thought, until I hit the river, and then turned right, the first city I came to would be Allahabad, and the second Varanasi. That was the best I could do without waiting for Neil to air-mail me the correct maps.

On 6 January, with the road atlas across my knees, I set off from Bhopal. The atlas was primitive, and showed only roads, railways and very big rivers. The first three hours were uneventful, but then I became aware of the engine labouring. It was not bad to begin with, a sort of chugging noise as if she was choking. Engine revs dropped to below 5,500, enough to maintain height, but not enough to climb or to get out of emergencies such as sinking air. There were no airfields nearby that I could see, and of course the map did not show any.

The problem could only get worse, and I decided to land while I still had power to play with. Through the mist, the countryside was full of small fields and hills, and I descended from 5,000 feet, looking for a suitable road. After ten minutes and down to 2,000 feet, I found one, a dirt track linking one village to another, with no traffic and approximately into wind. I circled downwind and descended, heading towards what I thought was a safe way in. As soon as I was low and almost committed, I saw the way was blocked by telephone lines.

Even though full power was not available, I opened the throttle and staggered on towards the road, and then decided I would not be able to get past a big tree. 'Can't do it! Can't do it!' I shouted, and wallowed through the air, over the road, and into a skidding circle with just enough power to keep me flying and just enough speed to stay in the air. All around the circle I chose places to land in case the power failed, but they would all have smashed the Flyer even if I could have got out unscathed. It was touch and go all the time – at one time perhaps fifty feet above the trees, in a detached cold sweat – but I made it back to line up on the roads again, scraped close to the tree, and slipped in, landing safely. With a hollow bump, the Flyer slowed on the dirt road as I jammed on the brakes and stopped.

As usual, I was alone for a while before villagers streamed in from all directions. A choking engine indicated a fuel problem, and I stripped the carburettor and checked all the jets. They were clear. When I reassembled it, the engine still sounded as though it was being strangled. Twice more, I stripped the carburettor, having little faith in my own mechanical work, but each time I started the engine it sounded poorly. Then I stripped the fuel pump, looked it over and reassembled it, but still no luck. Finally I tried the fuel filter, and when I released it a small trickle of fuel emerged. That was it! Eve had said cardboard filters were no good, but they had worked well until Abu Dhabi. It seemed that there was something in the fuel east of Suez that destroyed them. There was a spare filter in my bag, and I replaced it.

By this time, hundreds of villagers were sitting around my aircraft. They all had to touch it, and stroke it, and poke it, and I got ratty as hell and shouted at them to lay off. A man who seemed to be the chief took charge and drove away the children, who were only curious, not deliberately destructive. We all baked under the sun; sweating and curious, hundreds of eyes following every move I made. Once a bus arrived, the only traffic in an hour, and detoured into the fields to allow me to continue my work.

With the new filter fitted, I tested the engine; it roared healthily. The villagers clapped. One of them spoke a few words of English, and he asked me to stay for tea. I said I must fly on, and showed him my silly road atlas and asked where I was. He could not tell from the map, but one town name looked familiar. I asked him to clear the road, got into the Flyer, and started up. The villagers lined up along both sides of the road. Then a dog trotted into the middle of the road. I stopped the engine.

'Get rid of the dog!' I shouted, thinking someone would grab it and lead it away. Instead, three hundred sticks and stones started flying at the poor mutt, which went yelping and leaping all the way down the road. I started the engine again, closed the canopy, and revved up. At that moment, in the distance, a bus appeared.

If I go now, I thought, I will be in the air before it reaches me.

If I go a bit faster, the Indian bus driver must have thought, then I will soon find out what that strange object is in the distance. His dust cloud increased.

We hurtled towards each other. After a few seconds the Flyer's nose was in the air. I could not see the bus and I hoped I would make it. I hauled her into the air just above mushing speed, and staggered up over a tree, keeping her low to gain speed. When I circled back, there was the bus where I had taken off, with the driver getting out to ask what was happening.

For a while I climbed in circles, then headed northeast again. The mist and fog became worse when I reached the Ganges, but by that time the Panics had begun; the worst part of the flight, and the nearest I got to throwing in the towel, because of fears that I had lost my nerve.

Chapter Fourteen
The Panics

It is only in the last few years that I have become afraid of flying. It does not happen all the time, only on occasions, often when nothing else is going on. Falling out of the sky in 1978 did not help, and I had had to wind myself up a great deal to get back into powered flight.

Other pilots get frightened. There is a lot of toleration of fear in hang-gliding, my main experience of aviation. Johnny Carr, for example, one of the greatest of British pilots, had a daft fear about height. Circling at 1,900 feet he was happy as a lark. But whenever he went above 2,000 feet he started to look at the bits and pieces on his hang-glider and worry whether they would come apart on him. As he said, laughing about it, it will make your eyes water just as much to fall from 1,900 feet as from above 2,000, so fears were silly. They were with him for a long time, but he must have conquered them because he has flown at 15,000 feet in California's Owen's Valley, just up from Death Valley (and known to pilots as 'Scareyourgordoff'), and is still a competitive pilot after ten years at the top.

Dick Francis writes perceptively about fear in horse racing, and the nerve necessary to overcome it. Jump jockeys sometimes lose their nerve overnight, and never run a race again. Something snaps. Everyone in the game knows it happens. Ross Smith acknowledged his own fears in his book about the Australian flight, *Fourteen Thousand Miles Through the Air*. He said to a friend the real title should have been, *To Australia with the Wind Up*.

Until India, my own fears had never, quite, been crippling. They were not something I would acknowledge to anybody. By not going down various corridors of my mind, I could stop it affecting me, although if I couldn't help going down those corridors, I would become nervous and sweaty. I imagined myself falling out of the sky and remembered the exact sensation of hitting the ground in my 1978 crash. The rational part of my brain would argue the truth, that hang-gliders and microlights are now safe flying machines, and if there are accidents it is always the pilot's fault. But the animal part was still afraid.

There were various tricks I had developed to overcome fear. One was that I always chewed gum whenever I was in the air, though on the ground I rarely touched the stuff. I hated to fly if I had no chewing gum, and if I had to go up without it, I was more nervous than usual.

In a way, the Dalgety Flight painted me into a corner with my fear and said cope with it. The showdown came in India because there were no other distractions. The actual flying between Bhopal and the Ganges was easy, so I had time to rummage in my mind and drift unthinkingly down various corridors. Then I opened one door, and out jumped a djinni and screamed at me, Get down *now*!

At that point, the River Ganges had just come into view, 5,000 feet below me in the mist. There was no turbulence, the engine droned sweetly, and I had a lot of fuel and daylight left. All I needed to do was turn right along the river and get to Varanasi, and I was done for the day.

The djinni said, 'Throw open the canopy and stand on the nose and get off now!'

I said, 'No, I can't do that, I'll be killed.'

I was overwhelmed with fright.

The djinni conjured up pictures of the Flyer in pieces on Kythira, the joints repaired by stuffing glue into holes and cracks.

I imagined vividly the quarter-inch of fibrelam beneath me, and under that, the skin of one-eighth of an inch of wood, and then below that, five thousand individual feet of air to the safety of the earth.

Every movement of the aircraft paralysed me, and in my mind she crumpled up and fell, twisting out of the sky, and I looked down and saw the exact spot where we would hit the ground.

The Panics

The canopy hemmed me in. There was no room for movement right or left, and only space in front to shake my arms. I wanted to lash out and be free. My legs were constrained with only three inches for movement, and I wanted to kick and kick until the cockpit was destroyed but I would be free again to move.

And all the time the djinni screamed at me, 'Get out! Get out! Get out now! Get out! Get out!'

With a shaking but rigid hand I reached for my radio, and tuned in to a VOR frequency. The djinni retreated. I tried to find first Allahabad and then Varanasi. During this time the djinni's screams were still there, but muted. I picked up the VOR at Varanasi unclearly, which normally indicated that I was too far away and should get closer. But once I had absorbed this information and looked up, the djinni's screams returned as loud as ever . . . 'Get out! Get out! Push the control stick forward and get to earth and that way you will be on the ground, quickly!'

And I replied, 'I will die, I will die; I can't do that. I will die!'

To push the djinni behind the door again I struggled to think of other things, anything, just to stop him. The volume of his screams lowered whenever I could find a job that needed doing, but I spent hours sitting in the Flyer doing nothing except pointing her in the right direction and keeping her there. Without maps, there was no reference point on the ground, a road or railway or town that I could look at which would engage the front of my brain and turn the djinni off.

In this abject state of terror, rigid with fright and confined in the tiny cockpit of the Flyer, I came upon a big city below. The Ganges flowed through the middle, and turned left and then right. Between the two turns was a big bridge. The city was either Allahabad or Varanasi. I tried Allahabad's frequency and there was no reply, but when I called Varanasi there was an answer. It *had* to be Varanasi below.

There followed an hour of black farce.

I asked Varanasi ATC to guide me to their aerodrome. They asked if I could see the bridge. I said I could. They told me to fly on a bearing of 330 degrees, follow a railway line, and after eighteen miles I would see the aerodrome on the left. Could I see a railway line? I could, and I followed it. But the line turned left away from the 330 bearing, and when I followed the bearing I was soon out over another river, this one dried out. I turned around and went back to the bridge, and then tried following the railway line. After ten miles I was heading at ninety degrees to the 330 bearing.

When I called Varanasi again, they said go back to the beginning. This I did, and followed the 330 bearing, and once more a dried-up river appeared.

If I had been less terrified I would have been able to think clearly, and work out that heading north from a bridge and meeting another river meant that I was over Allahabad. Two rivers meet at Allahabad, the Ganges and the Yasmuna, and even without a detailed map I could see that. But I was fighting with the djinni all the time, and was using any radio contact I had to put him out of my mind. He always leapt back when I was unaware, screaming at me again, 'Get out, get out!'

The rational part of my brain started to worry about darkness. Visibility was bad anyway, and getting worse, and when I could not find the aerodrome after an hour I started to look for somewhere else to land. I could not take being in the air much longer.

Varanasi ATC kept trying to send me on the 330 bearing, until I finally told them I thought I was over Allahabad. From my primitive map I saw there was an airfield southwest of Allahabad, and tried flying that way, but found nothing. Circling the river, I was looking at the dried sandy bed for a place to land when a strange voice broke in.

'Golf Mike Tango Kilo Sierra, transmit for bearing, transmit for bearing!'

'This is Golf Mike Tango Kilo Sierra,' I replied. 'I am circling at a thousand feet above a safe place to land.'

'GolfMikeTangoKiloSierra!' the voice said, very excitedly. 'Steer 224 degrees, steer 224 degrees!'

The airfield at Allahabad was run by the Indian Air Force, which had heard my plight and scrambled four helicopters. But I had been tuned into Varanasi's frequency, fifty miles away. Allahabad did not want to chance losing touch with me, so one helicopter linked up between me, Varanasi, and his own station, Allahabad. Every time I broadcast, they picked up my signal and gave me a bearing to fly to their field.

By this time I was weary and sick of ATC, and was thinking longingly about being on the ground, on the spot I had selected on the river bed, but I decided to follow the helicopter's instructions. Every thirty seconds I was asked to transmit and was nudged along the 224-degree course. After only five minutes a big airfield appeared out of the mist below. Thankfully, I flew around the circuit and landed.

The djinni haunted me for three days.

That first night I had nightmares, and slept very badly. On the way to Calcutta the next day, I nearly turned around after takeoff to land and call the whole flight off. The djinni kept urging me to push the control stick forward, dive down and find anywhere to land. He did not care where I put down, or if I was killed doing what he wanted. I fought him, despairing that I was going to lose, and tried everything to put him off.

I imagined trying to explain to Fiona, Jamie and Tracey, but especially to Jamie, my son, how I had just had enough and could not take any more . . .

In my head I explained to Mike Atkinson that I had lost my nerve, and waited for his answer, but could not imagine what he would say. The worst thing was that he would probably understand.

Neil Hardiman in London had put six months of his life into the flight.

Tony Spalding at Dalgety . . . Terry Pryce . . . Sir Peter Carey – all their faith in me. Simon Newlyn . . . Patti Hewstone . . .

I imagined the contempt of people who would not have any interest in me succeeding and would laugh at my failure. I tried telling myself there was nothing to live for if I walked away from this, and how could I live with myself afterwards?

None of this worked.

The djinni ignored them all and carried on screaming, 'It does not matter, it does not matter! Get down, get down! Go on, jump!'

Mike Atkinson had been told before the flight that if I looked as though I was not going to make it, he had to stop me flying. When he saw me in Calcutta, grey with fatigue, he thought I was finished. That evening, in a diffident way, I told him about the Panics, but not in any detail because I was ashamed. He says now that he was very close to telling me to stop flying, and maybe continue later. Somehow he did not do it.

The Panics, I believe, were caused by fear of heights, by claustrophobia in the confined space of the cockpit, by fatigue from flying without a halt all the hours of daylight, and from plain old-fashioned fear of dying. This is a rational explanation, which occurs later, when the blood has cooled. At the time, the image of the djinni was real and horrible.

Leaving Calcutta, still in mist and fog, the djinni came back to me over the mouth of the Ganges, full of life and energy, screaming and frightening me half to death. It could not continue for very much longer. But the solution, such as it was, was bizarre.

Where the thought came from in that situation, I do not know, but I thought of a woman I had fancied, and imagined making love to her. The djinni stopped screaming. I thought of another woman, and then another, and lined up about a dozen. They were women I had seen, women I worked with, women I just knew. It was fantasy sex.

Flying over the Bay of Bengal, where the great Australian aviator Charles Kingsford-Smith had died during a storm, I lined up women one at a time in my mind, whenever I heard the djinni scream, and made love to them. It was desperate, and extremely frustrating, in a cramped cockpit at 5,000 feet. But it worked. The djinni was more interested in the women than he was in trying to kill me. He was, thank God, a dirty old man.

By the time I reached Rangoon I had him behind a closed door again, and about three corridors away from my conscious mind. From time to time I could hear him screaming faintly, but I knew not to go down that corridor. If, in the dozy dreamworld of flying a microlight for eight hours at a time, I slipped down the wrong corridor and heard him scream more loudly than I could bear, I always had a woman in my mind on standby to distract him, and it always worked.

When I half told this strange story later, an Australian reporter called Larry Anderson asked, 'Will you name these women?'

I laughed, and said, 'Never!'

Chapter Fifteen
Allahabad to Phuket

At Allahabad on 6 January, I was back on the route taken by Ross Smith. If his ghost and I had started our flights together in Karachi, from then on we would have raced neck and neck to Australia. Allahabad, one of the first RAF stations in India, was now run by the Indian Air Force, and though I had no permission to land there, I was greeted kindly, and the Flyer stowed away safely for the night.

Group Captain R. H. Desmukh invited me to eat at the officers' mess and stay the night on the camp rather than find a hotel. Washed out and very tired, I was also curious. The first glimpse of life there reminded me of the RAF, in which my father had served for thirty years. The mess walls were lined with the crests of squadrons, the long bare tables were as polished as I remembered them from visiting my father's squadron mess in the early 1950s, and the atmosphere was very familiar. But everyone, of course, was Indian.

A dashing wing commander called Pushi Singh was one of my hosts. He was slim, with a big moustache, and that air of rakishness which fighter pilots everywhere cultivate. Pushi had been born in 1951, four years after the British had left India, and we were talking about the 1971 war when he said abruptly, 'You left too early.'

'We had to go,' I said. I knew immediately what he was talking about. 'We had lost all moral right to be here. Once that happened, we had to leave, whether it was early or not. We no longer believed in our right to govern here.'

'Nevertheless you left too early. We were not ready,' said Pushi. 'Look at what happened between us and Pakistan! You should have taken longer and prepared us better.'

'The last people who could say you were not ready for independence would be the British,' I said.

It turned into a fascinating conversation. Pushi was incensed about the inertia of the Indian Civil Service, and the corruption of Indian politicians. He seemed to look back on British rule as an age of enlightenment, when India was more able to move with the times. But he did admit that he came from an upper-class family, and in the old days would have had a privileged position.

On the morning of 7 January, I was held up for a couple of hours while senior officers of the IAF inspected the Flyer. The most senior was Air Marshal N. C. Suri, AOC Central Air Command, who sat in the cockpit and said the Indian Air Force should consider using Shadow microlights as trainers. Despite the previous night's nightmares and very poor weather, I was impatient to go, but waited quietly for the air marshal to dictate three paragraphs of greetings to Australia in the Birthday Book. No one else had dictated an entry.

Group Captain Desmukh had found some of his old topographical maps which covered the ground from Allahabad to Calcutta and had given them to me. We were like two scheming schoolboys as neither of us thought that what he had done was permissible. The maps were superb.

'Surely you cannot fly in this fog?' asked Pushi.

The 470 miles between Allahabad and Calcutta – which I wanted to do in one flight – was further than I had flown in one hop on the trip so far, and I was pessimistic about my chances. But Pushi's 'fog' was really a mist, and I thought that once I was in the air I would be able to see where I was going. I did not really want to fly, because I was afraid, but the only way to cope with that fear was to get into the air and face it out on my own. At 9.25 am I got away and climbed in circles over the airfield until at 1,000 feet it disappeared. Then I turned east for Varanasi and Calcutta.

The flight itself was uneventful, which gave the Panics all the time necessary to frighten me. By some miracle I had a following wind, and made it straight through to Calcutta. When I landed after six hours, I was very shaky.

Mike Atkinson was there to greet me. He was in no great state either, constantly being sick. When I had left Karachi, Mike had taken a scheduled flight to Bombay and stayed there two days, both nights dining with local hang-glider pilots. He had gone down with a severe case of Bombay belly, and at Calcutta was on a distilled water diet. He is a very hard man, and does not admit to having limits. But I was also suffering from the effects of Eastern food. We were a couple of crocks.

Calcutta was the only place in India where we came across a corrupt official. Even then, it was mild by the standards of other countries. A customs officer was incautious enough to sign the Birthday Book before 'requesting' some American dollars for seeing us through customs. We gave him $10, which must have worked because I was able to get away early next day.

The engine had a case of morning coughs leaving Calcutta. It was soon after takeoff, but not bad enough for me to chicken out and land. Mike was not so lucky leaving India. He had brought the ITN camera into the country, given it to me in Calcutta, and I had flown away with it. When Mike tried to leave he was asked to produce the camera, and held up for a day with the formalities of getting ITN to confirm it was theirs. As a result, I missed seeing him in Rangoon, and he went on to Bangkok.

Back in London, Neil was jubilant about the progress I was making. Since the jump from Muscat I had flown to plan. Each day I told him where I would get to the following day, and each day I completed the flight. Ross Smith had taken four days crossing India. So had I. From Rangoon, Ross Smith had flown to Akyab, and that was my destination. It looked as if my original ambitions were achievable.

But Neil was not able to communicate his joy to the newspapers. Every day, dozens of journalists would ring to ask how things were going.

'Wonderfully,' said Neil. 'He has just completed his flight to Calcutta, the longest of the whole trip, and there are no problems.'

'No crashes? No incidents? Can't he land in the sea again?' they asked, and printed nothing. The Flyer was being pushed further and faster than any other microlight in history. If you ever wonder why the only news you ever heard of the Dalgety Flyer was when I was in trouble . . .

The PR professionals, Tony Spalding and Simon Newlyn,

watched my steady progress, and knew they had to wait until something else went wrong before I became 'news' again. I hated being a news story for that reason, but I am a realist about news values too.

On 8 January I jumped to Akyab, flying east for a hundred miles along the Bay of Bengal, in calm and misty weather. I flew over a corner of Bangladesh, turned right at Chittagong, and from then on headed more south than east until I crossed the equator. Akyab was halfway down the coast of Burma, half a mile from the sea.

The Akyab airport manager was U San Swe Maung (U being Burmese for Mister), an intelligent and cultivated man with an air of grave courtesy. He had petrol organised from a big fifty-gallon drum on the back of an old truck, and drove me to a local guesthouse to spend the night.

It is possible that the last European in Akyab was Eve Jackson, who had had to land there with engine problems. It was the only place not visited by Alexander Frater, the *Observer* journalist who revisited the former Imperial Airways stopover and wrote about it in a book called *Beyond The Blue Horizon*. Akyab itself, now called Sittwe, was built of rush huts, and the only solid concrete buildings were leftovers from the days of British rule. It had been occupied by the Japanese during the war.

U Maung found two small cans of beer that evening, which cost me $5 each. The official rate of exchange was six kyats to the American dollar, compared with the black market rate of thirty-six kyats. This caused the most pervading corruption.

U Maung, for example, had an income of 700 kyats a month, well above the Burmese average of 300 kyats. At the official rate of exchange, he earned $117 a month, but the black market reflected more clearly the true value of Burmese currency, putting his real earnings at $19.44 a month. For what it cost me to buy a beer, I could have paid U Chaung a week's wages, but he was better off than the average Burmese, for whom two weeks' work would buy a can of beer.

The Burmese people I met were kind and gentle and I liked them personally. But the system imposed upon them – the so-called Socialist Republic of the Union of Burma – is junk.

Once, I found U Chaung looking wistfully at my strip map of his country, and asked him what was wrong. He told me he had never seen a topographical map of Burma, only political ones. When asked why not, he said the government was worried about rebels and had banned maps which showed mountains, rivers, towns and roads. I thought back to the detailed maps of all the countries of the world which I could buy freely in London, and offered to send him a map of Burma. He said he would get into deep trouble if I did, but I could see how much he wanted one.

When I took off from Akyab on 9 January it was a clear day and I could see for miles. At 500 feet I turned right over the coast, and looked back at the airfield. There, to the right, running parallel and etched out faintly in the grass, was the ghostly outline of the old runway, the one where Ross Smith and Amy Johnson must have landed. With tingles down my spine, I circled, savouring the view of golden beaches and frothy white surf, rush huts, green tropical trees and aviation history, and then headed south for Sandaway and Rangoon.

In my logbook, I have '2HF' marked against the flight to Rangoon. They occurred after the coastal flight and the trip over the jungles and mountains to the Irrawaddy valley. The heart failures were caused by the engine losing power abruptly, as if one piston had stopped working. The Irrawaddy was in sight when they happened and in each case I descended and picked out a track to land on, but then power came back and I flew on to Rangoon, landing at 2.30 in the afternoon.

If I was irritated in Akyab, I became almost homicidal in Rangoon. All the money I possessed – notes, travellers' cheques, coins, every scrap of foreign currency – was laid out on a counter at immigration, and counted out in front of an official and a hundred fascinated spectators. This was to ensure that I accounted for all the Burmese currency I bought at the ridiculous rate of six kyats to the dollar, patently a rip-off. It took hours to buy fuel and handle the formalities.

When I got to the hotel that evening for a shower, I thought I had been bitten by bedbugs. They were, I later discovered, saddle sores from sitting in the Flyer so many hours a day. Downstairs, the beer was watery. To buy a gallon of two-stroke oil would have cost me, if I had paid, $60. But Eve Jackson had given me the name of an official guide called Victor, and he toured the city for me to find oil at a more reasonable price. I snapped at anyone who spoke to me, and wished the evening would end quickly so I could fly out of Burma first thing the following day.

Rangoon to Bangkok, the next stage of my flight, had put paid to the chances of the two Frenchmen, Poulet and Benoist, in 1919, and had nearly done for Ross Smith as well. There is a hundred miles of sea to cross to Moulmein, and then the formidable Thai mountains west of Bangkok. Ross Smith had flown in cloud for an hour to get over those mountains, and I had worried about how I would do. Eve Jackson made her longest flight on this part of the journey – seven hours in the air – and had landed short of Bangkok, the fuel tanks of her Shadow nearly empty.

Ratty from the runaround to get fuel and change money, I left Rangoon at 8.30 am on 10 January, flying east over a flat, calm sea and mist and following a compass course to pick up the VOR at Moulmein. West of town, I circled once in memory of Poulet and Benoist, and then started climbing from 2,000 feet up to the 9,500 feet required by Bangkok ATC. Post Kythira, I was not certain that the Flyer would get that high, but after an hour's steady climbing I was above the clouds and ready to turn left over the mountains.

The ground over which I flew was extremely inhospitable, mountainous, covered in trees and with no roads. For at least two hours I saw nowhere to land out if the engine failed. But at that height the air was smooth, and there were no heart failures. I came out of the mountains north of my intended track, and then flew in to Bangkok following a VOR radio beacon, still in mist but able at least to see the ground below, even if there was no horizon.

Mike met me at Bangkok, and I was glad to see him. We had grown very like brothers on the flight, and I crawled out of bed happier in the morning if I knew I would see him that evening. The Flyer was parked at the end of a long line of big jets, looking incongruous. Her engine was due for a service, so Mike dismantled it on the apron and took it in a bag to the luxurious airport hotel, mercifully only a short walk from the airport tarmac. We asked the hotel staff for some old cardboard to protect their carpets, and that evening, while I slept, Mike did a fifty-hour service.

He could not know that a copper tang on one of the earthing wires to a coil was close to breaking.

The following day, for reasons I cannot explain, I was extra wound up. No breakfast, as usual, in deference to my churning stomach, just a cup of tea and a stick of chewing gum. We got to the Flyer early. The weather had changed from mist and calm air, and it was now fairly windy, coming from the east, across the runway. Jets were landing and taking off every couple of minutes, and somehow I had to slot the Flyer in without getting blown away.

In the middle of the morning, after hours of prevarication, I tried for a takeoff and was cleared on to the runway. But when I had lined up, it felt as though I would be blown over by the crosswind, and I bottled out and returned to the apron. If I took off from the apron it would at least be into wind. It would have taken only thirty seconds and I could have been away safely, but I could not persuade ATC of my intentions. I believe they didn't want to understand my request. It was noon before I got away safely.

My flight path took me over the city of Bangkok and down the east coast of the Malay peninsula. That day's destination was Si Thammarat, not as long a flight as Ross Smith had made to Singora, but my aircraft was slower than his Vimy. Ross had run into rainstorms all down the coast, and had then been held up for a day because of an inadequate runway and flooding. Even though his ghost was now crossing the outback and heading for Sydney, I was hoping to catch a day on him.

There was a slight following wind and my groundspeed was 64 mph, but as I watched the sun cross the sky, I realised I would not make my goal. There were a number of options on the map, one of which was a town called Phuket, on the west coast. Phuket! Why not? I could cross the peninsula and get there before darkness. Local people pronounce the town's name 'Poo-ket', but American pilots who fly in have a more Anglo-Saxon pronunciation.

My new route took me through a region of small ragged mountains covered in trees and greenery. The weather, typical for that time of year, had deteriorated in the afternoon, and I was now under cloud, with some rain fogging the canopy. By six o'clock I could see the sea in the west, and, with hindsight, should have headed straight there and turned left to go down the coast. Phuket was only twenty miles away. Instead, unaware of any danger, I carried on through the mountains, below the peaks, dodging left and right to pass the underhanging bellies of cloud. Then a wall of cloud loomed up, which I watched without panicking, until – whiteout!

With the engine screaming on full power, I tried to climb out of the cloud. Nothing changed. Then the compass swung to the right. I corrected with the rudder and the compass stopped and started swinging the other way. The vario registered more than a thousand down – falling at a thousand feet a minute! – and airspeed climbed to more than ninety knots. Velocity Never Exceed (VNE) on a Shadow is ninety-four knots, and Peter Davies had told me a horrifying tale of skin cracking on the leading edges at speeds above this when he had been test-flying the prototypes. I pulled back the throttle, and the speed dropped, but I did not know where I was, whether I was upright, turning left or turning right, or which direction I was facing . . . and I had started off below the peaks of the surrounding mountains!

Twice more in those terrifying five minutes, I reached VNE. At any moment, I thought, I would see an instant of mountain, and then be in pieces all over it. After an age of sweating and trying to balance the instruments, I saw a darker patch to my right, almost above me. I kicked right rudder and came out of the cloud, and saw where I was again. Shakily, I descended into the valley and picked my way to the coast.

Never, *never*, I resolved, would I go into cloud again.

It became slightly tense at the airfield that evening when I refuelled. Their petrol meter read twenty per cent above true, which I discovered when I filled four twenty-five litre cans and was charged for 120 litres. It was not the money I objected to, just the idea that I should be cheated so obviously. The airport manager, Mr Pote-hamer, was not involved in the fiddle, but stood loyally by his staff for a long time, until we did an independent test of the capacity of my mixing tank. He had insisted on the test, and conceded graciously.

In the Birthday Book for Phuket, I have a note from Sutin Orvatana, the taxi driver who took me to and from the airport. 'I found Brian Milton oil, and didn't cheat him.'

The hotel I stayed in at Phuket was, I believe, a whorehouse. There were a great many women thronging the bar and restaurant, and a steady stream of men came through and went off with them. Following a long shower, a beer and then another beer, I ate a wonderful Thai meal and was happy to be alone. Everyone should have a postcard from Phuket, I thought, and bought about thirty cards and wrote them all that evening. There was good reason to feel cheerful that night; I was on schedule again, nothing had gone wrong for days, and once more there was a possibility that I would get to Australia for the Bicentenary.

I remember writing on one postcard: 'Of course, things could go wrong again, tomorrow.' But secretly I thought I was past all that.

Chapter Sixteen
Malaysia: More Roads than
Runways

My engine died just as I was biting into a chocolate bar. It was 1.20 in the afternoon of 12 January, and the chocolate bar was my lunch. I was flying at 2,000 feet, following the coast from Phuket to Kuala Lumpur; I had been in the air four hours and twenty minutes.

A heavy crosswind had made for a difficult takeoff from Phuket at nine o'clock that morning. I had steered east over the sea, with fifty miles of water to cross before I reached the coast proper and turned south towards Malaysia. All this time, when failure would have meant a water landing again, the engine behaved perfectly. Various air-traffic controllers picked up my radio messages, and passed me on, one to another. I had flown into Malaysia and was established with Butterworth ATC when I lost power.

'Hello Butterworth,' I radioed. 'Golf Mike Tango Kilo Sierra. This is not an emergency, but I am having problems with my engine.'

Ever since my engine had stopped in the Lake District in rain, I had resolved never again to call a Mayday. It is so embarrassing to explain to air-traffic controllers that you are flying a microlight. In any case, the Flyer had lost power any number of times, and after a while it would come back. But there was a quality of steadiness in this power loss that told me, as I circled and descended, waiting for power to return, that this time it would not.

The countryside below was coastal, a long stretch of muddy-looking beach, then palm trees and thatched houses, and beyond these, paddy fields. There was a choice of two places to land; on the beach, or on a track in a paddy field. The beach looked the more dangerous, as if it was soft mud, and I had a vivid picture in my mind of tipping the aircraft up on its nose and over. The paddy field looked a better bet, crisscrossed by tracks, one of which led directly into wind. After two full circles, I made up my mind. Engine power was not lost completely, so I had a little time to think. But then I became aware of excited questions in my ear; Butterworth ATC were wanting to know what was going on.

'Please don't talk to me,' I radioed, 'I am very busy right now!'

The radio went quiet and I carried on circling, or maybe I just stopped listening. One more circle, I thought, not too far downwind because there are two big palm trees to fly between, S-turn left . . . now S-turn right, yes, about right. Turn left again, cut the throttle, stick forward to keep speed, past the trees and this had better work because I won't have a second chance . . . Look out! There are three cows on the right. Keep calm and ride it in, line up the wheels on the track, past the cows, down . . . down . . . hit the brakes . . . phew!

The frightened cows were plunging up and down on their tethers when I lifted up the canopy and inspected the aircraft. The track itself looked very insubstantial now that I was on the ground, and I felt pretty good to have got her down safely. Ten feet on either side and I would have been in water. I took out the ITN camera, lined it up on a rock, and did a piece to camera, full of breathless pauses.

As usual, there was a period when I was all alone, and then the villagers streamed in from all sides. One of them spoke English, and agreed to look after the Flyer. Another had a motorbike, and I cadged a lift to the nearest telephone. Butterworth would be worrying about me, and I wanted to reassure them. But when I got to the phone I heard helicopters, and leaping on to the motorbike, tore back to the Flyer. The helicopters had landed on the same track, and soldiers and ambulancemen carrying stretchers were looking for me.

Captain Tei Poey Eong had been manning the radar screen when my engine failed. He had watched me carefully, even though I had refused to send out a Mayday call, and had been horrified when my dot had disappeared on his screen. He called out the search-and-rescue helicopters, and for five minutes all the aircraft in the area were vectored to find out where I was. The previous year, a fighter aircraft had disappeared in the same way, and when the wreckage was found the pilot was dead. All this Captain Tei told me later.

The rescue teams on the helicopters needed reassurance that I was indeed unharmed, and a number of hands felt my arms and legs to see if anything was broken. Mike had left Bangkok that morning by scheduled flight to Kuala Lumpur, and I wanted to get hold of him. One of the officers detailed a group of soldiers to guard the Flyer, so I unpacked my luggage and was helicoptered out of the paddy field to RMAF Butterworth. On Kythira, I had failed to get moving pictures of the Flyer upside down, but this time I was able to get a helicopter shot of the Flyer as we left.

The commanding officer of Butterworth ATC, Major Yakub, greeted me with relief and also checked my arms and legs to make sure they were not broken. He wrote in the Birthday Book later that day, 'Almost had a heart attack when the blip on GMTKS disappeared from the radar screen. Got my heart back when the pilot came out of the SAR helicopter, smiling.'

Crossing the Saudi Desert, I had done any number of landings out and no one had taken a blind bit of notice. But Malaysia has an excellent radar system, which I was later to test to the full, doing more landings on roads than I did on airfields.

Thanks to Neil's invaluable 'bible', a loose-leaf notebook of information, I knew which hotel Mike would check into in Kuala Lumpur, and left a message for him to phone me. ATC officers brought tea and we sat around chewing the fat and waiting for my adrenaline level to fall. It struck me that instead of filming or taking photographs I should have removed the Flyer's engine and taken it with me in the helicopter. Mike could then have turned up that evening in a hotel in nearby Penang, fixed it, and we could have stuck it back on the following morning and flown away.

Arrangements were being made to go back to the Flyer when the phone rang. It was a Captain Hassan, from the Malaysian Civil Aviation Authority in Kuala Lumpur. What had happened to me was, in aviation jargon, a 'notifiable incident'. As such, he told me, I was not allowed to touch my own aircraft until it had been examined by the relevant officials.

'Look,' I said, 'I can take the engine off in half an hour and soon find out what is wrong with it.'

'You are not allowed to touch the aircraft until we say so, Mr Milton,' said Captain Hassan. 'I will be coming up tomorrow with two of my colleagues to see what damage your landing out has caused to it, and to examine it for airworthiness.'

My heart sank. It does happen, and it feels just like a huge weight sinking inside you. Examine it for airworthiness! High winds could flip me upside down, or the engine could stop and drop me in the sea, or sandstorms could put me into the desert; all this I could cope with. But when it came to officials, if you did not know the rules, you were lost.

'It is the law of our land,' said a pained Captain Hassan. 'You must comply with it. I will be there as soon as I can.'

In London, Patti and Neil were as alarmed as I was when I phoned, telling them what had happened, and that the CAA were going to examine the Flyer. After I had gone into the Persian Gulf, the British CAA had had doubts about the Flyer's airworthiness, and had phoned Neil for reassurance. Neil had learned that, if possible, the CAA were going to look at my aircraft in Malaysia, since there were close links between the British and Malaysian authorities. The worst possible country to land out, I thought, and I had chosen it.

Captain Hassan and his colleagues looking at the battered Flyer grew in my imagination; I could picture them throwing up their hands in horror at all her scars, and then grounding her. This ignoble end to the flight obsessed me for twenty-four hours. Neil and Patti worried in London, and I worried in Penang, where I booked a hotel for the night. I was thoroughly miserable when Mike flew in from Kuala Lumpur.

The next morning we went back to Butterworth and kicked our heels until noon, waiting for the officials. My mood was vile, and when I finally met them I was full of unexploded anxieties. There were three officials: Captain Hassan, who was a Malaysian, an Englishman called Jim Barry, and a third man, a Chinese whose name I never learned. They were formal but friendly, all that officials should be, but I saw them only as people who were going to ground me. We climbed into two separate cars, and with a third car full of pressmen, set off on an hour's journey over small roads to find the Flyer.

Mike told me I was getting paranoid as I walked around in tight circles, but I felt the flight was in mortal danger. Neil and Patti felt the same way in London. Tony Spalding, I heard later, had listened to their fears and then said, 'Right, if the Dalgety Flyer is grounded, I want you to find him another Shadow and air-freight it out immediately!' Peter Davies volunteered his aircraft, if it proved necessary. It turned my heart over when Neil told me this.

Then Captain Hassan came over and asked me how I had landed. I described the flight in, where the cows had been, and began reassuring him that the aircraft was perfectly airworthy, although the engine needed some repairs.

'We can see that for ourselves, Mr Milton,' he said dryly. 'You seem to have some idea that it is our job to ground you. That is the last thing we want to do. But the law says we must examine the aircraft before it flies again after yesterday's incident. We must all obey the law. You are not suggesting one law for you, and another for the rest of us, are you?'

If I had not been so relieved, I would have been ashamed of myself.

On a flight like mine you get obsessed with anything that looks like getting in your way. Gradually, I calmed down and stopped walking round in circles, and Mike went to the engine and stripped it.

He had thought, when I described what had happened the previous evening, that he had overjetted the engine in Bangkok, which had caused a hole to be blown in the piston. But the pistons were fine, and he had to look elsewhere for the problem. He found an earthing wire broken on the coil to the front piston, which had cut off the spark to one piston. It was a repair which meant taking off the engine, and it was fixed by 4 pm. There was no way we could have known about the wire before it happened. Meanwhile, I talked to the three officials and found that they were flyers themselves, and human, not the no-sayers my fevered imagination had made them.

We started the engine and she ran sweetly. To achieve an adequate takeoff run, I pulled the Flyer back to the two big palm trees through which I had flown on the way in, and lined her up. We warned the villagers to stand well back, and I closed the canopy and started up. The dirt track was broken and twisted ahead of me, but level enough for a takeoff, as long as I did not veer right or left into the paddy field. It was an exciting takeoff, and I wasn't absolutely certain about making it until she rose into the air. Mike filmed it on the ITN camera, and I did a little low flying, making playful passes just over treetop level, thankful to be flying once more.

'I knew you couldn't resist playing to the camera,' he said later.

It was too late to get to Kuala Lumpur, but I flew down the coast and landed at Penang International Airport. It was at Penang that Parer and Mackintosh had had an engine seizure, landing on a polo pitch in the middle of a game, and, according to an apoplectic British planter, 'without asking permission!' Eve Jackson had been there before me, and ATC remembered her fondly. Mike and I stayed at a good hotel, and went out to dinner with Captain Tei, the air-traffic controller who had watched my aircraft disappear from his screen. He took us to an amazing restaurant which consisted of tables and chairs in the middle of a square surrounded by stalls. We went from stall to stall and pointed out what we wanted, paying for it on the spot. Each stall was individually owned, and had to compete against other stalls. As a result, the quality of the food was superb. It was another evening where Mike and I agreed there was nowhere else in the world we wanted to be.

So absorbing were my fears about the Flyer being grounded that I had forgotten to recharge my two ICOM radios. When I set off from Penang island at 8.30 on the morning of 14 January, crossing the sea to resume course down the west coast of the Malay Peninsula, I was soon having difficulty talking to ATC. The charging unit for the battery at the back, which worked off the engine, had broken down, another casualty in the war of attrition between the Flyer and the world, which the Flyer was slowly losing. Though I nursed power as best I could in the radios, south of Kuala Lumpur they faded completely.

The weather worsened.

After five and a half hours, I had flown as far south as I was permitted to go on the west coast. Any further, and I would have been in Singapore airspace, where microlights are banned because they are too slow and not considered reliable. My proposed course took me directly east across southern Malaysia, and then, when I had passed to the north of Singapore, directly south to Batam Island in Indonesia. When I turned east I started to be afraid again. Cloud was reaching down to the jungle and plantations below, and it began to rain heavily.

After only fifteen minutes I found myself changing heights continuously, over one cloud, under another, left and right, heading east all the time. By 2.30 in the afternoon I could go no further east, and was flying in circles in a hole in the clouds. All around were rain and fog, blocking me from going anywhere else. 'Get her on the ground,' I said out loud. 'On a road or a track, because you can't stay up in this.'

At 500 feet I picked on one plantation, and lined up on a red-soil track, but as I was coming in to land I saw I would hit the wing against a high bank. Climbing away, I soon saw another track that looked better. I flew over it once, circled, and brought her down safely. It was raining hard when I opened the canopy, and walked around to calm down.

Half an hour later, having found a phone in a plantation building and let ATC sixty miles away know I was safe, I heard a helicopter. Not again! It was embarrassing. I ran back through the mud to the Flyer, and watched with a dozen locals as the helicopter landed.

The pilot was Captain Revi Chandran, who wrote in the Birthday Book: 'To Brian – may you complete your journey safely.' But he seemed to spend the rest of the day trying to kill me.

Chandran invited me to spend the night at his base. It was thirty miles away, but I was not sure where. He said I should follow him, and suggested I use a nearby road for takeoff. We pushed the Flyer along the track to the road, while Chandran flew away to fetch the local police. Hundreds of motorists stopped on both sides of the road, getting out of their cars to look at the Flyer, and soon there was an enormous traffic jam. It was very good-natured, except for me in the middle. The police arrived and joined in the general mêlée. I had to restrain myself from shouting with frustration.

Two English tourists, Martin Waldock and Liz Penney, both from Somerset, drove by in their car, and stopped in amazement, saying they had seen me take off from the Docklands on television in December.

Late that afternoon, still with low cloud and heavy rain, police cleared the crowds off the road for a couple of minutes, and I took off. Chandran asked me before I left what speed I flew at. Sixty knots, I told him. I circled over the road, watching the crowd disperse and Chandran taking off in his helicopter. My radios, of course, were dead and I could not communicate with him.

He tore off to the north, at eighty-five knots!

Though I made every effort to stay with him, he disappeared from view in the mist and rain. My canopy fogged up, and I did a lot of swearing. I did not know where I was, nor where he was going. Angrily, I circled another road and contemplated landing. After five minutes, Chandran appeared again and we circled before heading off to the north. Again, he flew at eighty-five knots, and again, he left me behind. I carried on flying to the north, but could not see any towns, or anywhere that looked like a helicopter base.

Soon I found another road, and a big plantation, and circled for half an hour, waiting for traffic to clear. I had been in the air for more than seven hours, and was low on fuel. When there was no traffic on the road, I swooped down and taxied to a kiosk.

'Please tell me the way to the nearest helicopter base,' I asked.

'See the road you are on?' said the shopkeeper. 'Go north on it for eighteen miles, until you come to a mountain on your right. You cannot miss it. Just after that, turn left at a T-junction, cross a railway line, and the helicopter base is on your right. It is called Kluang.'

He drew a makeshift map on the back of an envelope, and I thanked him. I then leapt back into the Flyer and took off before any more cars stopped. His directions were accurate, and I was relieved when the helicopter airfield came up on schedule. Two more minutes and I'll be on the ground, I thought, when suddenly the canopy fell in on me, crushed by an enormous force.

When it twanged out again, there, fifty feet ahead, in all his cretinous glory, was Captain Chandran and his helicopter. He was so overjoyed to see me again, having lost me twice, that he thought he would express his joy by banging me with his propwash. Bob Wills, one of the world's great hang-glider pilots, had been killed in this way ten years earlier. A helicopter displaces its own weight in air; any closer and he could have folded up the Flyer's wings. I do not think I would have survived the fall from 500 feet.

Incandescent with rage, I circled violently to signal him to go away. When I could not see him, I turned to land on the runway, but I was 100 feet off the ground when he flew in at right angles, right across my intended track. Thoroughly frightened and swearing loudly, I opened the throttle and circled away again. He can't mean to kill me, I told myself; he's a search-and-rescue pilot. It's just that he's thick as fifteen short planks; plain stupid. When he landed on the other side of the field, and I was certain he was not going to take off again and kill me, I wearily flew on finals and landed.

'We know you are very angry about what happened,' said Chandran's observer, Chiefy Nantha Kuman, later.

That evening I was given a beer to relax, just what I needed to mellow out. Then I was given a second beer, and a third . . . and a fourth. Everyone in the officer's mess wanted to buy me a beer. Not having eaten since the previous day, two beers were fine, but by eleven o'clock, still not having eaten, I was ready to wring necks. It was only by being absolutely forceful, getting a car, driving to a restaurant and ordering food, that I finally ate.

When I flew away the following day I thought it was safer for me to be in the air on my own in dreadful weather than be around Captain Revi Chandran for another day.

Chapter Seventeen
Chased by Thunderstorms: Kluang to Kupang

One feature of the tropics is that thunderstorms occur every after-noon, almost as regularly as clockwork. Days start fine and clear at dawn, but throughout the morning the sun burns into the wet earth, and the moisture rises into gigantic clouds, reaching thousands of feet high. By the early afternoon the atmosphere becomes oppressive, and rain lashes down. Lightning bolts are jagged and regular, not the sheet lightning we are used to in England. Thunderstorms had held up Ross Smith and the other competitors who had got as far as Indonesia, and to a microlight pilot they are fearful.

Storms and rain were the theme of the whole flight along the Indonesian islands.

There was more low cloud and rain when I left Kluang in Malaysia at 8.30 in the morning of 15 January. Because I had landed out twice on roads, I had to let the CAA know what had happened before I was allowed to continue. Jim Barry, the man I had met in the Penang paddy fields, asked me to ring him.

'What happened, Brian?'

'The weather was dreadful. I just couldn't get through, and it was more prudent to land where I did.'

'Can you assure me there is no damage to the aircraft?' he asked.

'Absolutely none.'

'Well, you have permission to fly on, and good luck, but one thing, Brian,' he warned. 'Get there, OK? Just get there. All right?'

I laughed. I liked civil servants like that.

The takeoff at Kluang gave me a fright. It was close to the equator, where for one reason or another, either gravity or the thick, sluggish quality of the air, it was more difficult to take off.

The Flyer was heavily loaded, and nearly did not get away at all. She clawed her way into the air, skidding around the sky, fighting for height and circling before I reached cloudbase at about 500 feet to turn east. Rain collected on the outside of the canopy and mist on the inside. I soon picked up a VOR beacon to the northeast of Singapore, and flew to it, talking to Singapore ATC on my newly recharged radios. First stop after turning right at the beacon was Batam Island, which I reached in an hour and a half. Customs formalities into Indonesia went very smoothly.

The airport manager told me that Batam Island had been down to 200-yards visibility the previous day, when I had been trying to get there, and that all my alternative airfields had also been closed by bad weather. I told him I had been lucky enough to find a safe spot to land, but did not alarm him with any details. It did not do to tell the Indonesian authorities any more than they needed to know about landings away from scheduled airfields.

Heading south again over the sea after only an hour on the ground, I crossed the equator at eleven o'clock, and the weather changed from low cloud to clear skies. Ross Smith had reported a mighty bump when he crossed the equator, and I wondered if it would happen to me, but it did not.

The middle stage of the flight to the east coast of Sumatra was delightful. All the cares of the flight seemed to drop away from me. I stopped being constantly frightened, the tension left my stomach, and though the terrain I was flying over – flooded paddy fields and jungle – was impossible to land on safely, I stopped caring. This was one of the rare times when I thought of Judy Leden's Sixth Commandment: 'Thou shalt pause at least twice a day to enjoy thyself and think, verily, this is a wonderful wheeze!' Too much that was unenjoyable had happened to me on the flight so far for me to take any time off to enjoy myself, but there was an hour over Sumatra when I did so. Then I noticed a huge build-up of cloud to the west, with a thick black sheet of rain underneath, and I reverted to my customary state of supercharged nervousness. The rain front was fifty miles long, and advancing on my intended track to Palembang.

The countryside below was waterlogged jungle or paddy field, none of it suitable for landing on. It was a four-hour flight from Batam to Palembang, and the last ninety minutes were spent sweating with fright. Palembang is in the middle of Sumatra next to a river; the airfield lies to the north of the town. When it came into sight, I was just scraping around the end of the rain front, and was relieved to land. Ten minutes later, the rain came bucketing down, and this was only the *outskirts* of the main downpour.

It rained all night, and it was raining when I turned up at the airfield the following morning, 16 January, ten days from Australia's Bicentenary. The local aviation authorities said I could not fly as I did not have the relevant permissions. In a bad mood, I wrote out Judy Leden's Ten Commandments in the Birthday Book and mooched around until, after a few telephone calls to Jakarta, I was allowed to fly on to the Indonesian capital. I took off at 9.30 am and headed south for the bottom of Sumatra, flying over water-soaked plantations and jungle, and worrying vaguely about what I would do if the engine stopped.

There was supposed to be a VOR radio beacon to mark the southern tip of the island, but it could not have been working that day. Navigation was primitive: fly to the end of the island and then turn left, out over the sea, making for Java Head and the main island of Indonesia. After four and a half hours in the air, dodging more thunderstorms, I arrived at the capital and landed in a strong crosswind, nearly tipping one wing in. Mike met me along with an efficient local agent, Tulus Budiarso, who had the clearances to allow me to fly on through Indonesia.

Mike and I stayed in a local hotel that evening, and managed to get a phone call through to London to say where we were. I was very tired, having flown for seventeen days in a row, often in conditions when I should never have been in the air. We went out on to the streets of the capital with the ITN camera to shoot scenes of local market life, following a request from Simon Newlyn at Shandwick PR. The ground steamed with the heat, and crowds of smiling people teemed around the stalls selling fruit and rather dubious-looking pieces of meat. A lot of people asked to be put on camera, though they would never see the resulting pictures. We were wary in case anyone asked for appearance money. Afterwards, it rained again, and we sat on the verandah, drinking beer and watching rivers of water running in the gutters.

I noticed I was now on the last and biggest of the strip maps I was using to navigate. At one end lay Jakarta. As I unrolled the map, other islands appeared: Bali, Lombok, Sumbawa, Timor. At the far end there was a big expanse of blue and then – Darwin!

'Michael, look!' I said. 'Australia is at the far end of the map.'

Australia had been a long way away ever since we had set off on 2 December. I did not want to be distracted now until the final day's flying took me there. Every evening, the only thing which mattered was where I would get to the following day. Seeing Australia on the map was so disturbing that I took out a knife, and cut that part off. When I needed to I would use it, but not before.

In Jakarta, I was back with Ross Smith's ghost again, and planned the same day's flying along the island of Java to Surabaya. There were fierce, thick clouds all over the sky at 10.15 am on 17 January. It was pouring with rain, and I was more nervous than usual. The takeoff run seemed to go on forever and she climbed slowly as I picked my way east, looking for a way above the cloud. An hour later I was at 7,000 feet, without having been caught in a whiteout, but only by the skin of my teeth. Cloud was becoming so thick over land that I was driven out to sea, where I descended into thinning cloud. From then on, I flew over the sea all the time, avoiding the huge cloud masses that were building up over land, and the great sheets of falling rain.

One of the rainstorms did catch me, and then the canopy became totally opaque. The experience was as terrifying as all my night-mares of it, even if it only lasted a few minutes. I had to fly a compass course to get away.

Ross Smith had nearly been wrecked at Surabaya, which was then a boggy landing ground. As I neared the town I could see why. I was lost for a while finding my way around one bank of cloud after another, and trying to fly past rainstorms, but I knew that if I kept heading east I would reach the coast, and then find Surabaya easily. Which is how it worked out: first fish farms, then the city itself, and finally the coast and a safe landing on a solid tarmacked runway that Ross would have given his eyeteeth for. Groggy with fatigue after nearly seven hours in the air, and having flown 410 miles, I nearly fell into Mike's arms. He had arrived by scheduled flight from Jakarta.

The Australian media were taking a bigger interest in the flight now that it looked as though I would arrive, and that evening I did a number of telephone interviews. The whole emphasis of the flight seemed to be falling away from Neil and Patti in London, transferring to a woman called Anita Lyons who worked for Shandwick in Sydney. It was she I now called at the end of every day, whenever communication was possible.

We had to live with the image the Australians wanted to pin on me; the mad pom crashing his way around the world to try to reach the Bicentenary. No one seemed to know anything about Ross Smith. They kept confusing him with another Australian aviator, Charles Kingsford-Smith.

By this time, forty-eight days after he had left London, Ross Smith's ghost was well south of Darwin, but his Vimy was in deep trouble. The manhandling it had taken in Surabaya had loosened all the flying wires, and chicken wiring was now looped over the wings and fuselage to hold it together. Its port propeller had broken and been glued together. As a result, the engine became unbalanced and blew up in a town called Charleville in Queensland. Locals called the Vimy the 'Flying Chicken Coop', and Ross was stuck at Charleville for fifty days while repairs were made.

He had beaten me fair and square to Darwin, but I wanted to beat him to Sydney. If he had all his problems in Australia, I dearly hoped I had all my problems behind me.

On 18 January, there was another row over a misreading fuel meter in Surabaya. The aviation suppliers did not want to have to admit to us that their meter was overreading, and they would not refuel using the Flyer's mixing can because they knew we would find out. We insisted. They walked off, and came back later when they had reset the meter to tell the truth.

The 420-mile flight from Surabaya to Bima was technically the most difficult of the whole trip. My route took me over water to the east of Java, and then across the north end of the islands of Bali and Sumbawa. When I passed Bali I took a minute, despite a threatening rainstorm, to circle once in memory of Matthews and Kay who crashed there in the 1919 race. Again, I stayed out to sea and apprehensively watched thunderclouds develop, hoping they would not catch me.

Sumbawa is a strangely shaped island, like a large pair of bollocks at the west end, and a woman's breasts at the east (to use Eve Jackson's phrase). It has two airfields. After five and a half hours I passed Sumbawa airfield, where I had permission to land, but I had filed a flight plan for Bima, an airfield at the far end of the island, and pressed on.

At a headland – the 'balls' of the island – thick black cloud developed in a line across my intended path, and wispy, evil-looking fingers reached down the sea. The cloud nearly sucked me in as I dived underneath, and I had to hold the stick well forward and cut the throttle to get away. When I looked back a few minutes later, the fingers had reached the sea and there was rain from horizon to horizon. No going back!

Ahead I could see a vague outline of the 'two tits', as Eve Jackson described the mountains which conceal Bima, but there were storm clouds everywhere. I flew up a long bay at 2,000 feet, trying to decide whether to go north around the island and slip into Bima that way, or climb over clouds to the south and then out to sea along the south coast of the island. I could have gone either way, but I chose to go south and I was glad I did; when I looked north half an hour later, I wouldn't have wanted to be there in an airliner.

On three-quarter throttle, climbing steadily, the Flyer took me up to 7,000 feet and delicately over the top of black and white swirling cloud to where I could see the south side of the island. Following the map features closely, I picked my way along, hoping that as I reached lower ground at the far end the cloud would clear enough for me to descend. Bima ATC called anxiously in my earphones, saying there were thunderstorms over the airfield, but I could hear their voices only faintly.

The southern approach to the airfield is between the two mountains. When I finally turned north to try to fly between them, cutting the throttle to descend below cloud, I had been in the air for more than seven hours. All the way down to 300 feet I looked at various tracks, mentally marking them as possible landing areas if the engine ran out of fuel. Cloudbase was 400 feet above the road; I dived underneath and threaded my way through the rain between the mountains to the bay at the far end. There I found sopping wet countryside, with the landmark bay in the distance. Angry black clouds bubbled just a hundred feet above me, and for what seemed a long time, there was no sign of the airfield. In a state of fright, I thought about landing on a road, but pressed on and finally found the landing strip. Ross Smith himself had sited this airfield when Indonesia was the Dutch East Indies.

As I put down on the tarmac, the wind changed abruptly and nearly tipped me over. I jumped out immediately, and pushed the Flyer into wind. When I looked at the ATC tower, dozens of men were running across the grass towards me. A siren wailed and a fire engine plus various vehicles started tearing around the airfield.

'No, no!' I shouted into the radio, 'I am all right. Don't worry, I'm all right.'

A couple of men held the wings as I taxied in to the parking apron, and about a hundred people milled around, smiling and shaking hands. It was the best of all welcomes because it was spontaneous. The airport manager, Mr Soewarno, drove me to the best hotel in town, where there was beer, peanut-covered meat, and a crackly phone connection to Mike in Surabaya. He was relieved I had arrived safely; he could now catch the scheduled service to Kupang, my next destination.

There was no petrol at Bima airport, only jet fuel, so I had to use ordinary gasoline from a car garage. The five cans Mr Soewarno dug up were sufficient to fill the Flyer's tanks, but they were so dirty inside that I took an extra hour and double-filtered the fuel through chamois leather. In the Flyer's back cockpit I had sufficient oil to get all the way through to Darwin, two-stroke oil being common in Indonesia.

There was no weather forecast worth reading at Bima. For some days now I had flown without getting a forecast. It was not much use whingeing about it.

The last airfield on the last island in Indonesia before Australia was Kupang in Timor, 355 miles from Bima. On 19 January, at 9 am, I took off and followed the southerly coast of a number of islands until, more than halfway through the day, I reached Ende. Conditions were easy, and somehow I never seemed to get the Panics over water. At Ende I turned right and took a course across 130 miles of water to Timor. It was monotonous flying for six and a half hours, but I was thankful for it. Forty miles out to sea, flying at 5,000 feet, I picked up the VOR at Kupang, and had a little excitement on the way in dodging my way around two persistent rainstorms. Mike had arrived there before me, but had gone to town to get more two-stroke oil.

That evening, we ate dinner in a deserted hotel near the airport and watched the rain fall heavily. This was the start of the infamous 'white-knuckle route' to Darwin. I had asked for a weather forecast, however little faith I had in it, and heard that not much wind was expected but that it would be easterly, a direction I did not want.

Michael and I bickered like an old, married couple. I wanted to go direct to Darwin, and thought I might chance it if the winds were light. Mike said I should be cautious and head for an island off the northern coast of Western Australia which Neil Hardiman had researched in London. It was called Troughton Island, was run by an oil company, and was closer to Timor than Darwin by 170 miles.

In the middle of our tired, crotchety but amiable argument, a phone call came through from London. Patti Hewstone put Dalgety's chief executive, Terry Pryce, on the line.

'We're all proud of you, Brian,' he said, 'but when you go tomorrow, please take great care. You have come so far and we don't want you to take unnecessary risks.' It was as though Terry had been listening, 9,000 miles away, to the conversation between Mike and me.

They were both right, of course. The distance between Darwin and Kupang was further than any microlight had ever flown over water, and I cannot think why I even contemplated flying there in a head-wind. But as I went to sleep, I hoped the weather would change enough for me to have a go.

Chapter Eighteen
The White-Knuckle Route: Timor
to Darwin

The Timor Sea is the last overwater stage of the London–Australia
flight, and the most terrifying one. It has unpredictable weather
with winds changing hourly, and the sea itself is full of sharks which
are not as friendly as those in the Persian Gulf. In the 1930s,
Imperial Airways had established a base at Kupang, on the southwest of the island, more than 500 miles from Darwin. It had been
their pilots who had dubbed the jump across the sea the 'white-
knuckle route'. Pilots as well as passengers had white knuckles.
Some aircraft had not made it.

When the island was part of the Dutch East Indies it had not
much mattered where the airfields were as long as the runways were
long enough. But ever since East Timor achieved independence
from the Portuguese in 1975, and was immediately invaded by
Indonesian troops, there has been a clampdown on news. There are
persistent rumours that genocide is being committed against the
indigenous people by the Indonesians. Eve Jackson gave it a miss
altogether, flying to islands further east and closer to the Australian
mainland before setting off for Darwin. I had thought I might
follow Eve's route, but the authorities said I must leave from
Kupang.

On 20 January, Dalgety sent an aircraft over from Darwin with
two television crews and some radio and newspaper reporters. If
Mike had had to rely on scheduled services, he would have had to
return to Surabaya or even Bali before catching a flight to Darwin.
By the time he arrived, I would have been well on my way across the
Australian outback. But now Mike could go to Darwin in Dalgety's
aircraft.

While I was delighted to see the Australian pressmen, I could not
understand why they were walking around as though on eggs,

talking to each other in urgent whispers. They were trying to hide their big television cameras, and asked me to confirm to the Indonesian authorities that they were employed by Dalgety, rather than the TV networks they really worked for.

'Why are you all creeping around?' I asked one of them.

He told me that a few years ago five Australian journalists had been shot to death by Indonesian soldiers while investigating genocide allegations in East Timor. It was cold-blooded murder, and a warning to other reporters not to get involved. Australian journalists took the shootings personally. They were also banned from being in Indonesia because of an article in one Melbourne newspaper about 'Mrs Five Per Cent', which detailed the corruption of the wife of President Suharto in Jakarta. This was the first visit by Australian journalists since the ban, which was still in force. No one knew for certain what the reaction of the Indonesian authorities would be.

The pilot of the Dalgety aircraft had maps and information for me. He told me that the weather forcast he had received in Darwin made it unlikely that I would be able to get there that day; he suggested taking a route directly south to Troughton Island.

'The Australian government won't be happy if you do that,' he said, 'but if you have no choice then I'm sure they'll understand.' He then gave me a radio frequency for the island, and said it was owned by Broken Hill Properties, the biggest company in Australia, who used it as a base for helicopters to supply oil rigs drilling in the Timor Sea.

'It hasn't got a VOR,' he said, 'but twenty miles before you get to the Australian mainland there's a big reef which you can't miss. It sticks out like dogs' balls. Troughton Island is between the reef and the mainland.'

There was loose, wet-looking cloud gathering over Timor, and the wind was a southeasterly, but it looked quite light. With all the wind information I could gather, I plotted my course and arrived at a heading of 146 degrees for Troughton. But I actually filed a flight plan to Darwin, because I was not allowed to acknowledge that I was entering Australia through Troughton, which had no customs and immigration facilities.

The pressmen did their interviews, still feeling threatened, although money changed hands somewhere to calm things down. They provided the first home-grown Australian signatures in the Birthday Book: Larry Anderson of Australian Associated, Keith Loveard of ABC, Gary Kinna of Film North, and the comment by Simon Breer of Channel 10 Network: 'You'd better make Australia, I'm telling everyone you will!'

Ever since the idea of flying to Australia had first been suggested, I had worried about crossing the Timor Sea, but now that I was actually doing the crossing, I wasn't frightened. If I had sat down and thought about it, turned the idea over in my mind, tried to see how I felt inside, I would have been afraid. But the experiences of the last seven weeks had blunted my sensibilities. Fear was confined to a part of the mind I never visited. It was only when I was immediately threatened that I became worried. Long-term threats, by which I mean those more than an hour away, did not concern me. If I made it, well and good. If the engine stopped and I went into the sea, conditions that day looked similar to those in the Persian Gulf on Christmas Day.

Inch'Allah.

All the formalities of leaving the country were completed by nine o'clock and I taxied out, making the usual long takeoff run that characterised flying near the equator. Climbing was a slow, painful process, a series of S-turns to avoid hitting the rising ground to the south. At 2,000 feet I had enough height to get over the hills. The VOR beacon doesn't work very well for southerly aircraft, and I soon lost it. The Dalgety aircraft would, I hoped, catch me over the water and confirm the course I was flying, but I did not see it again.

Back in London, it was still the previous night. Simon Newlyn set up a camp bed next to the downstairs telephone to avoid waking his wife, and prepared a big flask of coffee. He insisted on being told as soon as I got across the Timor Sea or, if I didn't make it, what had happened to me.

As I looked down at the coast of Timor, I was poignantly aware of the long sea flight ahead. This is the air Ross Smith flew in, I thought, and I looked east to where they had flown, feeling close to them. Like them, I had to make the crossing on a compass course.

The White-Knuckle Route: Timor to Darwin

There were no navigation aids that would guide me into Troughton. As long as I didn't run out of fuel, I was eventually going to find Australia, but when I did I would have to identify where I was, and then find a tiny island ten miles off the coast. Troughton is only one kilometre long, half a kilometre wide, and twenty feet high.

This was the flying I had set out to experience.

The Timor coastline disappeared slowly behind me. Settling on my compass course, I climbed to 3,000 feet and looked for signs of life. Every hour, I changed my chewing gum. Above me the sky was blue and clear, but I saw no aircraft, not even high above me making condensation trails. Like all the other pilots before me, I kept an eye on the sea for sharks, but saw none.

Once I picked up a faint radio signal from the pilot of the Dalgety plane at Timor, saying he had given me the wrong frequency for Troughton Island. He transmitted the correct one. I acknowledged the change, but he was too far away to hear my radio, and kept transmitting the new frequency. I was very lucky indeed to hear that signal.

Inside the cockpit of the Flyer, I had found eight separate places to sit on my bum. These I changed infrequently, and prolonged the experience by first anticipating it, then making the change, then comparing it favourably to the previous position. Because I rarely used the rudder, I had found I could lie half on my right side and fly a straight course. My bed sores had disappeared.

About a week before the Timor Sea flight, I had discovered the joys of crossing my legs in flight, but had to ration this experience to get the best out of it. For arm exercise, I held the control stick with my right knee and stretched my hands as far away as possible, wagging them vigorously.

When I wasn't exercising, I fell into a dream. Part of my brain watched the compass and the altimeter, but especially the rev counter; I had to stay below 5,500 revs to get the best performance from the engine. This did not take a lot out of me. The air was smooth, and I could see twenty miles in the haze. Where was the usual Timor Sea weather of fresh, gusty winds and storms? I droned on, dreaming.

Three and a half hours out from Timor, and still following a heading of 146 degrees, I saw to my right some small dots on the sea. They resolved into a big oil rig towed by three tugs, two ahead and one behind. They were not going to pass directly underneath me, and for a while I just looked at them and thought I would fly by. But I had seen nothing for hours so I altered course to overfly them and tuned into the new frequency the Dalgety pilot had given me for Troughton Island. I circled the rig and called.

'Is there anybody out there?'

A voice came back immediately.

'I know you, you're the Dalgety Flyer and we're expecting you at Troughton Island!'

The voice belonged to Neil Stuart, the pilot of a Troughton Island helicopter, fifteen miles away from the oil rig and heading towards it. The rig was called the SEDCO 708, and it was 130 miles from Australia.

'Can you see the oil rig?' radioed Neil.

'I am circling it now.'

Neil said he would join me, and told me to keep circling. After a few minutes I looked over to my left, and there was a helicopter, flying in formation with me, with much more concern for my welfare than my recent experience with Ravi Chandran in Malaysia.

'Am I on the right course for Troughton Island?'

Neil asked what course I was steering. After I told him, there was a few seconds' silence while he worked things out.

'No,' he radioed back. 'You're too far to the west. If you continue this way you will end up somewhere between Troughton and Perth! Try steering 130 degrees, and that should get you there.'

The wind had obviously changed since I made my calculations that morning from the weather forecast. Making one more circuit, I thanked him and headed off on 130 degrees. Neil said he would see me later that evening. As I left him and the rig disappeared from view, I thought of the odds against coming across the oil rig the way I had. I was less than ten degrees off course but I could see no airfield on the map if I had continued and reached Australia. I would then have had to put down on a beach somewhere, and radioed on the emergency 121.5 channel until someone replied.

But little changed for the next two and a half hours. The scenery was the same: sea from horizon to horizon. Once a ship came into view, heading from east to west, and I watched it for twenty minutes. It didn't do anything, signalled nothing, made no change of course and I saw no human beings on it. But because it was the only thing worth looking at, I looked at it until I could hardly see it any more.

After six hours in the air, and without seeing the reefs that 'stuck out like dogs' balls', I slowly became aware that there was a difference in the view ahead. From time to time, there had been shallow banks of clouds ahead, but now the clouds began climbing into great towers. The sea was no longer a uniform blue with plankton streaks but multi-coloured. Gradually the outline of land became clear.

Australia!

But where in Australia? I scanned the million-scale map, and compared what I was seeing through the canopy with where I should be. After a few minutes I concluded I was looking at the coast of Cape Bougainvillea, a distinctive knuckle of land facing north, with little bays between each knuckle. Troughton Island, by my calculation, should be off to my left. When I looked there I could see nothing but seaweed. I tuned into the Troughton Island frequency and picked it up clearly enough to talk to them, but I still could not see the island. But the more I compared my map with what I could see, the more certain I was that I was approaching Cape Bougainvillea.

So where was Troughton?

Back out to sea, I looked all over the place, and after twenty minutes I decided to investigate a patch of seaweed. As I got closer, I saw from 5,000 feet that it wasn't seaweed at all, but a tiny island.

'Can you see that towering cumulus on the coast?' radioed Troughton. 'That is exactly southeast of us.'

'I can see you now,' I replied, 'and you are a welcome sight.'

A few people came out of buildings as I circled a couple of times and descended. As I turned on finals I was conscious that there were pilots down there watching me, and I said a little prayer not to cock up the touchdown. At 3.30 pm, the Flyer's wheels rolled smoothly on to the dirt strip and I taxied in.

'Welcome to Australia!' said a large man with a spray can, who disinfected all three wheels.

That night I was guest of the small island community – seventeen men and one woman, all pilots or engineers working on contract for BHP. They wrote good wishes in the Birthday Book, and drew little pictures. I particularly cherished the message from one of the Troughton pilots, Allan Mackenzie (and Robert Burns):

Here's to us,	(Here's to us,
wha's like us,	Those like us,
few ae us,	Few of us,
an' they are all deid!	And they are all dead!)

Inside myself, I felt at peace for the first time in a long time, as if I had really completed the flight. But I still had to make Darwin the following day, and I was thinking of racing on to Sydney. Only one thing spoiled it, and that was not the fault of the small Troughton community, but BHP policy. Broken Hill Properties, the largest company in Australia, did not want to take the chance that any of its pilots would be the worse for drink. My first landfall in Australia had no beer! It was a dry island.

Before I went to sleep, I spent a few minutes looking south in the darkness. The coast of Australia was lit up by frequent flashes of lightning, and if I listened carefully I could hear the distant thunder. That was the sort of weather I would now have to fly in.

On 21 January, visibility was good, but the wind had swung more to the east – still a headwind. With a borrowed camera, having given mine to Mike, I took photographs of the Flyer on Australian soil. Her fuel tanks were refilled, free of charge, courtesy of BHP, and at 7.30 am I climbed away from Troughton. My course was easterly, first to cross the northern coast of Western Australia, and then across Joseph Bonaparte Gulf.

(Just south of the route I took, a German pilot called Hans Bertram force-landed in his Junkers seaplane in 1932, having flown from Timor by night. He was forty-one days in the outback before being found, and later wrote a book called *Flight into Hell* about his experiences. ABC TV made a programme about Bertram's adventures which involved building a brand-new Junkers. Bertram himself is one of the few pioneers from the heroic age of aviation still alive. He is a revered figure in German aviation circles, still thriving at the age of eighty-nine.)

To get to the headland which led north to Darwin I had to cross 150 miles of sea. It was another smooth flight, hour after hour following the same compass course, but gut-tightening nerves in the middle when all land disappeared and I felt as though I was heading into a void.

I crossed the coast about thirty miles north of Port Keats, south of my intended track, and then picked my way north over Anson Bay and the Finnies River, where I was bumped around by summer thermals. Darwin came within radio range at 1.30 in the afternoon, after six hours in the air, and I heard helicopters being vectored to my position. Three helicopters, each with a TV crew, kept me company as I crossed the estuary over the city itself. ATC asked me to circle twice, for the cameras, and then I made for the airfield, where I put down at exactly two o'clock.

There was a big reception committee and a lot of reporters, but they were all told to stand back while three very forceful officials completed the formalities to admit me into Australia. I signed a paper agreeing to pay $9,000 in import taxes if the Flyer remained in Australia for more than a year. When I went out to talk to the pressmen, Mike appeared with a beer.

'I can't drink,' I said. 'I'm taking off to go to Katherine in an hour.'

'No, you're not,' he said, grinning.

For the next seven hours, until I collapsed, shivering with exhaustion in a suite in the Darwin Sheraton, I did press interviews. Anita Lyons, a very bright, intense, slightly bossy girl, methodically worked through a long list of interviews. Her phone bill that evening was $900, even though many of the calls were incoming. She guided me between one phone and another with fifteen-second briefings.

'This is a station in Melbourne . . . Second biggest in the city . . . Followed your flight regularly . . . His name is John.'

'Hello, John, Brian Milton . . .'

. . . Hour after hour, after hour . . .

In between interviews with the press, I snatched time to talk to Fiona in Bristol, who was relieved and proud that I had made it. Jamie and Tracey were curiously blasé about the whole flight, as if every child had a father who flew to Australia in a microlight. They had had no fears at all for my safety. It was as though they saw the whole flight as an extension of my previous television job. Everyone knows adventures on TV are not real.

'Didn't you worry about me?' I asked.

'Look Daddy, you've been in lots of scrapes before, and none of them have harmed you,' said Jamie.

'You always get out of them,' said Tracey.

But of course, it wasn't over yet.

Cartoon by Wil Mitchell in the *Queensland Times*, 23 January 1988.

The Dalgety Flyer in Australia

This cartoon was drawn in Australia to lampoon the excessively bureaucratic Australian Department of Aviation which, as soon as I landed in Sydney and was out of the public eye, reminded me that I was flying a restricted aircraft. These restrictions included bans on flying above 500 feet and on crossing any roads! After an acrimonious argument, I managed to get permission to fly on around Australia to write this book, but was banned from flying into Adelaide, where Ross Smith's Vimy is preserved at the airport itself. I had to land fifty miles away and be helicoptered to see the Vimy. I was never able to show the Flyer the aircraft whose ghost we had chased across the world.

But the above cartoon could as easily apply to the British Microlight Aircraft Association back home. Published comment within the British microlighting community was extremely hostile to the Dalgety Flight, and very effective too. A year after I landed in Sydney, and nine months after I returned to England, I had been a guest speaker at a number of places, including the famous 617 'Dambuster' Squadron annual dinner, but not one British microlight club thought the flight worthy enough to invite me to talk about it.

Cartoon by Jock McNeish.

Chapter Nineteen
GABA
(Great Australian Bugger All)

I resolved to race to Sydney.

The stopover at Darwin had cost me dearly in time, but I had lost a great many days already, in Greece and Abu Dhabi. There was a slim chance I could make it through to Sydney in five days for the Bicentenary on 26 January – if luck didn't turn against me, and I flew all the hours of daylight. It was in my favour that I was now in a southern hemisphere summer with long hours of daylight. But for hours on end I also had to cope with the vicious thermals of the Australian outback summer.

It was much later that I learned that the Australian Army had crossed the continent the previous year using microlights, and had taken four and a half weeks doing it. Two of the ground crew were killed in the attempt.

Mike spent the hours I was being interviewed looking for a suitable vehicle to chase me across the country. We were going into the outback proper, where there would be hundreds of miles between one airfield and another. The first-class air ticket that had stood him so well was no longer enough. He found a Japanese Toyota Hiace van, caravan-equipped and with a long-distance tank. He also asked all the Darwin journalists if any of them wanted to accompany us to Sydney. If he had to follow me, he needed someone to spell him with the driving. A television cameraman accepted, but was pulled out on the first day. The ABC radio journalist, Larry Anderson, stuck with us all the way through.

In the nine days they knew each other, Mike and Larry became friends, but they were not what each would have chosen for a friend in less difficult circumstances. Larry was thirty, a tough, cynical journalist who freelanced for a number of radio stations. He is independent and a left-winger. Mike thinks all politics is rubbish.

But Larry decided our flight was a story worth covering when the editors he worked for did not agree. He said later that the experience he went through changed his life completely.

At four o'clock on the morning of 22 January I was woken by the hotel operator, packed, and was downstairs in the hotel lobby to meet Anita by quarter to five. Having arrived in Australia, I was full of energy and adrenaline, despite having flown for twenty-one days without a rest. The odds were against getting to Sydney in five days, but I wouldn't have been a journalist if I hadn't seen the value of the story of the race, and the benefits it could bring Dalgety. They had stuck by me with great corporate courage, and I owed them an enormous debt.

Anita took me to two television stations, one for *Good Morning, Australia*, the other for a programme called *Today*, both based in Sydney. After those interviews, plus a couple with radio stations, we drove to the airport, where we pulled the Flyer out of the hangar. Mike arrived with his yellow van, accompanied by Larry Anderson. We fuelled up, and at eight o'clock, I took off.

My logbook records an 'uneventful flight, changing terrain, Mike chasing in van, very hot, hassle-free fuel.'

Darwin is in a subtropical region, but heading south over hills the countryside soon changes to scrub and desert. I followed a road, as I was to follow roads or railways almost all the way to Sydney. Who would want to go into the outback on a compass course in a microlight?

It was, by the standards of the Big Flight, a short trip: three hours to the town of Katherine, the first of the old Imperial Airways staging posts across Australia. Like all Australian towns, Katherine is laid out in a square grid pattern, none of the interesting, winding roads that English villages have. What was striking about the place names I flew over – Hughes, Livingstone, Gould, Macdonald, Batchelor – was their Britishness. The faces of the people I met were of British stock. It was eerie to think of them, or for them to think of themselves, as foreigners.

At Katherine, I was an hour on the ground refuelling. Mike had kept with me all the way in the van, which indicated I was bucking a headwind. Just after noon I set off again, and followed the road south for hours. To get to Sydney on time I had to make it to Tennant Creek that day, but if I succeeded this would be the longest leg of the whole trip: 577 miles from Darwin. If I fell short, it would have to be well short, somewhere like Elliot, otherwise I would have to spend a night in the desert.

As I left Katherine, a voice said on the radio: 'Earthquake at Tennant Creek,' but I did not take a lot of notice. I was back in my familiar tunnel vision mode; all I cared about was getting to Tennant Creek, earthquake or no earthquake.

At four o'clock I flew over the tiny village of Daly Waters and landed on the old airstrip. The great names of aviation – Amy Johnson, Bert Hinkler, Kingsford-Smith – had landed at Daly Waters when it had been another Imperial Airways staging post, but now it had only a pub and twenty inhabitants. There was a rusting car on the airfield and the remains of a microlight inside the hangar. I could hear the creak of a door and the wind whistling through holes. In the gloom at the back there were banks of what must have once been radio equipment. I stretched my legs, had a pee, and dreamed . . . and used up twenty minutes I dearly regretted later.

Back in the air, I couldn't raise Mike on the radio. At the time he was behind me, but he overtook me on the road to Elliot, where I in turn flew over him. Happy in a dozy way, I headed south, hour after hour holding the control stick.

When Fear came back I thought I had forgotten about it. But it was a familiar feeling.

Clouds had been building all afternoon. Now, in the distance, I could see that they were letting down rain, and the rain looked thick and black. The clouds moved slowly from left to right, and I adjusted my course to dodge them. They increased in number, and great jagged streaks of lightning linked them to the ground. If I was caught by them, I could be killed.

It was 7.30 in the evening, and on my right the sun was going down. Lightning storms were everywhere. If I was driven out into the desert to skirt one, I scuttled back to the road immediately afterwards, wishing I could go faster, and then dodged another one. There were television relay masts every twenty miles, and I judged my speed over the ground by counting them. Air-traffic control at

Tennant Creek reported more storms, and heavy rain on the airfield.

At 7.45, I saw a large motel over a crossroads. I could, I thought, land there. But there was a light blinking in the distance.

'Is that your beacon I can see, Tennant Creek?'

'That is affirmative, Dalgety Flyer.'

'Have you runway lights?'

'Affirmative, Dalgety Flyer, and they are switched on.'

With one more look at the motel and a go-for-it kind of feeling, I set off over the desert towards the blinking light. On either side of the light were lightning storms, and bolts hit the ground every ten to fifteen seconds. It was a race between me and the storm on the left. After five minutes, I couldn't see my instruments, and I watched the light, praying it would not go off. My altimeter showed 2,500 feet before I ceased to see it in the gloom, enough height to get over the hills just north of Tennant Creek. Looking down, I seemed to crawl over the countryside.

After what felt like a long time, I cleared the hills and saw the airfield to my right. I looked left and calculated I was ahead of the next storm by five minutes. Get her down, I said to myself, and put everything else out of your mind except landing safely.

'Turning final to land,' I called Tennant Creek ATC.

'We can't see your lights,' they replied.

'Negative lights,' I radioed.

There was silence at *that* news. Cutting the throttle, I slipped down through the night air, looking left and right to judge my height and distance from the runway. I mistook the bright lights at the beginning of the runway for the runway itself. They were lights set on poles to guide pilots to the threshold of the runway, and if I had landed on them I would have destroyed the aircraft. But then I saw what they were, opened the throttle, and floated over them. Once over the threshold, I cut the throttle again and felt my way down until the lights were almost level. Then I pulled the control stick back, and waited. The wheels hit the ground and I let out my breath and thought how lucky I was. When I opened the canopy, I could see nothing.

More by watching light patches in the gloom than by anything else, I felt my way along the taxiway towards the parking apron. A small crowd of people was waiting to see me. When I stopped the engine, someone pulled the top off a beer bottle and handed it to me.

'We've all heard that's what you need when you land,' he said, to the sound of laughter.

Tennant Creek is a town of 3,500 people, and the first 'big' town north of Alice Springs. It was there that I met the first of the small army of people in Australia who work for Dalgety. Neville Chalmers was assistant manager of Dalgety in Alice Springs, a mere 300 miles away over a rough, single-track tarmac road. He had driven that distance just to say hello. I was slightly bewildered that someone I didn't know would do that.

It rained very heavily just after I landed. We all drank beer, and people queued up to sign the Birthday Book, including two delightful little girls called Rebecca and Karen Walker who went out with me in the rain to tie the Flyer down. Rebecca wrote: 'Very small cockpit but good. Have luck for the rest of the flight and forever.'

After an hour Mike still had not arrived, so I checked into a motel and left messages with ATC as to where I was. At 9.30 in the evening, I was just starting my dinner when the ground shook heavily.

Earthquake!

I had been in one before, in Cape Town in 1969. Fiona and I had been in a restaurant the night before I was expelled from the country, when the quake hit. What is frightening about them is the way the previously solid earth is no longer reliable. But the South African earthquake was much smaller than the one in Tennant Creek, which was the biggest earthquake in Australia for 100 years. There had already been two major shocks that day, and by common consent the second had been much worse than the first.

The lights above me swung wildly. Across the room a party was going on; everyone stopped what they were doing and looked up. Four or five seconds passed. Then, as one, we all got up, trooped out of the restaurant, and stood in the dark. The trembling went on for a few more seconds, and then stopped. We went back inside and resumed our meal.

There were quakes all through the night. I was asleep when

my shoulder was shaken, and Mike whispered hoarsely in the gloom:

'We broke down on the road south of Elliot. Fixed it but don't think it will last. Setting off for Mount Isa after a meal,' he said.

I mumbled something in reply: 'OK.'

'Did you fly through those thunderstorms?' he asked.

I said I had managed to avoid them.

'They were bloody awful,' he said. 'First the bushes were thrashed around in the wind right across our path, and we couldn't see where we were going. Then the van was nearly blown off the road by the wind. When the rain started, we couldn't see anything.'

I was thankful I had missed them, but fell asleep at once. All through the night I was wakened by earth tremors. It was the next morning when I realised that Mike had gone out into the outback in a dodgy van.

When I paid the motel bill at Tennant Creek at 5 am I noticed that even though it was dawn there were groups of people in the street. Hardly anyone had slept through the night, but had lain in bed with their children and half an ear cocked for the next tremor, ready to run out of the building if the earth started quaking again. There were understandable delays getting fuel, but I was into the air at 8.45 am, heading north to the crossroads where I had nearly landed the previous night, and then east.

The first thermal hit me at 9.30 am. For the next five hours, I was bashed around in the roughest leg of the whole flight. The Flyer was tossed like a ping-pong ball, sometimes slewing seventy degrees left or right as hot air bubbled off the desert. I didn't like flying high, where the air is smoother, because I'm nervous of heights, but with a 10,000-foot ceiling I think I would still have been thrashed. My average altitude was 2,000 feet, and I stayed there even though it was rough.

The aircraft shook in bad thermals, and the tail juddered. The worst thermals were the 'headbangers', when I was thrown up, hitting my head on the canopy. Other thermals were dubbed 'jumpers' in my mind, when I was lifted bodily and banged down again in the seat. I thought back to David Cook's words when he sold me the aircraft – 'I can't think of any conceivable weather which would break the Shadow' – and hoped he was right. It was the severest test of the repairs made in Kythira.

Since India I had carried two litres of water in the cockpit, but usually drank only two or three mouthfuls a day. My toilet facilities were primitive – a bottle to pee in – and I did not like doing it. Every morning my takeoff time was determined by when I went to the toilet, and I always had a last pee before getting into the cockpit, sometimes just before I lined up for takeoff. But on the flight from Tennant Creek to Mount Isa, I needed to drink constantly because of the heat and the sun baking the canopy. Though I worried about peeing I still drank, and used the whole two litres by the time I arrived. It was all dry-sweated out of me.

The highway I followed was called the Barkly, which went over the Barkly Tablelands of the Northern Territory and into Queensland. Every twenty miles there was a tower with microwave aerials, and by counting these I judged my groundspeed. At 10.30 I flew over the Barkly Roadhouse, buildings set down in the middle of a vast, arid, red plain. Eve Jackson had landed on the road and taxied to the roadhouse for fuel – a nice gesture. Every microlight pilot dreams of a road landing, taxiing into a petrol station for fuel, and it would have been even more appreciated in the isolated roadhouse. But, again, I did not have the time. I flew on, wondering how anyone would go there in the first place. How they could look around and say, this is where my roots will be?

The last few miles to Mount Isa were particularly gruelling, with both headbanger and jumper thermals. It was a relief to look along a mountain valley and see the city after flying a total of 370 miles in six and a half hours. The air-traffic controller who saw me in was called Bill Makin, and by a weird chance we had last met in 1959 at RAF Hornchurch for aircrew selection.

The temperature at Mount Isa was over 100°F, and hadn't been below that for eleven days. The Flyer's engine needed a fifty-hour service, and I wanted to go on to Cloncurry, fifty miles further, before darkness.

Mike and Larry were in the hangar housing the Flying Doctor aircraft. They looked terrible. Their faces were grey with fatigue, and their eyes were curiously bright, surrounded by white patches. I had seen faces like those in films: German prisoners taken from the ruins of Monte Cassino, Canadians at Dieppe, British soldiers at Dunkirk, US marines in Guadalcanal. Mike had his hands in the van's engine, and was putting on a new alternator.

He told me that after they had left Tennant Creek, they had spelled each other driving in the dark, and had been bounced all over the place trying to sleep. The engine's water-temperature gauge had hovered in the red and had twice boiled over. The air-conditioning unit had failed and they had been cooked in the van. Opening the windows had been like putting their faces into an oven. At dawn, the engine had stopped again. Mike and Larry waited and suffered. Larry said people had died within six hours in the outback in similar conditions. Mike, a former paratrooper and deep-sea fisherman, and twelve years a hang-glider pilot, felt he had never been closer to death. But then a truck had come by, and they waved it down.

The truck towed them on a short rope for 300 kilometres over a one-track road, in a van which had servo-assisted brakes, and the servo unit did not work. The truck stopped every hour to let Mike change places behind the wheel with Larry. A headlight had broken and the windscreen had cracked in a number of places. Arriving at Mount Isa, they had had no reserves left. Yet Mike had found a new alternator and put it on.

Then I had turned up looking for sympathy about my own flight.

'I think we ought to go on to Cloncurry after I refuel,' I said, 'and my engine needs a fifty-hour service.'

I was lucky not to get flattened.

Michael told me he was in no state to continue following me. He said I should stay in Mount Isa, and I would be able to fly through to Charleville the following day. But we both knew I had to have the engine serviced. The last time it had been stripped was in Bangkok, and it should have been done at Troughton Island. Mike didn't get to Troughton, and we'd been in such a hurry at Darwin that there hadn't been any time. The engine had done seventy hours without being looked at.

Mike took it off and serviced it that night at the motel. It was a measure of his toughness and determination to keep the Flyer going.

Despite our tiredness, we all went off to the Irish Club at Mount Isa, centre of the town's social life. It was mainly for the prospect of looking at European women again after so many weeks without the sight of one.

When I woke the following day, 24 January, two days short of the Bicentenary, I thought I would have a thick head, but instead I felt as fit as a flea. We checked the wind, and wonder of wonders, it was a northwesterly! I was heading southeast; finally the wind would be helping me on my way. Mike put the engine back on, we refuelled, and I took off just before 8 am. I saw Larry and Mike pull out on to the road and follow me, but I went too fast for them and did not see them for the rest of the day.

Over the mountains to Cloncurry I followed roads again, and then took the Landsborough highway via Winton to Longreach. Winton is where the Australian airline Qantas was founded (Qantas standing for Queensland and Northern Territory Aeronautical Services). Longreach was the site of the first Qantas office, set up in 1920. In my logbook I noted the trip as 'joyous flying, the longest day', but it was only the first part that was joyous.

For the past two days I had been flying over GABA – Great Australian Bugger All. But now the countryside over which I passed was showing some signs of life: trees and shrubs and more settlements, with names like Hampden Downs, Broadlands, Fairymead, Penrith, all truly English names, but mixed together with Aborigine ones – Mount Booka Booka, Kooroora, Congewoi. At 1.30 in the afternoon I landed at Longreach and refuelled.

Dalgety had organised a small crowd of people to meet me, but there was hardly time to say hello to anyone. I said I had to get to Sydney, and at 2.45 took off again for Charleville, via Barcaldine and Blackall. Ross Smith's ghost was still stuck at Charleville, and I hoped that evening finally to catch him.

Mike and Larry tore into Longreach at five o'clock. A clearly exhausted Larry hoped that I was going to stay in Longreach. He asked Mike, 'What if Brian has flown on to Charleville?'

'Then that's where we're going,' said Mike.

Larry groaned.

East to Barcaldine I followed the road, chased by a rainstorm, and then turned south for Blackall. If I had taken a route directly southeast from Longreach I knew I could have saved time, but I could not chance missing Blackall. From there, I had two choices: to follow the road to Charleville, via Tambo and Augathella, or to cut across the outback on a compass course and hope to pick up the experimental VOR which was said to be working at Charleville.

Two factors influenced the decision. One, it was getting late in the afternoon, the road took a detour and was considerably longer than a straight line; I did not want to be stuck out in the bush when night came. Two, thunderstorms were now occurring at regular intervals, and I had to dodge them. But, I had to get to Charleville, I just had to. I took a deep breath and, abandoning all my previous warnings about leaving outback roads, set off to follow a compass course.

Just south of Blackall there were two storms, one either side of my intended track, but they met in the middle high above me. Evil, black cloudy fingers reached down towards the ground, and lightning bolts closed in on each other. It was like curtains being pulled across the sky. Beyond the cloud and rain there was blue sky, and I thought that if I dived at the curtains and got through, I would be OK through to Charleville. I descended to 700 feet and ran for it.

The rain lashed at my canopy but only for a couple of minutes. When I was through, I looked back a little later and it was black from east to west. I had only just made it. What I did not know until a couple of hours later was that the storms marked a distinct wind shift, from behind me to a headwind, and when I found out it gave me a terrible fright. There was a real chance that I would be still flying over the trackless bush when the light faded.

Four hours after leaving Longreach I was still over bush country. It stretched flat, as far as the eye could see, and was thin forest, bush, or bare red soil. There were the occasional homesteads. Some time before darkness I picked up the VOR for Charleville and established contact with ATC, but the sun started to go down and I still could not see the airfield. Counting off all the places I could land if it came to it, I became seriously nervous. All the time I was talking to Charleville ATC they were reassuring, urging me to stay in the air, keep on course, and follow the VOR signal, which was very strong.

I did not want to land in the dark again.

When I passed over a road and saw a house, I radioed: 'I can see a road I can land on. If I do not see you in the next two minutes I am turning back to it.'

'OK, Dalgety Flyer, we copy your message. Can you see our beacon yet?'

'No, I cannot see anything. I would like confirmation once again about the time of sunset.'

They said there was another fifteen minutes until it was officially dark, but looking out of my canopy, it was *unofficially* dark as far as I was concerned. Then, music . . .

'Dalgety Flyer, we have a visual, we have a visual, you are heading towards the airfield!'

It was as if, suddenly, a wonderful panorama was spread before me when I pushed the nose down. One moment all I could see was bush country, the next, I could see the airfield and the lovely runway with its familiar white marks at one end and a flashing beacon. Was I glad to arrive! It was 7.25 in the evening when I touched down, and I had five minutes of daylight left. I had been in the air for more than ten hours that day.

The Bicentenary was two days away, but from Charleville it was possible to fly to Dubbo the following evening, and Sydney the next afternoon. After all the alarms and scares, I was poised to make it to the scene of the first European colony in Australia. But I made a decision that evening that I now think was a mistake. I went instead to Brisbane.

I can only plead exhaustion.

The flight of the Dalgety Flyer was an official Bicentenary event, endorsed as such by the British–Australian Committee in London. It had always been my intention to make it to Sydney, but for a long time it had looked as though I wouldn't even make Australia. Now, after risking a great deal, especially in the three days of Australian flying, my resolution faltered.

It was only partially because the authorities told me I should not fly into Sydney on 26 January.

The Bicentenary organisation in Sydney had to cope with an expected two million people, the tall ships, and thousands of small boats. In the air, virtually the whole of the RAAF would be taking part in a fly-past, and fifty helicopters were expected to be fluttering around Sydney Harbour Bay.

If I brought the Dalgety Flyer into the middle of this, it was suggested, I would probably be trodden on. No one would do it deliberately, of course, but the Flyer was so small, and so subject to the whims of the wind, that I couldn't guarantee what time I would get there. A twenty-five-knot southerly wind was forecast, which would really slow me down if I headed south.

There were other factors. Many Australians might say, if I knocked at the door on the evening of the event, that even though I had been told there was no room for me, I had come a long way and should be let in. Others, though, might say that this was an Australian event, and ask who was this pom gate-crashing it after being told he was not welcome? I had to worry about Dalgety's image, which I thought was pretty good at the time, and which I could ruin by one wrong action.

The PR people in London and Sydney said go to Sydney. They agreed that there would be no real welcome there, and that Brisbane had opened its arms to the Flyer. But Sydney, they said, was the only place in Australia to be on 26 January.

In London, Dalgety were determined not to put me under any pressure after I had reached Darwin, and they said they had no opinion either way. If Terry Pryce or Tony Spalding had felt strongly that I should go to Sydney, then I would have. But they did not. I knew no one at Dalgety Australia at that time.

On the night of 24 January I knew I could make Sydney, but I wanted to be welcomed, not gate-crash the event. As a result, I opted to go to Brisbane instead. Perhaps I could creep into Sydney later, when everyone was suffering from party hangovers, and have my five minutes' joyous circling over the Opera House then.

I now think I made a mistake. The PR people were right. Even if I didn't gate-crash the Bicentenary, I should have hovered on the fringes of Sydney until I was allowed in, whether on 26 January or later.

On 25 January, the wind was southerly and as strong as the forecast said it would be. Mike, Larry and I pottered around the airfield, preparing the Flyer. That day I was set to go Toowoomba, about sixty miles west of Brisbane, and then fly into Brisbane for the Bicentenary itself. An old man came up and gave me some grapes as refreshment to fly with. He also told me that his wife had flown in the aircraft which had been there in 1920.

'Did she fly with Ross Smith?' I asked, incredulously.

'Yes, she was a girl of eleven at the time,' he said.

I went over to meet Alice Mae Maclennan.

Alice Mae was eighty years old. When she was eleven, she said, she had been one of two children taken for a flight by Ross Smith when he celebrated fixing the engine at Charleville. Today was the day that I overtook him as his ghost still struggled to put the Vickers Vimy together a few kilometres out of town. Having someone who had touched his aircraft, and then, sixty-eight years later, touched mine, was a very moving experience. If I could have taken Alice Mae for a flight I would have, but I asked her to sign the Birthday Book.

The two-hour flight east from Charleville to Roma was uneventful; only the nature of the countryside changed. The further east, the better the farming. It was a luxury to be savoured, to be in the air for only two hours at a time. At Roma I refuelled and had a sandwich, waited for Mike and Larry to catch me, and then set off for Toowoomba. There was a frisson of excitement on the way in as I dodged more thunderstorms, but by now I was confident I could do it and they caused no problems. Wayne Buckley from Dalgety met me there, and said I looked ragged with exhaustion, but I didn't feel that way.

The Bicentenary Day itself was a letdown. I was wound up and nervous as I flew over Brisbane on a wonderful summer's day, following the river and landing at the international airport. Mike arrived, and we took the wings off the Flyer and trucked her to a park where a big party was going on. No arrangements had been made to display the aircraft, and as we watched the pile of empty beer cans reach the height of small mountains, both of us were apprehensive for her safety. We took her to pieces early, trucked her to Archerfield airport, and left her in a hangar.

At the Brisbane Hilton that evening, Larry sent a note to two pretty girls. 'Come and join us,' he wrote, along with a lot of stuff about travellers from the outback. They smiled and wrote back, 'Sorry, better luck next time.'

'I'm not giving up,' he muttered, and wrote a second note full of even more romantic sentiments. The girls, Tina Southerland and Kathy Reardon, came over to say hello. Tina was a nurse, Kathy a teacher.

Larry had developed a taste for expense-account living, and ordered champagne. At around eleven o'clock I went to bed as I had to fly to a golf course the following morning, setting the alarm for four o'clock. Mike and Larry took the girls swimming at 2 am, and at 2.30 am booked the Hilton's tennis courts. With a racket in one hand, and a glass of champagne in the other, the four of them played tennis until they lost all the balls, somewhere in the streets of Brisbane far below. Kathy went home. Mike had half an hour's sleep, until I woke him to take me to the airfield.

Larry and Tina lay down chastely in Larry's room, fully clothed, and fell asleep. Larry was woken by telephone at 8.20 am on 27 January, because I had to tell him a story.

'I'm on a golf course on the Gold Coast with a broken under-carriage,' I said. 'The last pilot to land here was Bert Hinkler. It's your story for the next half-hour.'

Chapter Twenty
Sydney, Via a Golf Course

The *Today Show* is an Australian breakfast television programme on Channel 9, a bit like the old BBC *Breakfast Time* used to be with Frank Bough and Selina Scott. On Bicentenary Day, one of the producers called our hotel. He asked if I had seen the invitation to appear on the programme the following day, and told me I had to land at a golf course in Surfers' Paradise before 7.40 am, when the Great White Shark, Greg Norman, teed off for a competition. The invitation I received read:

'0730: BM to fly to Surfers' Paradise, eighty kilometres south of Brisbane, and land at the Palm Meadows Golf Course for interview with *Today Show*.

'Directions: Fly due south to Surfers' Paradise and look out for Jupiter's Casino, which is a large, glass, ritzy building, then fly to the right of the building and look out for a racecourse. The golf course adjoins the racecourse.'

The key word in the invitation is 'racecourse'.

Mike and I drove through the darkness before dawn from the Hilton to Archerfield airport in Brisbane, where we pulled the Flyer out of a hangar. She had ample fuel on board for the flight. I got away easily enough, if a bit worried about more headwinds, and Mike drove back to the Hilton. He was looking for Larry Anderson when the receptionist there said, 'Sorry about the crash.'

Mike thought he was being teased about previous exploits on the flight, and took no notice. It was only when he called a recently awakened Larry that he heard about my golf-course landing.

My route out of Archerfield was due south, away from built-up areas and then southeast over coastal mountains. By 7.15 am, because of the headwind, I still had not reached Surfers' Paradise and had the throttle wide open, looking at my watch all the time.

But the racecourse was marked clearly on my map and, when I finally got there just after 7.25, I looked for a golf course.

There were three of them!

Which was the right one? The only solution was to fly over all three, measure them with my eye, and choose the nearest one. There was little activity down below, but it was coming up to 7.30 and Greg Norman could be anywhere. I circled once over the club building, losing height, and saw the main fairway was clear of people and long enough for a landing. The Flyer whistled in, fifty feet above the clubhouse, and settled in a fast run down the fairway. With a sigh of relief, as always, that I was down safely, despite a strong crosswind, I started to look for Mr Norman and the television cameras.

In the distance there was a man working with a machine on a putting green. However hospitable they are, I thought, no one will be happy with tyre tracks on the green, so I hit the brakes. The front nose-wheel leg, which had been weakened on Kythira, broke in two, and a divot about a foot long was gouged in the fairway. The Flyer rocked on to its nose and stopped, and I got out. When I saw what the damage was to the aircraft, I stopped worrying, because it was easily repairable. I was more worried about the fairway.

But it was the wrong fairway, on the wrong golf course.

My directions, on consideration, were pretty naff. To an Englishman, a racecourse is where horses go around in circles. When I asked a representative sample of Australians, that was what they thought too. But someone in the *Today* programme used the word racecourse, when in fact they meant a car racing track. The racing track was four miles to the east of the racecourse, and it had been on the nearest golf course to the track that I had been supposed to land.

There was a *sotto-voce* apology from the *Today Show* later in the day, *sotto voce* because, like all journalists, they thought my golf-course landing was a much better story and why let the facts get in the way of a good story?

The story acquired its own piquant flavour when I discovered that the last pilot to land at the Southport Golf Club had been the lone Australian aviator Bert Hinkler in 1928. Hinkler had done London–Darwin in fifteen days, solo. He had landed his single-engined DH Moth at the golf course because, in his opinion, the field that had been set aside for him was too small to land on. There was a faked-up picture of him driving a golfball in the clubhouse, his aircraft in the background.

Mike, naturally, had heart failure when he saw the news on television and thought of the serious repairs to be done. In fact, the nose-wheel leg was repaired by a local handyman, Ted Westbrook, and ended up far stronger than the original leg because Ted had no worries about weight. When Mike arrived at 10.30 the repairs had been completed. But the wind had risen to twenty-five knots and the sky was looking bad, so we took the Flyer to pieces and transported her to a nearby airfield.

There followed a procession of tough young women journalists who filmed the Flyer while all this was happening. Four of them stood around, speculating cheerfully on the mundane ways I was going to die, since I had escaped uninjured from far more obvious ways of leaving this world.

The Australian press had been yearning for something like the golf-course landing to occur. They had heard from international news agencies that I had 'crashed' all over the world, a 'crash' being any landing away from an airfield. To them, however I might argue it was a narrow view of my flight, that was the 'story'. When I had set off from Darwin and flown to Brisbane in four and a half days, faster than any previous microlight over the same distance, no one had wanted to know.

One journalist had even sidled up and suggested it would be a better story if I could land on a road somewhere to refuel. I had considered it, but I was in such a hurry to get to Sydney that I could not afford the time. I think I was lucky, though, to find that Bert Hinkler had landed on the course before me, because Hinkler was a certified Australian hero. Few Australians were going to slag out Hinkler. I had done a Bert Hinkler, so I didn't receive the slagging off I might have.

We stayed the night at Surfers' Paradise, but saw nothing of the wild nightlife for which the area is famous. I went to bed early and we were up before dawn; I was airborne by 5.45, trying to reach Sydney on 28 January.

Sydney, Via a Golf Course

It was a rotten-looking day, full of loose, wet cloud that seemed to pile up out of the sea to the east and south, the direction in which I was heading. Over Southport airfield, I climbed to 6,500 feet, trying to find a way through clouds. They had breaks in them, which kept me technically legal in that I could see the ground.

Passing over one huge cloud I found the coast, and started tracking down it. The cloud soon thickened and I was forced out to sea to avoid it. Trying to go south and to stay over land, I dodged showers, but I was inexorably forced out to sea. After two hours in the air I calculated that I was fifteen miles out to sea, with no land in sight. I was in a huge hole, with clouds all around.

It was frightening, and I was also very irritated. Not expecting to fly over more water, I had no lifejacket, although there was a dinghy in the back. To find a way to get back to the coast, I tried flying at different heights, but there was no way through. Then I circled, watched the wind on the sea, and saw that it was blowing from the east. If I continued to circle, the hole in the cloud would be blown over Australia, and I would be blown with it. Which is what happened.

When I saw the coastline again I quickly identified it as a stretch south of Ballina, itself just south of Byron Bay, the most easterly point in Australia. Tracking up the coast in the rain, I headed for the old airfield marked on the map. When I found it to the west of town, it didn't look much, but I circled and landed at 8.30 am, throwing out sprays of water from the wheels and stopping halfway down the field.

Opening the canopy, I discovered that I was six feet short of an electric cattle fence, rigged right across the runway.

Mike and Larry were chasing me in the van, and when I phoned Anita from a nearby motel I heard they were just leaving Ballina. I rushed out on to the road to intercept them, but a newspaper journalist called, alerted by Anita, and I went in and missed them pass me by. The local police chased them and brought them back.

Then the rain eased off and conditions looked flyable, so I taxied up the runway and tried for a takeoff. Halfway along the strip, the nose of the Flyer was still on the ground. Mike said it looked as though I was water-skiing because I was throwing up so much water. It was slowing me down, and I couldn't reach flying speed. I couldn't fly on a second attempt. When I turned the engine off, Mike discovered big chunks of wood had been gouged from the propeller by the rain and grass.

As it happened, Dalgety's luck struck again. Whenever anything went wrong with the Flyer, it was Dalgety's luck that the means were at hand to repair it. In this case, we needed either a new propeller, or the old one rebuilt. A hundred yards away from where I landed was the workshop of one of the young geniuses of the Australian Ultralight movement, Scott Winton. He had a number of designs to his credit, including a flying wing called the Opal which weighed 100 kilogrammes, and which he claimed was the fastest-climbing piston-engined aircraft in the world. He said it would go up at 5,000 feet a minute! Scott offered to rebuild my propeller, and did so in under three hours. It was perfect when he handed it back, and he would take no payment.

Rain bucketed down on Ballina. We were soaked to the skin as we dismantled the Flyer and put her on a trailer supplied by another Ultralight manufacturer, LiteWing. They drove us to the new airport on the other side of town, so new it wasn't marked on the map. Still in lashing rain, we reassembled the Flyer, laughing wildly as the rainwater plastered our clothes to our bodies. Anita in Sydney was changing press releases hourly. I phoned her at 2.40 to say I was on my way again, took off, and continued south.

The next fifty-five miles took an hour and fifty minutes, which gives you some idea of how slowly I was going over the ground, yet my airspeed was 70 mph. It was frustrating, but as always, there was nothing I could do about it. Sydney was obviously out for the day (which pleased Larry, who was miserable the story was ending), but I resolved to get as far as possible. I had filed a flight plan for Coffs Harbour, but then I started worrying that I wouldn't have enough fuel to make it.

The fuel gauge had not worked for weeks, but we always had a reasonable excess of fuel in the tanks for any journey, even if, as now, the wind was against me. It began to prey on my mind that fuel was getting low. I imagined crossing over a town, the engine dying, and having nowhere to land. The ideal landing place is an airfield, but in case that failed, I started to look at the beaches below me for somewhere near a garage, and picked on a small town called Minnie Water. There was a beach to the north which was firm, and a beach to the south which was soft. Without knowing which was the firmer, I landed on the beach to the south.

If I hadn't broken the nose-wheel leg at Southport golf course, I would have broken it there, but she landed without damage, though pulled up abruptly.

Down towards the sea the sand was firm, so I pulled the Flyer there and started hauling her back up the beach, helped by a growing number of local people who came streaming down from the town. Disc jockeys on local radios up and down the coast had proclaimed a coastwatch for the Dalgety Flyer, and everyone was delighted that I had landed at Minnie Water. I climbed a small cliff and hitched a lift to a nearby garage for five gallons of petrol and some oil. Back on the beach, there was a crowd around the aircraft, and a lot of helping hands refuelling.

Takeoff had to be in a stiff crosswind, so I lined up close to the sea, watched the tide wash up ahead of me, and, as it retreated, opened the throttle. Takeoffs are always a wind-up when they are not on runways, and this was as tense and exciting as any I had done. As soon as the nose wheel was off the ground she started crabbing left, and I hauled her into the air just above stalling speed. Then, keeping her low at first to gain airspeed, I climbed over Minnie Water, waggled wings, and set off again for the south, making it to Coffs Harbour by six o'clock that evening.

By this time I had been flying, or dismantling and reassembling the Flyer, for fourteen hours, and I dearly wanted to stay in Coffs Harbour. The mayor invited me to, and it looked a lovely little town. But there was more than an hour of daylight left, and thanking him for the invitation, I threw in some more fuel, took off again and headed for a town called Kempsey, about forty-five miles to the south and inland by ten miles. It was another one of those flights where I had my heart in my mouth, watching the sun going down and hoping I had not miscalculated. But I made it with a few minutes of daylight to spare, and waited for Mike and Larry to catch up.

The Dalgety Flyer

We were all tired that evening. I had been going non-stop from London for fifty-eight days, and had flown every one of the last thirty days. My dearest wish was to get to Sydney and wake up the following morning knowing that the Flyer was safe and I didn't have to get into her and fly her that day. I just wanted to lie down and sleep.

On 29 January, three days after the Bicentenary and 230 miles north of Sydney, we lost our way at dawn trying to find the airfield at Kempsey. We were horrified to hear ABC radio news at 6.30 am saying I was already in the air and heading for Sydney. When we found the airfield, we quickly fuelled up and at ten minutes to seven I was airborne. I felt apprehensive about the weather ahead of me; low clouds were coming in from the sea, with rain showers around Port Macquarie and Forster, but once past there the sky cleared, and I fairly raced over the ground. I had to descend to 500 feet to get under the airway into Williamstown airport at Newcastle, and liked the experience so much that I stayed at 500 feet down most of the coast.

Heading for Sydney, I kept hearing the words 'Dalgety Flyer' on my radio. My earphones were broken and I was using a hearing aid with the radios, but I had to scrunch up in the seat and hold the aid tight in my ear to be able to make out what was being said to me. Helicopters chartered by television stations were being vectored to find me, and soon I had four of them accompanying me. This is always frightening to a microlight, and was particularly so when one helicopter, looking for a good shot, went right over the top of me. I shut my eyes and thought, 'Oh, God, this is it!' but the downwash missed me.

The famous Australian adventurer, Dick Smith, who had flown around the world by helicopter, came out in his helicopter to say hello. By that time I was shell-shocked, and could only half hear my radio. Much of what was said to me I had to guess at. As most people talking to me were TV people, and I was a journalist myself, it was not difficult to deduce what they were asking, and I busked the usual thirty-five-second reply I knew they wanted. But I mistook Dick Smith for another TV interviewer, and gave him the same old stuff I had given everyone else. I apologised later when I met him.

Sydney, Via a Golf Course

Sydney Harbour is one of the most beautiful harbours in the world. To see it from the air, as I did that morning, was staggering, with the sun sparkling off the water, the yachts, the Opera House itself and the great bridge. Linked to air-traffic control through a nearby helicopter, I was guided to the Opera House, which I circled once as I looked down at what had been my goal for the past fifty-nine days.

I was glad I had made it, and had not died.

Happy Birthday, Australia!

(Sorry I was a bit late.)

Appendix I
The Dalgety Flyer's Timetable

		Duration (hrs/mins)	Distance (miles)	Speed (mph)
02.12.87	London – Le Touquet	3.30	107	30
02.12	Le Touquet – Mondidier	1.45	72	41
02.12	Mondidier – Beauvais	0.30	25	50
03.12	Beauvais – Chalon	5.30	230	42
04.12	Chalon – Valence	5.25	130	24
05.12	Valence – Valence	0.30	–	–
05.12	Valence – Valence	1.30	–	–
06.12	Valence – Albenga	2.45	228	83
06.12	Albenga – Forli	3.25	205	60
07.12	Forli – Brindisi	5.45	387	67
08.12	Brindisi – Kirkira	3.10	130	41
08.12	Kirkira – Kefallinia	2.55	110	37
09.12	Kefallinia – Kythira	4.15	192	45
15.12	Kythira – Iraklion	2.15	130	58
16.12	Iraklion – Alexandria	6.25	400	62
16.12	Alexandria – Cairo	1.45	112	64
17.12	Cairo – Aqaba (via Sinai)	5.45	370	64
19.12	Aqaba – Safi	2.00	103	51
20.12	Safi – Amman	1.30	62	41
21.12	Amman – 'Ar' ar	5.25	300	55
22.12	'Ar' ar – Shoba	4.50	265	55
23.12	Shoba – Al Qaysumah	1.40	90	54
24.12	Al Qaysumah – Dhahran	3.15	275	85
25.12	Dhahran – Sea off Abu Dhabi	3.50	255	67
30.12	Abu Dhabi local – test flight	0.10	–	–
31.12	Abu Dhabi – Muscat	3.15	250	77
01.01.88	Muscat – Muscat	4.30	–	–
02.01	Muscat – Gwadar	4.15	270	64
03.01	Gwadar – Karachi	6.15	305	49

The Dalgety Flyer's Timetable/Ross Smith's Timetable

		Duration (hrs/mins)	Distance (miles)	Speed (mph)
04.01	Karachi – Ahmadabad	6.25	367	57
05.01	Ahmadabad – Bhopal	5.35	295	53
06.01	Bhopal – Allahabad	6.55	315	46
07.01	Allahabad – Calcutta	6.15	470	75
08.01	Calcutta – Akyab (Sittwe)	5.35	420	75
09.01	Akyab – Rangoon	5.40	330	58
10.01	Rangoon – Bangkok	6.50	400	61
11.01	Bangkok – Phuket	6.15	400	64
12.01	Phuket – Malay Paddy field	4.20	230	53
13.01	Paddy field – Penang	0.30	20	40
14.01	Penang – Kluang	6.30	330	51
15.01	Kluang – Batam Island	1.40	92	55
15.01	Batam Island – Palembang	3.55	276	70
16.01	Palembang – Jakarta	4.35	292	64
17.01	Jakarta – Surabaya	6.45	410	61
18.01	Surabaya – Bima	7.30	420	56
19.01	Bima – Kupang	6.30	355	54
20.01	Kupang – Troughton Island	6.30	295	45
21.01	Troughton Island – Darwin	6.30	350	54
22.01	Darwin – Tennant Creek (2 stops)	10.25	577	55
23.01	Tennant Creek – Mount Isa	6.30	370	57
24.01	Mount Isa – Longreach	5.30	372	68
24.01	Longreach – Charleville	4.40	273	58
25.01	Charleville – Roma	2.15	156	69
25.01	Roma – Toowoomba	3.20	213	64
26.01	Toowoomba – Brisbane	1.40	73	44
27.01	Brisbane – Southport golf club	1.05	50	46
28.01	Southport – Ballina	2.45	65	23
28.01	Ballina – Coffs Harbour	2.45	105	38
28.01	Coffs Harbour – Kempsey	0.55	55	60
29.01	Kempsey – Sydney	4.25	230	52

Total flying time (minus Valence, Muscat): 241 hours 20 minutes
Total distance flown: 13,607 statute miles
Average ground speed: 56 mph
Average air speed: 70 mph
Average headwind: 14 mph

The Dalgety Flyer

Number of flying days: 44

Number of flying days:	44
Total number of days elapsed:	59
Average time in air on flying days:	5 hours 40 minutes
Average daily distance, including stops:	231 miles
Average daily distance, flying days only:	309 miles

Ross Smith's Timetable

		Duration (hrs/mins)	Distance (miles)	Speed (mph)
12.11.19	London – Lyons	6.20	500	79
13.11	Lyons – Pisa	4.45	380	80
15.11	Pisa – Rome	3.20	180	54
16.11	Rome – Taranto	2.35	260	101
17.11	Taranto – Suda Bay	5.40	520	95
18.11	Suda Bay – Cairo	7.20	650	89
19.11	Cairo – Damascus	4.10	450	108
20.11	Damascus – Ramadie	6.00	420	70
21.11	Ramadie – Basra	3.30	350	100
23.11	Basra – Bandar Abbas	7.40	630	82
24.11	Bandar Abbas – Karachi	8.30	730	86
25.11	Karachi – Delhi	9.00	720	80
27.11	Delhi – Allahabad	4.25	380	86
28.11	Allahabad – Calcutta	5.00	470	78
29.11	Calcutta – Akyab (Sittwe)	4.45	420	88
30.11	Akyab – Rangoon	4.15	330	78
01.12	Rangoon – Bangkok	6.00	400	67
02.12	Bangkok – Singora	6.00	470	78
04.11	Singora – Singapore	6.20	480	76
06.11	Singapore – Kalidjati (Java)	9.00	640	71
07.11	Kalidjati – Surabaya	4.20	350	81
08.11	Surabaya – Bima	5.00	420	84
09.11	Bima – Atambua	5.30	440	80
10.12	Atambua – Darwin	6.30	470	72
13.12	Darwin – Warlock Ponds	4.20	220	51
14.12	Warlock Ponds – Cobbs Creek	5.30	300	54
17.12	Cobbs Creek – Anthony's Lagoon	0.15	20	80

The Dalgety Flyer

		Duration (hrs/mins)	Distance (miles)	Speed (mph)
18.12	Anthony's Lagoon – Brunette Downs	1.00	50	50
19.12	Brunette Downs – Avons Downs	2.45	180	65
20.12	Avons Downs – Cloncurry	3.00	230	77
22.12	Cloncurry – Longreach	4.40	300	64
23.12	Longreach – Charleville	3.40	330	90
12.02.20	Charleville – Bourke	4.00	260	65
13.02	Bourke – Narromine	3.00	230	77
14.02	Narromine – Sydney	4.15	200	47

Total Flying time:	172 hours 20 minutes
Total distance:	13,380 statute miles
Average ground speed:	78 mph
Average air speed:	95 mph
Number of flying days:	35
Total number of days on flight:	95
Average time in air/flying day (Darwin):	5 hours 40 minutes
Average daily distance, including stops:	141 miles
Average daily distance, flying days only:	382 miles
Average daily distance (London – Darwin):	395 miles
Average daily distance, flying days only (London – Darwin):	481 miles

Appendix II
Myths and Paperwork

When I decided to make the Australia flight there was a lot I didn't know. There were only two people in England at the time, Richard Meredith-Hardy and Eve Jackson, who had made long flights in a microlight. From them I learned of others I should talk to, though most of the digging for information was done by Neil Hardiman.

Before Neil took the job, I had dinner with Richard Meredith-Hardy, who had flown a microlight from London to Cape Town over a six-month period. Richard is an old Etonian, and appears to have private means. He is of wiry build, with black hair and a thick scraggy beard, and he dresses in tatty old clothes. His hands always seem to be covered in oil. He has the air of a cheerful, manic Pigpen from the cartoon strip, 'Peanuts'. But he is a brilliant pilot who has gone on to become British, European and now World microlight champion.

Richard arrived for dinner in Camden Town with his girlfriend, Nicki Lindsay-Smith. Nicki had followed him across Africa in a supply vehicle and knew a lot of the tricks to get past frontier posts. The most important source of information for pilots like us, Richard told me, was the AIS, the Aeronautical Information Service, then at Pinner in Middlesex. The AIS had a civil servant called Barry Davidson who was a sort of patron saint of madmen. If you told Barry you intended to fly upside down across Russia in a balloon, singing 'Rule Britannia' and playing bongo drums, Barry would give you all the regulations covering your flight the following day. He was a civil servant who said 'yes!' and, said Richard, I would be an idiot not to consult him about everything.

Richard made a number of points, then and later to Neil, some of which I accepted, and some which I should have taken more notice of:

— Arriving in a country, I would be required to go through a customs-designated airport. To arrange for customs inspection to be done early in the morning before leaving, it might be necessary to pay the customs inspectors a small 'fee' to get them to turn up on time. But I had to be diplomatic in volunteering to pay any 'fees' as many people could not accept a blatant bribe. (This was not true of Egypt.)

— The American dollar was the universal currency, and I should carry a wad of one-dollar bills for fees. It would be much more impressive to give ten one-dollar bills than a single ten-dollar bill.

— Before leaving the last airport in a country, a pilot has to arrange customs and immigration and file a flight plan, although a flight plan isn't always required for flight within a country. If an aircraft is forty-five minutes behind its estimated time of arrival, the airport is obliged by international law to start a search.

— If possible, I should wear a captain's uniform with lots of 'scrambled eggs' on the lapels.

— I shouldn't tell airports before I arrived that I was flying a microlight. I should just say I was flying a CFM Shadow, and they wouldn't admit to ignorance. If I asked for official permission to land a microlight they would almost certainly say no.

— There could be big problems if I lost my temper with local airport officials. This should not happen!

— If I carried a camera I would need special permission to take it in to every country, and some places, like Saudi Arabia, would say no.

— Richard recommended I should make a 'Permit for Everything' paper which looked very official, giving permission for everything I could think of. I should also make an official nonsense stamp for use in emergencies, and carry headed notepaper.

— In choosing fuel, Richard recommended high-quality Avgas (Aviation Gasolene) which has the water filtered out at the pump. His piston rings had gummed up in the Sudan, but he said that it wasn't the petrol but the oil he used that caused it. There is also a fuel carnet system which can be used to pay for Avgas. He recommended the Shell carnet for this.

– Like Richard's, my engine was a two-stroke Rotax. I should choose the oil carefully, but it could be either synthetic or natural. The Rotax normally uses a 50:1 mixture, but synthetic oil can be run at ratios as high as 100:1, though 80:1 is safer. I should always choose good-quality oil.

– The engine should have a top-end stripdown every fifty hours, preferably with a change of the small-end bearings where the piston rod connects to the piston itself. Mike should carry a complete spare engine (this would weigh approximately thirty-five kilogrammes).

– Richard thought I should carry an ADF – an Automatic Direction Finder – since an ADF transmitter is relatively simple and the electronics to interpret it are in the aircraft. ADFs are common throughout the world. He was disparaging about a VOR – VHF Omni Rangefinder – believing they could become unreliable.

(Eve Jackson carried an ADF and came to exactly the opposite view. She said her ADF sometimes picked up mountains, other aircraft, flocks of birds, and if she was lucky, the beacon she was trying to find. She recommended a VOR. I used a hand-held ICOM A20, which included a VOR, and it saved my life on at least half a dozen occasions. It always worked and would guide me in from forty miles.)

– On his African trip, Richard's fuel consumption averaged 9.3 litres per hour. In competition, with no extra weight to carry and being very frugal, Richard could cut down to 5.33 litres an hour. He had a 147-litre tank with a duration of more than fifteen hours and a range of 800 miles at a groundspeed of 50 mph. *He said that the slower you go, the further you get.*

– Richard did not use clearing agents, but suggested it might be wise for me. In every country these are agents who complete the formalities for you, for a fee. In some places, like Indonesia, they are mandatory. He thought we would have more problems with Mike Atkinson carrying the spare parts than with the aircraft.

– One-million-scale maps would be best for navigation, even though quarter million are available. The cockpit in a microlight is so tiny, there is no room for bigger maps. In any case, I would have to cut them into strips to use them.

– 'It is definitely possible to make Australia in thirty days but Brian will have to bloody go for it!'

Because my travels would take me through a different part of the world from Richard's own flight, some of his advice was not relevant. Obviously, I had to choose my route to go through customs, but outside of Calcutta and Alexandria I was never required to pay bribes. As for the other advice from Richard, I came to the following conclusions:

– I did carry $1,500 in American bills, from one- to twenty-dollar notes, and I needed all the funds I carried in this form.

– I did buy a pilot's shirt, and wore bars on my epaulettes, but took them off in embarrassment when I landed at an air force base in India, and never wore them again.

– In Western countries and Australia, air-traffic controllers know what a microlight is. In other countries they don't. But I took Richard's, and later Eve Jackson's, advice, and never pointed out the status of my aircraft in radio signals.

– I lost my temper a number of times, especially in Burma when my goods were being pawed over, but did not suffer for it. Mike had a spectacular loss of temper in India, which he says did him a lot of good. But we were both reacting to exhaustion and the pressure of time.

– Cameras were a worry, but only before I went. I carried two stills cameras which were lost in the Persian Gulf, but I bought another and continued on with it to Australia. I also carried an ITN Sony 8 movie camera. At no time did I wave the cameras around, but neither did I have problems with them.

– I didn't carry a 'Permit for Everything', but having driven through Africa, I can see how it would have been useful for Richard. Thanks to Neil's work, I never needed one.

– Bad fuel, wrong fuel, and just procuring fuel were among the worst practical problems I faced daily on my flight. As for the right quality oil, how could I know what I was getting? To quote Eve: 'When it's written in Urdu, you don't ask questions, you just put it in and pray.'

– Mike stripped the engine every fifty hours, and the decision to take a complete spare engine saved the Dalgety flight. On the other hand, it invalidated any thought of any official record for the flight since the FAI rules governing records require one to fly with the same engine from start to finish.

– My fuel consumption on the World Distance Record in September had come to just under two gallons, or nine litres an hour. On the big flight, the engine normally ate upwards of twelve litres an hour. The problem, which I did not appreciate until much later, was that I was flying too fast. I wish I'd underlined and stuck exclamation marks after Richard's comment, 'The slower you go, the further you get!'

– Neil cleared me through most countries, with Barry Davidson's help. We used clearing agents in Indonesia, but I wish I had used them in Egypt as well, before I arrived there and was rooked. Maybe I would have been rooked anyway.

– The Shell carnet was only accepted on two airfields.

– The one-million-scale maps were perfectly adequate outside Europe, but flying across France and Italy I preferred a half-million scale.

– The phrase 'Brian will have to bloody go for it' haunted me all across the world, as I sat under the rain and fog in Valence, as a bundle of nerves on Kythira, crossing from Cairo to Aqaba, the Saudi Desert, Muscat to Gwadar, India, Malaysia . . . It caused all my problems too, of course.

One of Neil's first actions was to talk to John Harwood, the London contact for Eve Jackson. They had dinner in the middle of July, while Eve was still finding her way south across the outback from Darwin to Sydney. These were his comments before I left England:

– Eve's original budget was for £123,000, but although she tried for three years she failed to secure a sponsor. They had paid a professional agent £500 to find a sponsor but the agent had failed and they felt they had been ripped off by him. Her preparation costs had been about £20,000, and the expense of the flight at that stage had reached about £25,000. She had been given a lot of help by the CFM factory, as well as free instruments. Pan American Airways flew David Cook out to India for free when her engine needed repairing. Royal Jordanian Airlines came through with money after she met King Hussein.

– Eve had problems with the aircraft's undercarriage. She broke it twice, but was able to weld it together again. CFM have now modified it. She carried no parachute, and a life raft only after Jordan.

– On long water crossings she would work out the point of no return in case the engine cut. She flew as high as possible, once up to 12,000 feet.

– John thought our target of four hundred miles a day was optimistic, bearing in mind pilot fatigue and sandstorms. One day in three, he said, would probably be unflyable. I should fly early, or late, crossing the desert since the midday heat can melt tyres.

– To navigate, Eve used an ADF and a compass, and disliked the ADF. IFR is aircraft jargon for Instrument Flight Rules, but when Eve used IFR, she meant I Follow Roads, and that is how she crossed most of the world. John did not recommend a VOR, as he believed (wrongly) that beacons were very scarce after Egypt.

– The Rotax engine interferes with a radio and needs special screening.

– Eve found Avgas was reliable but not always available. She found two-stroke oil was sometimes impossible to obtain, and once used engine oil.

– Eve did not carry a transponder to identify herself automatically on a radar screen, but thought it a good idea.

– She thought the Shadow's claimed performance was an underestimate.

In contrast, my budget was less than Eve wanted, but more than she spent. Dalgety were my sole financial sponsor, though ICOM (UK) supplied me with an HF radio (which worked wonderfully until it went into the Persian Gulf, and was sent back wet). I paid the retail price for every item I bought from the CFM factory, and all expenses plus a fee for David Cook to help when I went down in Kythira in Greece.

– I had no problems with the undercarriage. Like Eve, I carried no parachute, but I hired a life raft and sent it back months later.

The life jacket I wore was the same one that went into the English Channel with me in 1977 when I was picked up by the Russians. I inflated it again for the Persian Gulf. It is now in the Powerhouse Museum in Sydney.

– On long water crossings I just set off. If the engine stopped I didn't care if I had to descend from 10,000 feet or 2,000 feet; I was going in. I hated flying high and only reached 10,000 feet (the absolute ceiling of my aircraft) three times. That was going over the French and Italian Alps, and the mountains of Thailand. Otherwise I flew at 2,000 feet.

– Our daily target distance of 400 miles *was* optimistic, but not if the winds behaved themselves. With a prevailing wind, which I had once in India, I had no difficulty in beating 400 miles. In the summer months, with long hours of daylight and a bit of grit, 400 miles is a reasonable target, and 600 miles quite possible on many days. Ross Smith averaged less than 400 miles a day getting to Darwin.

– I flew every day, whether it was flyable or not. Mike Atkinson reckoned that of the thirty-six flying days I took to get to Darwin, only ten of them were actually flyable. On the other twenty-six days a prudent pilot wouldn't have been in the air, but then it's hardly prudent to set off for Australia in a microlight in the first place. In a race, you have to keep going, whatever the weather.

– I Followed Roads, like Eve did, but relied on my trusty VOR as well. There were enough VOR stations across the world for me to use.

– I screened the Rotax and had no problems with interference with the radio, except for the last day of the flight into Sydney.

– My experiences trying to find two-stroke oil were similar to Eve's.

– I carried a transponder, and when that was ruined in the Persian Gulf, I bought another one. It was invaluable in calming the fears of big-city radar operators.

– I don't think I was a good enough pilot to know whether or not the Shadow's performance was an over- or an underestimate. It did what I expected, except over the Persian Gulf, and I was grateful.

– One further point concerned paperwork. When aircraft fly from one country to another, the pilot has to fill in a General

Declaration, known as a Gen Dec. This is a description of how many crew and passengers are on board, and so on. Gen Decs are second nature to airline pilots. I carried a large number of Gen Dec forms, but was not required to use them until Pakistan. From there, it was Gen Dec madness.

In Burma, for example, I had to fill out twelve separate Gen Decs on the evening I arrived at Rangoon, and twelve more when I left the following day. As I was the only crew, and had no passengers and no goods embarking or disembarking, I just wanted to fill in one form and photocopy the rest. There was no photocopier in the airport, and I was reduced to grinding my teeth and writing out the daft forms myself.

I had known I would have paperwork problems. I didn't realise until I was in the middle of them how stupid they often were . . .

Neil and I met Barry Davidson, the civil servant who likes to say yes, at AIS in Pinner at the end of August and were briefed on the sort of reception I was likely to get in each country. We collected a number of opinions, and I include them all since they obviously affected the way we approached the flight.

– We expected no problems in France or Italy. France turned out to be probably the most air-minded nation I passed through. Italy was a rude awakening, but only on my test flight to Pisa in November, which turned into a nightmare. Greece we expected to be OK for paperwork. It was in Egypt we thought the first problems would occur.

– Cairo was known, internationally, as a time-wasting airport, probably because of Egyptians wanting to find the best way to take the most money off you. If I decided to go south to Luxor I was to be wary of one particularly infamous bureaucrat. I could be forced to change $500 into worthless Egyptian currency just to pay for fuel.

(One result of this advice was to limit my stay in Egypt to one day – a day too long.)

– Jordan was thought to be westernised, and if we could interest King Hussein in our flight, it ought to be an oasis of peace. Patti Hewstone sent letters to the Royal Palace in Amman, but had no response. We had no idea of the problems I would face in Jordan without the backing of the Palace. She kept trying, and also tried to get through to Prime Minister Rajiv Gandhi of India, a former airline pilot, but again, had no success.

— Saudi Arabia was a big worry. Barry suggested we emphasise the idea of the Birthday Book, have dual approaches from the Australian and British Embassies, and use whatever business contacts Dalgety had. Eve had visa problems in Saudi and was forced to follow airways. The safety altitude over the desert was said to be at least 8,000 feet, much higher than I was prepared to go.

— Barry said Eve ran into problems in Saudi, and elsewhere, for two reasons. The first was because she was a woman, the second because she had no official backing. I was not a woman, and I had official backing (of sorts).

— On no account was I to take alcoholic drinks into Saudi.

— Abu Dhabi was portrayed, truthfully, as an oasis of sanity in the Middle East, as was Muscat.

— Pakistan, said Kevin Hoban, a pilot in the Paris–Peking air race, was a 'hellhole of bureaucracy'. All fees have to be paid in the local currency, which is awkward when you are restricted by the amount of currency you can take in. Barry Davidson agreed with this assessment.

— India was also bureaucratic. A French microlight pilot called Patrice Franceschi was given permission to land at one airfield, but when he did so was told he would have to go to Delhi for permission to take off again. It took him two weeks to get that permission!

— In Burma, all fuel had to be prearranged.

— Bangkok should be OK, but I had to watch out for afternoon thunderstorms. The same applied to Malaysia. Indonesia needed special care, said Barry. I should use a professional agent to handle all the paperwork, permissions, customs, immigration, fuel and accommodation.

All of these problems were taken care of by Neil Hardiman, and there were no hiccups in his area of expertise during the Dalgety Flight.

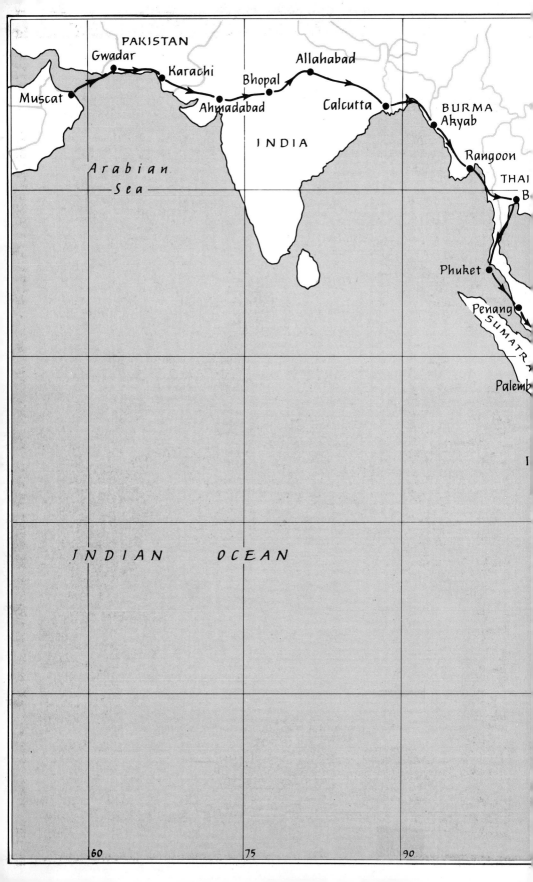